Mumford/32.00

OC 27 '04

AMERICAN IDEALS

AMERICAN IDEALS

EDITED BY

NORMAN FOERSTER, 1887-

AND

WILLIAM WHATELY PIERSON, Jr.

Essay Index Reprint Series

BOOKS FOR LIBRARIES PRESS
FREEPORT, NEW YORK

PREFACE

"BEFORE our war we were to Europe but a huge mob of adventurers and shopkeepers. Leigh Hunt expressed it well enough when he said that he could never think of America without seeing a gigantic counter stretched all along the seaboard."

It is the Civil War that James Russell Lowell referred to in this passage; it is the Civil War that revealed once more, as the War of Independence had also revealed, the idealism of those remote forbears of ours who came to this continent "not to seek gold, but God." But after the Civil War, our material prosperity grew apace, until our ideals seemed gradually to become dimmer and, in the view of many observers, both foreign and American, faded away altogether. And now, having accepted our responsibilities in world affairs, we believe that we shall reveal once again some of the ideals we have cherished in the past and some of the new ideals that the age calls for.

It is the function of this little book to bring together certain essays, addresses, and state papers that express, from the point of view of American statesmen and men of letters, these ideals, past and present. A final chapter of "Foreign Opinion of the United States" regards a few of the same subjects from an interestingly different angle.

One who reads these utterances reflectively will come to the conclusion that they exhibit a marked nobility of will and mind. For that the reader was amply prepared. But at the same time one cannot but confess that these expressions of the ideals that have guided us in the past and are animating our action in the present are somewhat deficient in clarity of purpose. Emerson said that "America is another word for Opportunity," and the phrase has often been repeated — but who inquires, "Opportunity for what?" There is another sentence of Emerson's that is even more deserving of repetition: "It is not free institutions, it is not a republic, it is not a democracy, that is the end, — no, but only the means." If Emerson is right, what *is* the end — what, at bottom, has the American tradition as its goal? This question cannot be answered now; but a more intimate knowledge of our professed ideals and policies, our spiritual and political tendencies, will perhaps bring us to an earlier answer than we should otherwise attain.

It need scarcely be said that, in collecting these expressions of our national and international consciousness, the editors have been obliged to omit, from so small a book, many significant utterances. Perhaps it likewise goes without saying that in arranging the selections under certain topics, the editors have sometimes assigned positions arbitrarily. These defects will not be serious so long as the total impression is reasonably near the truth. In the choice of matter to be included, a number of friends have generously assisted, particularly J. G. de Roulhac Hamilton, Professor of History, and James H. Hanford, Associate Professor of English, both of the University of North Carolina. Professor Hanford not only cooperated with the editors in drawing up the plan of the book, but also read the whole *corpus* of proof-sheets.

N. F.
W. W. P., Jr.

August, 1917.

CONTENTS

I. LIBERTY AND UNION

Liberty Speech . . . . *Patrick Henry*   3
The Declaration of Independence . . . . . *Thomas Jefferson* . .   7
The Adoption of the Declaration of
   Independence . . . . *Daniel Webster*   9

II. STATE AND NATION

The Nature of the Union . . . . *Daniel Webster* 17
The Nature of the Union . . . . *John C. Calhoun* . . . 27
Second Inaugural Address . . . . *Abraham Lincoln* . . 45
How to Preserve the Local Self-Gov-
   ernment of the States . . . . *Elihu Root* 48

III. AMERICAN DEMOCRACY

DEFINITION AND ILLUSTRATION

First Inaugural Address . . . . *Thomas Jefferson* . . 59
Gettysburg Address . . . . *Abraham Lincoln* . . . 65
Abraham Lincoln . . . . *R. W. Emerson* 66
Contributions of the West to American
   Democracy . . . . *F. J. Turner* 72
The Present Crisis . . . . *J. R. Lowell* 98
Rise, O Days, from Your Fathomless
   Deeps . . . . *Walt Whitman* 104
Thou Mother with Thy Equal Brood . *Walt Whitman* 107
A Charter of Democracy . . . . *Theodore Roosevelt* . 114

EDUCATION

The American Scholar . . . . *R. W. Emerson* 133
Democracy in Education . . . . *P. P. Claxton* 156

THE SUPREME TEST

Can Democracy be Organized? . . . . *Edwin A. Alderman* 158
Conscription Proclamation . . . . *Woodrow Wilson* . . . 175
Americanism and the Foreign-Born . . . . *Woodrow Wilson* . . . 178

IV. AMERICAN FOREIGN POLICY

IDEAL OF ISOLATION

Counsel on Alliances ....*George Washington* . 185

IDEAL OF INTER-AMERICAN ASSOCIATION

The Monroe Doctrine ....*James Monroe*..... 190
The Emancipation of South America..*Henry Clay*........ 194
Pan-Americanism..................*Robert Lansing* 200

IDEAL OF INTERNATIONAL ASSOCIATION

A League to Enforce Peace..........*A. Lawrence Lowell*. 207
The Monroe Doctrine and the Program
    of the League to Enforce Peace.....*George G. Wilson*... 224
The Conditions of Peace.............*Woodrow Wilson*... 233
War for Democracy and Peace ....*Woodrow Wilson*... 242

V. FOREIGN OPINION OF THE UNITED STATES

The Sovereignty of the People........*Alexis de Tocqueville* 257
General Tendency of the Laws.......*Alexis de Tocqueville* 261
The Activity of the Body Politic .....*Alexis de Tocqueville* 267
The German and the American Temper.*Kuno Francke*..... 273
The "Divine Average".............*G. Lowes Dickinson* 282
The Frame of National Government...*James Bryce*....... 285
Criticism of the Federal System......*James Bryce*....... 301
Merits of the Federal System........*James Bryce*....... 312
The Coöperation of English-Speaking
    Peoples ....*Arthur J. Balfour* .. 322

AMERICAN IDEALS

I

LIBERTY AND UNION

OUR FIRST CENTURY [1]

GEORGE EDWARD WOODBERRY

It cannot be that men who are the seed
Of Washington should miss fame's true applause;
Franklin did plan us; Marshall gave us laws;
And slow the broad scroll grew a people's creed —
Union and Liberty! then at our need,
Time's challenge coming, Lincoln gave it pause,
Upheld the double pillars of the cause,
And dying left them whole — our crowning deed.
Such was the fathering race that made all fast,
Who founded us, and spread from sea to sea
A thousand leagues the zone of liberty,
And built for man this refuge from his past,
Unkinged, unchurched, unsoldiered; shamed were we,
Failing the stature that such sires forecast!

[1] From *Poems*, 1903. Reprinted through the generous permission of The Macmillan Company.

AMERICAN IDEALS

LIBERTY SPEECH[1]

PATRICK HENRY

MR. PRESIDENT: No man thinks more highly than I do of the patriotism, as well as abilities, of the very worthy gentlemen who have just addressed the House. But different men often see the same subject in different lights; and, therefore, I hope that it will not be thought disrespectful to those gentlemen, if, entertaining as I do, opinions of a character very opposite to theirs, I shall speak forth my sentiments freely and without reserve. This is no time for ceremony. The question before the House is one of awful moment to this country. For my own part I consider it as nothing less than a question of freedom or slavery; and in proportion to the magnitude of the subject ought to be the freedom of the debate. It is only in this way that we can hope to arrive at a truth, and fulfill the great responsibility which we hold to God and our country. Should I keep back my opinion at such a time, through fear of giving offense, I should consider myself as guilty of treason toward my country, and of an act of disloyalty toward the Majesty of Heaven, which I revere above all earthly kings.

Mr. President, it is natural to man to indulge in the illusions of hope. We are apt to shut our eyes against a painful truth, and listen to the song of that siren, till she transforms us into beasts. Is this the part of wise men, engaged in a

[1] The speech delivered before the Virginia Convention of Delegates, March 23, 1775.

great and arduous struggle for liberty? Are we disposed to be of the number of those who, having eyes, see not, and having ears, hear not, the things which so nearly concern their temporal salvation? For my part, whatever anguish of spirit it may cost, I am willing to know the whole truth; to know the worst and to provide for it.

I have but one lamp by which my feet are guided; and that is the lamp of experience. I know of no way of judging the future but by the past. And judging by the past, I wish to know what there has been in the conduct of the British ministry for the last ten years to justify those hopes with which gentlemen have been pleased to solace themselves and the House? Is it that insidious smile with which our petition has been lately received? Trust it not, sir; it will prove a snare to your feet. Suffer not yourselves to be betrayed with a kiss. Ask yourselves how this gracious reception of our petition comports with these warlike preparations which cover our waters and darken our land. Are fleets and armies necessary to a work of love and reconciliation? Have we shown ourselves so unwilling to be reconciled, that force must be called in to win back our love? Let us not deceive ourselves, sir. These are implements of war and subjugation; the last arguments to which kings resort. I ask gentlemen, sir, what means this martial array, if its purpose be not to force us to submission? Can gentlemen assign any other possible motives for it? Has Great Britain any enemy, in this quarter of the world, to call for all this accumulation of navies and armies? No, sir, she has none. They are meant for us; they can be meant for no other. They are sent over to bind and rivet upon us those chains which the British Ministry have been so long forging. And what have we to oppose to them? Shall we try argument? Sir, we have been trying that for the last ten years. Have we anything new to offer on the subject?

Nothing. We have held the subject up in every light of which it is capable; but it has been all in vain. Shall we resort to entreaty and humble supplication? What terms shall we find which have not been already exhausted? Let us not, I beseech you, sir, deceive ourselves longer. Sir, we have done everything that could be done to avert the storm which is now coming on. We have petitioned; we have remonstrated; we have supplicated; we have prostrated ourselves before the throne, and have implored its interposition to arrest the tyrannical hands of the Ministry and Parliament. Our petitions have been slighted; our remonstrances have produced additional violences and insult; our supplications have been disregarded; and we have been spurned, with contempt, from the foot of the throne. In vain, after these things, may we indulge the fond hope of peace and reconciliation. There is no longer any room for hope. If we wish to be free — if we mean to preserve inviolate those inestimable privileges for which we have been so long contending — if we mean not basely to abandon the noble struggle in which we have been so long engaged, and which we have pledged ourselves never to abandon until the glorious object of our contest shall be obtained, we must fight! I repeat it, sir, we must fight! An appeal to arms and to the God of Hosts is all that is left us.

They tell us, sir, that we are weak; unable to cope with so formidable an adversary. But when shall we be stronger? Will it be the next week, or the next year? Will it be when we are totally disarmed, and when a British guard shall be stationed in every house? Shall we gather strength by irresolution and inaction? Shall we acquire the means of effectual resistance by lying supinely on our backs, and hugging the delusive phantom of hope, until our enemies have bound us hand and foot? Sir, we are not weak, if we make a proper use of the means which the God of nature hath placed in

our power. Three millions of people, armed in the holy
cause of liberty, and in such a country as that which we
possess, are invincible by any force which our enemy can
send against us. Besides, sir, we shall not fight our battles
alone. There is a just God who presides over the destinies
of nations; and who will raise up friends to fight our battles
for us. The battle, sir, is not to the strong alone; it is to
the vigilant, the active, the brave. Besides, sir, we have no
election. If we were base enough to desire it, it is now too
late to retire from the contest. There is no retreat but in
submission and slavery! Our chains are forged! Their
clanking may be heard on the plains of Boston! The war is
inevitable — and let it come! I repeat, sir, let it come!

It is in vain, sir, to extenuate the matter. Gentlemen may
cry peace, peace — but there is no peace. The war is actually begun! The next gale that sweeps from the North will
bring to our ears the clash of resounding arms! Our brethren
are already in the field! Why stand we here idle? What is it
that gentlemen wish? What would they have? Is life so
dear, or peace so sweet, as to be purchased at the price of
chains and slavery? Forbid it, Almighty God! I know not
what course others may take; but as for me, give me liberty,
or give me death!

THE DECLARATION OF INDEPENDENCE

In Congress, July 4, 1776

THOMAS JEFFERSON

WHEN in the Course of human Events, it becomes necessary for one People to dissolve the Political Bands which have connected them with another, and to assume among the Powers of the Earth, the separate and equal Station to which the Laws of Nature and of Nature's God entitle them, a decent Respect to the Opinions of Mankind requires that they should declare the Causes which impel them to the Separation.

We hold these Truths to be self-evident, that all Men are created equal, that they are endowed by their Creator with certain unalienable Rights, that among these are Life, Liberty and the Pursuit of Happiness. — That to secure these Rights Governments are instituted among Men, deriving their just Powers from the Consent of the Governed, That whenever any Form of Government becomes destructive of these Ends, it is the Right of the People to alter or to abolish it, and to institute new Government, laying its Foundation on such Principles and organizing its Powers in such Form, as to them shall seem most likely to effect their Safety and Happiness. Prudence, indeed, will dictate that Governments long established should not be changed for light and transient Causes; and accordingly all Experience hath shown, that Mankind are more disposed to suffer, while Evils are sufferable, than to right themselves by abolishing the Forms to which they are accustomed. But when a long Train of Abuses and Usurpations, pursuing invariably the same Object evinces a Design to reduce them under absolute Despotism, it is their Right, it is their Duty, to throw off such Government, and to provide new Guards for their future security. Such has been the patient Sufferance of these Colonies; and such is now the Necessity which constrains them to alter their former Systems of Government. The History of the present King of Great Britain is a History of repeated Injuries and Usurpations, all having in direct Object the Establishment of an absolute Tyranny over these States. . . .

We, therefore, the Representatives of the United States of America, in General Congress Assembled, appealing to the Supreme Judge of the World for the Rectitude of our Intentions, do, in the Name, and by the Authority of the good People of these Colonies, solemnly Publish and Declare, That these United Colonies are, and of Right ought to be, Free and Independent States; that they are Absolved from all Allegiance to the British Crown, and that all political connexion between them and the State of Great-Britain, is, and ought to be, totally dissolved; and that as Free and Independent States, they have full Power to levy War, conclude Peace, contract Alliances, establish Commerce, and to do all other Acts and Things which Independent States may of right do. And for the support of this Declaration, with a firm reliance on the Protection of Divine Providence, we mutually pledge to each other our Lives, our Fortunes, and our sacred Honour.

THE ADOPTION OF THE DECLARATION
OF INDEPENDENCE [1]

DANIEL WEBSTER

LET us, then, bring before us the assembly, which was about to decide a question thus big with the fate of empire. Let us open their doors and look in upon their deliberations. Let us survey the anxious and careworn countenances, let us hear the firm-toned voices, of this band of patriots.

Hancock presides over the solemn sitting; and one of those not yet prepared to pronounce for absolute Independence is on the floor, and is urging his reasons for dissenting from the Declaration.

"Let us pause! This step, once taken, cannot be retraced. This resolution, once passed, will cut off all hope of reconciliation. If success attend the arms of England, we shall then be no longer Colonies, with charters and with privileges; these will all be forfeited by this act; and we shall be in the condition of other conquered people, at the mercy of the conquerors. For ourselves, we may be ready to run the hazard; but are we ready to carry the country to that length? Is success so probable as to justify it? Where is the military, where the naval power, by which we are to resist the whole strength of the arm of England, — for she will exert that strength to the utmost? Can we rely on the constancy and

[1] From the "Oration on Adams and Jefferson," 1826. Regarding the famous imaginary speech of John Adams, Webster wrote, in 1846, "The speech was written by me in my house, in Boston, the day before the delivery of the discourse in Faneuil Hall; a poor substitute, I am sure, if we could now see the speech actually made by Mr. Adams on that transcendently important occasion."

perseverance of the people? or will they not act as the people of other countries have acted, and, wearied with a long war, submit, in the end, to a worse oppression? While we stand on our old ground, and insist on redress of grievances, we know we are right, and are not answerable for consequences. Nothing, then, can be imputed to us. But if we now change our object, carry our pretensions farther, and set up for absolute Independence, we shall lose the sympathy of mankind. We shall no longer be defending what we possess, but struggling for something which we never did possess, and which we have solemnly and uniformly disclaimed all intention of pursuing, from the very outset of the troubles. Abandoning thus our old ground, of resistance only to arbitrary acts of oppression, the nations will believe the whole to have been mere pretence, and they will look on us, not as injured, but as ambitious subjects. I shudder before this responsibility. It will be on us, if, relinquishing the ground on which we have stood so long, and stood so safely, we now proclaim Independence, and carry on the war for that object, while these cities burn, these pleasant fields whiten and bleach with the bones of their owners, and these streams run blood. It will be upon us, it will be upon us, if, failing to maintain this unseasonable and ill-judged declaration, a sterner despotism, maintained by military power, shall be established over our posterity, when we ourselves, given up by an exhausted, a harassed, a misled people, shall have expiated our rashness and atoned for our presumption on the scaffold."

It was for Mr. Adams to reply to arguments like these. We know his opinions, and we know his character. He would commence with his accustomed directness and earnestness.

"Sink or swim, live or die, survive or perish, I give my hand and my heart to this vote. It is true, indeed, that in

the beginning we aimed not at Independence. But there's
a Divinity which shapes our ends. The injustice of England
has driven us to arms; and, blinded to her own interest for
our good, she has obstinately persisted, till Independence
is now within our grasp. We have but to reach forth to
it, and it is ours. Why, then, should we defer the Declaration? Is any man so weak as now to hope for a reconciliation with England, which shall leave either safety to the
country and its liberties, or safety to his own life and his
own honor? Are not you, Sir, who sit in that chair, — is
not he, our venerable colleague near you, — are you not
both already the proscribed and predestined objects of pun-
ishment and of vengeance? Cut off from all hope of royal
clemency, what are you, what can you be, while the power
of England remains, but outlaws? If we postpone Independence, do we mean to carry on, or to give up, the war? Do
we mean to submit to the measures of Parliament, Boston
Port Bill and all? Do we mean to submit and consent that
we ourselves shall be ground to powder, and our country
and its rights trodden down in the dust? I know we do not
mean to submit. We never shall submit. Do we intend to
violate that most solemn obligation ever entered into by
men, that plighting, before God, of our sacred honor to
Washington, when, putting him forth to incur the dangers
of war, as well as the political hazards of the times, we
promised to adhere to him, in every extremity, with our
fortunes and our lives? I know there is not a man here,
who would not rather see a general conflagration sweep over
the land, or an earthquake sink it, than one jot or tittle of
that plighted faith fall to the ground. For myself, having
twelve months ago, in this place, moved you, that George
Washington be appointed commander of the forces raised,
or to be raised, for defence of American liberty, may my
right hand forget her cunning, and my tongue cleave to the

roof of my mouth, if I hesitate or waver in the support I give him.

"The war, then, must go on. We must fight it through. And if the war must go on, why put off longer the Declaration of Independence? That measure will strengthen us. It will give us character abroad. The nations will then treat with us, which they never can do while we acknowledge ourselves subjects, in arms against our sovereign. Nay, I maintain, that England herself will sooner treat for peace with us on the footing of Independence, than consent, by repealing her acts, to acknowledge that her whole conduct towards us has been a course of injustice and oppression. Her pride will be less wounded by submitting to that course of things which now predestinates our Independence, than by yielding the points in controversy to her rebellious subjects. The former she would regard as the result of fortune; the latter she would feel as her own deep disgrace. Why then, why then, Sir, do we not as soon as possible change this from a civil to a national war? And since we must fight it through, why not put ourselves in a state to enjoy all the benefits of victory, if we gain the victory?

"If we fail, it can be no worse for us. But we shall not fail. The cause will raise up armies; the cause will create navies. The people, the people, if we are true to them, will carry us, and will carry themselves, gloriously, through this struggle. I care not how fickle other people have been found. I know the people of these Colonies, and I know that resistance to British aggression is deep and settled in their hearts and cannot be eradicated. Every Colony, indeed, has expressed its willingness to follow, if we but take the lead. Sir, the Declaration will inspire the people with increased courage. Instead of a long and bloody war for the restoration of privileges, for redress of grievances, for chartered immunities, held under a British king, set before them the glorious object of entire Independence, and it will breathe into them anew the breath of life. Read this Declaration at the head of the army; every sword will be drawn from its scabbard, and the solemn vow uttered, to maintain it, or to perish on the bed of honor. Publish it from the pulpit; religion will approve it, and the love of religious liberty will cling round it, resolved to stand with it, or fall with it. Send it to the public halls; proclaim it there; let them hear it who heard the first roar of the enemy's cannon; let them see it who saw their brothers and their sons fall on the field of Bunker Hill, and in the streets of Lexington and Concord, and the very walls will cry out in its support.

"Sir, I know the uncertainty of human affairs, but I see, I see clearly, through this day's business. You and I, indeed, may rue it. We may not live to the time when this Declaration shall be made good. We may die; die colonists; die slaves; die, it may be, ignominiously and on the scaffold. Be it so. Be it so. If it be the pleasure of Heaven that my country shall require the poor offering of my life, the victim shall be ready, at the appointed hour of sacrifice, come when that hour may. But while I do live, let me have a country, or at least the hope of a country, and that a free country.

"But whatever may be our fate, be assured, be assured that this Declaration will stand. It may cost treasure, and it may cost blood; but it will stand, and it will richly compensate for both. Through the thick gloom of the present, I see the brightness of the future, as the sun in heaven. We shall make this a glorious, an immortal day. When we are in our graves, our children will honor it. They will celebrate it with thanksgiving, with festivity, with bonfires, and illuminations. On its annual return they will shed tears, copious, gushing tears, not of subjection and slavery, not of agony and distress, but of exultation, of gratitude, and of joy. Sir, before God, I believe the hour is come. My judgment approves this measure, and my whole heart is in it. All that I have, and all that I am, and all that I ever hope, in this life, I am now ready here to stake upon it; and I leave off as I began, that live or die, survive or perish, I am for the Declaration. It is my living sentiment, and by the blessing of God it shall be my dying sentiment, Independence *now*, and INDEPENDENCE FOREVER."

And so that day shall be honored, illustrious prophet and patriot! so that day shall be honored, and as often as it returns, thy renown shall come along with it, and the glory of thy life, like the day of thy death, shall not fail from the remembrance of men.

II
STATE AND NATION

THE NATURE OF THE UNION [1]

DANIEL WEBSTER

I MUST now beg to ask, sir, Whence is this supposed right of States derived? Where do they find the power to interfere with the laws of the Union? Sir, the opinion which the honorable gentleman maintains is a notion founded in a total misapprehension, in my judgment, of the origin of this Government, and of the foundation on which it stands. I hold it to be a popular Government, erected by the people; those who administer it responsible to the people; and itself capable of being amended and modified, just as the people may choose it should be. It is as popular, just as truly emanating from the people, as the State Governments. It is created for one purpose; the State Governments for another. It has its own powers; they have theirs. There is no more authority with them to arrest the operation of a law of Congress, than with Congress to arrest the operation of their laws. We are here to administer a Constitution emanating immediately from the people, and trusted by them to our administration. It is not the creature of the State Governments.

This Government, sir, is the independent offspring of the popular will. It is not the creature of State Legislatures; nay, more, if the whole truth must be told, the people brought it into existence, established it, and have hitherto supported it, for the very purpose, amongst others, of imposing certain salutary restraints on State sovereignties. The States cannot now make war; they cannot contract alliances; they cannot make, each for itself, separate regula-

[1] From Webster's " Reply to Hayne," January 26, 1830.

tions of commerce; they cannot lay imposts; they cannot coin money. If this Constitution, sir, be the creature of State Legislatures, it must be admitted that it has obtained a strange control over the volitions of its creators.

The people then, sir, erected this Government. They gave it a Constitution, and in that Constitution they have enumerated the powers which they bestow on it. They have made it a limited Government. They have defined its authority. They have restrained it to the exercise of such powers as are granted; and all others, they declare, are reserved to the States, or the people. But, sir, they have not stopped here. If they had, they would have accomplished but half their work. No definition can be so clear as to avoid the possibility of a doubt; no limitation so precise as to exclude all uncertainty. Who, then, shall construe this grant of the people. Who shall interpret their will, where it may be supposed they have left it doubtful? With whom do they repose this ultimate right of deciding on the powers of the Government? Sir, they have settled all this in the fullest manner. They have left it with the Government itself, in its appropriate branches. Sir, the very chief end, the main design, for which the whole Constitution was framed and adopted, was to establish a Government that should not be obliged to act through State agency, or depend on State opinion or State discretion. The people had had quite enough of that kind of government under the Confederation. Under that system, the legal action, the application of law to individuals, belonged exclusively to the States. Congress could only recommend; their acts were not of binding force till the States had adopted and sanctioned them. Are we in that condition still? Are we yet at the mercy of State discretion and State construction? Sir, if we are, then vain will be our attempt to maintain the Constitution under which we sit.

But, sir, the people have wisely provided, in the Constitution itself, a proper, suitable mode and tribunal for settling questions of constitutional law. There are in the Constitution grants of powers to Congress, and restrictions on these powers. There are also prohibitions on the States. Some authority must, therefore, necessarily exist, having the ultimate jurisdiction to fix and ascertain the interpretation of these grants, restrictions, and prohibitions. The Constitution has itself pointed out, ordained, and established that authority. How has it accomplished this great and essential end? By declaring, sir, that "the Constitution and the laws of the United States, made in pursuance thereof, shall be the supreme law of the land, anything in the Constitution or laws of any State to the contrary notwithstanding."

This, sir, was the first great step. By this the supremacy of the Constitution and the laws of the United States are declared. The people so will it. No State law is to be valid which comes in conflict with the Constitution, or any law of the United States passed in pursuance of it. But who shall decide this question of interference? To whom lies the last appeal? This, sir, the Constitution itself decides also, declaring "that the judicial power shall extend to all cases arising under the Constitution and laws of the United States." These two provisions cover the whole ground. They are, in truth, the keystone of the arch! With these it is a Government; without them, a Confederation. In pursuance of these clear and express provisions, Congress established, at its first session, in the judicial act, a mode for carrying them into full effect, and for bringing all questions of constitutional power to the final decision of the Supreme Court. It then, sir, became a Government. It then had the means of self-protection; and but for this it would, in all probability, have been now among things which are past. Having constituted the Government, and declared its powers, the people have further said that since somebody must decide on the extent of these powers, the Government shall itself decide, subject always, like other popular Governments, to its responsibility to the people. And now, sir, I repeat, how is it that a State Legislature acquires any power to interfere? Who or what gives them the right to say to the people, "We who are your agents and servants for one purpose, will undertake to decide that your other agents and servants, appointed by you for another purpose, have transcended the authority you gave them!" The reply would be, I think, not impertinent, "Who made you a judge over another's servants? To their own masters they stand or fall."

Sir, I deny this power of State Legislatures altogether. It cannot stand the test of examination. Gentlemen may say that in an extreme case a State Government may protect the people from intolerable oppression. Sir, in such a case the people might protect themselves without the aid of State Governments. Such a case warrants revolution. It must make, when it comes, a law for itself. A nullifying act of a State Legislature cannot alter the case, nor make resistance any more lawful. In maintaining these sentiments, sir, I am but asserting the rights of the people. I state what they have declared, and insist on their right to declare it. They have chosen to repose this power in the General Government, and I think it my duty to support it like other constitutional powers.

For myself, sir, I do not admit the competency of South Carolina or any other State to prescribe my constitutional duty, or to settle, between me and the people, the validity of laws of Congress for which I have voted. I decline her umpirage. I have not sworn to support the Constitution according to her construction of the clauses. I have not stipulated by my oath of office or otherwise to come under any responsibility, except to the people, and those whom they have appointed to pass upon the question, whether laws, supported by my votes, conform to the Constitution of the country. And, sir, if we look to the general nature of the case, could anything have been more preposterous than to make a Government for the whole Union, and yet leave its power subject, not to one interpretation, but to thirteen or twenty-four interpretations? Instead of one tribunal, established by all, responsible to all, with power to decide for all, shall constitutional questions be left to four-and-twenty popular bodies, each at liberty to decide for itself, and none bound to respect the decisions of others; and each at liberty, too, to give a new Constitution on every new election of its own members? Would anything, with such a principle in it, or rather with such a destitution of all principle, be fit to be called a Government? No, sir. It should not be denominated a Constitution. It should be called, rather, a collection of topics for everlasting controversy; heads of debate for a disputatious people. It would not be a Government. It would not be adequate to any practical good, or fit for any country to live under.

To avoid all possibility of being misunderstood, allow me to repeat again in the fullest manner that I claim no powers for the Government by forced or unfair construction. I admit that it is a Government of strictly limited powers; of enumerated, specified, and particularized powers; and that whatsoever is not granted is withheld. But notwithstanding all this, and however the grant of powers may be expressed, its limit and extent may yet, in some cases, admit of doubt; and the General Government would be good for nothing, it would be incapable of long existing, if some mode had not been provided in which those doubts as they should arise might be peaceably but authoritatively solved. . . .

The honorable gentleman argues that if this Government be the sole judge of the extent of its own powers, whether that right of judging be in Congress or the Supreme Court, it equally subverts State sovereignty. This the gentleman sees, or thinks he sees, although he cannot perceive how the right of judging in this matter, if left to the exercise of the State Legislatures, has any tendencies to subvert the Government of the Union. The gentleman's opinion may be that the right ought not to have been lodged with the General Government; he may like better such a Constitution as we should have under the right of State interference; but I ask him to meet me on the plain matter of fact. I ask him to meet me on the Constitution itself. I ask him if the power is not found there, clearly and visibly found there?

But, sir, what is this danger, and what are the grounds of it? Let it be remembered that the Constitution of the United States is not unalterable. It is to continue in its present form no longer than the people who established it shall choose to continue it. If they shall become convinced that they have made an injudicious or inexpedient partition and distribution of power between the State Governments and the General Government, they can alter that distribution at will.

If anything be found in the National Constitution, either by original provision or subsequent interpretation, which ought not to be in it, the people know how to get rid of it. If any construction, unacceptable to them, be established so as to become practically a part of the Constitution, they will amend it at their own sovereign pleasure. But while people choose to maintain it as it is, while they are satisfied with it, and refuse to change it, who has given, or who can give, to the Legislature a right to alter it, either by interference, construction, or otherwise? Gentlemen do not

seem to recollect that the people have any power to do anything for themselves. They imagine there is no safety for
them any longer than they are under the close guardian-
ship of the State Legislatures. Sir, the people have not
trusted their safety, in regard to the general Constitution,
to these hands. They have required other security, and
taken other bonds. They have chosen to trust themselves,
first, to the plain words of the instrument, and to such construction as the Government themselves, in doubtful cases,
should put on their powers, under their oaths of office,
and subject to their responsibility to them, just as the people of a State trust their own Governments with a similar
power. Second, they have reposed their trust in the efficacy
of frequent elections, and in their own power to remove
their own servants and agents whenever they see cause.
Third, they have reposed trust in the judicial power, which,
in order that it might be trustworthy, they have made as
respectable, as disinterested, and as independent as was
practicable. Fourth, they have seen fit to rely, in case of
necessity, or high expediency, on their known and admitted power to alter or amend the Constitution, peaceably and quietly, whenever experience shall point out defects or imperfections. And, finally, the people of the United
States have at no time, in no way, directly or indirectly,
authorized any State Legislature to construe or interpret
their high instrument of government, much less to interfere, by their own power, to arrest its course and operation.

If, sir, the people in these respects had done otherwise than
they have done, their Constitution could neither have been
preserved, nor would it have been worth preserving. And
if its plain provisions shall now be disregarded, and these
new doctrines interpolated in it, it will become as feeble
and helpless a being as its enemies, whether early or more
recent, could possibly desire. It will exist in every State

but as a poor dependent on State permission. It must borrow leave to be; and will be, no longer than State pleasure, or indiscretion, sees fit to grant the indulgence, and to prolong its poor existence.

But, sir, although there are fears, there are hopes also. The people have preserved this, their own Constitution, for forty years, and have seen their happiness, prosperity, and renown grow with its growth, and strengthen with its strength. They are now, generally, strongly attached to it. Overthrown by direct assault, it cannot be; evaded, undermined, NULLIFIED, it will not be, if we, and those who shall succeed us here, as agents and representatives of the people, shall conscientiously and vigilantly discharge the two great branches of our public trust, faithfully to preserve and wisely to administer it.

Mr. President, I have thus stated the reasons of my dissent to the doctrines which have been advanced and maintained. I am conscious of having detained you and the Senate much too long. I was drawn into the debate with no previous deliberation, such as is suited to the discussion of so grave and important a subject. But it is a subject of which my heart is full, and I have not been willing to suppress the utterance of its spontaneous sentiments. I cannot, even now, persuade myself to relinquish it without expressing once more my deep conviction that since it respects nothing less than the Union of the States, it is of most vital and essential importance to the public happiness. I profess, sir, in my career hitherto to have kept steadily in view the prosperity and honor of the whole country, and the preservation of our Federal Union. It is to that Union we owe our safety at home, and our consideration and dignity abroad. It is to that Union that we are chiefly indebted for whatever makes us most proud of our country. The Union we reached only by the discipline of our virtues in the severe school of adversity. It has its origin in the necessities of disordered finance, prostrate commerce, and ruined credit. Under its benign influences these great interests immediately awoke, as from the dead, and sprang forth with newness of life. Every year of its duration has teemed with fresh proofs of its utility and its blessings; and although our territory has stretched out wider and wider, and our population spread farther and farther, they have not outrun its protection or its benefits. It has been to us all a copious fountain of national, social, and personal happiness.

I have not allowed myself, sir, to look beyond the Union, to see what might lie hidden in the dark recess behind. I have not coolly weighed the chances of preserving liberty when the bonds that unite us together shall be broken asunder. I have not accustomed myself to hang over the precipice of disunion, to see whether, with my short sight, I can fathom the depth of the abyss below; nor could I regard him as a safe counsellor in the affairs of this Government, whose thoughts should mainly be bent on considering, not how the Union may be preserved, but how tolerable might be the condition of the people when it should be broken up and destroyed. While the Union lasts we have high, exciting, gratifying prospects spread out before us, for us and our children. Beyond that I seek not to penetrate the veil. God grant that in my day, at least, that curtain may not rise! God grant that on my vision never may be opened what lies behind! When my eyes shall be turned to behold for the last time the sun in heaven, may I not see him shining on the broken and dishonored fragments of a once glorious Union — on States dissevered, discordant, belligerent; on a land rent with civil feuds, or drenched, it may be, in fraternal blood! Let their last feeble and lingering glance rather behold the gorgeous ensign of the Republic, now known and honored throughout the earth, still full high advanced, its arms and trophies streaming in their original lustre, not a stripe erased or polluted, not a single star obscured, bearing for its motto no such miserable interrogatory as "What is all this worth?" nor those other words of delusion and folly, "Liberty first and Union afterward"; but everywhere, spread all over in characters of living light, blazing on all its ample folds, as they float over the sea and over the land, and in every wind under the whole heavens, that other sentiment, dear to every true American heart — Liberty *and* Union, now and forever, one and inseparable!

THE NATURE OF THE UNION [1]

JOHN C. CALHOUN

Resolved, That the people of the several States composing these United States are united as parties to a constitutional compact, to which the people of each State acceded as a separate and sovereign community, each binding itself by its own particular ratification; and that the Union, of which the said compact is the bond, is a Union *between the States* ratifying the same.

Resolved, That the people of the several States thus united by the constitutional compact, in forming that instrument, and in creating a General Government to carry into effect the objects for which it was formed, delegated to that Government, for that purpose, certain definite powers, to be exercised jointly, reserving, at the same time, each State to itself, the residuary mass of powers, to be exercised by its own separate government; and that, whenever the General Government assumes the exercise of powers not delegated by the compact, its acts are unauthorized, void, and of no effect; and that the said Government is not made the final judge of the powers delegated to it, since that would make its discretion, and not the Constitution, the measure of its powers; but that, as in all other cases of compact among sovereign parties, without any common judge, each has an equal right to judge for itself, as well of the infraction, as of the mode and measure of redress.

Resolved, That the assertions that the people of these United States, taken collectively as individuals, are now, or ever have been, united on the principle of the social compact, and, as such, are now formed into one nation or people, or that they have ever been so united, in any one stage of their political existence; that the people of the several States composing the Union have not, as members thereof, retained their sovereignty; that the allegiance of their citizens has been transferred to the General Government;

---

[1] From the reply of Calhoun to Webster, on the resolutions offered by the former respecting the rights of States; delivered in the Senate, February 26, 1833. Considered in its entirety, this was perhaps Calhoun's most powerful speech in defense of State sovereignty.

that they have parted with the right of punishing treason through their respective State Governments; and that they have not the right of judging, in the last resort, as to the extent of powers reserved, and, of consequence, of those delegated, are not only without foundation in truth, but are contrary to the most certain and plain historical facts, and the clearest deductions of reason; and that all exercise of power on the part of the General Government, or any of its departments, deriving authority from such erroneous assumptions, must of necessity be unconstitutional — must tend directly and inevitably to subvert the sovereignty of the States — to destroy the federal character of the Union, and to rear on its ruins a consolidated government, without constitutional check or limitation, which must necessarily terminate in the loss of liberty itself.

I WILL now return to the first resolution, to see how the issue stands between the Senator from Massachusetts [Webster] and myself. It contains three propositions. First, that the Constitution is a compact; second, that it was formed by the States, constituting distinct communities; and, lastly, that it is a subsisting and binding compact between the States. How do these three propositions now stand? The first, I trust, has been satisfactorily established; the second, the Senator has admitted, faintly, indeed, but still he has admitted it to be true. This admission is something. It is so much gained by discussion. Three years ago even this was a contested point. But I cannot say that I thank him for the admission: we owe it to the force of truth. The fact that these States were declared to be free and independent States at the time of their independence; that they were acknowledged to be so by Great Britain in the treaty which terminated the War of the Revolution, and secured their independence; that they were recognized in the same character in the old Articles of the Confederation; and, finally, that the present Constitution was formed by a convention of the several States — afterwards submitted to them for their respective ratifications, and was ratified by them separately, each for itself, and each, by its own act, binding its citizens, — formed a body of facts too clear to be denied, and too strong to be resisted.

It now remains to consider the third and last proposition contained in the resolution — that it is a binding and a subsisting compact between the States. The Senator was not explicit on this point. I understood him, however, as asserting that, though formed by the States, the Constitution was not binding between the States as distinct communities, but between the American people in the aggregate; who, in consequence of the adoption of the Constitution, according to the opinion of the Senator, became one people, at least to the extent of the delegated powers. This would, indeed, be a great change. All acknowledge that, previous to the adoption of the Constitution, the States constituted distinct and independent communities, in full possession of their sovereignty; and, surely, if the adoption of the Constitution was intended to effect the great and important change in their condition which the theory of the Senator supposes, some evidence of it ought to be found in the instrument itself. It professes to be a careful and full enumeration of all the powers which the States delegated, and of every modification of their political condition. The Senator said that he looked to the Constitution in order to ascertain its real character; and, surely, he ought to look to the same instrument in order to ascertain what changes were, in fact, made in the political condition of the States and the country. But, with the exception of "We, the people of the United States," in the preamble, he has not pointed out a single indication in the Constitution, of the great change which, as he conceives, has been effected in this respect.

Now, sir, I intend to prove that the only argument on which the gentleman relies on this point, must utterly fail

him. I do not intend to go into a critical examination of the
expression of the preamble to which I have referred. I do
not deem it necessary. But if it were, it might be easily
shown that it is at least as applicable to my view of the
Constitution as to that of the Senator; and that the whole
of his argument on this point rests on the ambiguity of
the term thirteen United States; which may mean certain
territorial limits, comprehending within them the whole
of the States and Territories of the Union. In this sense,
the people of the United States may mean *all* the people
living within these limits, without reference to the States
or Territories in which they may reside, or of which they
may be citizens; and it is in this sense only that the expression gives the least countenance to the argument of
the Senator.[1]

But it may also mean, *the States united*, which inversion
alone, without further explanation, removes the ambiguity
to which I have referred. The expression, in this sense, obviously means no more than to speak of the people of the
several States in their united and confederated capacity;
and, if it were requisite, it might be shown that it is only
in this sense that the expression is used in the Constitution.
But it is not necessary. A single argument will forever
settle this point. Whatever may be the true meaning of
the expression, it is not applicable to the condition of the
States as they exist under the Constitution, but as it was
under the old Confederation, before its adoption. The Constitution had not yet been adopted, and the States, in or-
daining it, could only speak of themselves in the condition
in which they then existed; and not in that in which they
would exist under the Constitution. So that, if the argu-

[1] Calhoun did not know then, as he did later, the true history of the
opening phrase in the preamble of the Constitution, — that in the form
framed by the drafting committee the names of the States were enumerated and that this form was modified when Article VII was adopted.

ment of the Senator proves anything, it proves, not (as he supposes) that the Constitution forms the American people into an aggregate mass of individuals, but that such was their political condition before its adoption, under the old Confederation, directly contrary to his argument in the previous part of this discussion.

But I intend not to leave this important point, the last refuge of those who advocate consolidation, even on this conclusive argument. I have shown that the Constitution affords not the least evidence of the mighty change of the political condition of the States and the country, which the Senator supposed it effected; and I intend now, by the most decisive proof, drawn from the instrument itself, to show that no such change was intended, and that the people of the States are united under it as States and not as individuals. On this point there is a very important part of the Constitution entirely and strangely overlooked by the Senator in this debate, as it is expressed in the first resolution, which furnishes conclusive evidence not only that the Constitution is a compact, but a subsisting compact, binding between the States. I allude to the seventh article, which provides that "the ratification of the conventions of nine States shall be sufficient for the establishment of this Constitution *between the States* so ratifying the same." Yes, "*between the States.*" These little words mean a volume — compacts, not laws, bind *between* States; and it here binds, not as between individuals, but between *the States;* the States *ratifying;* implying, as strong as language can make it, that the Constitution is what I have asserted it to be — a compact, ratified by the States, and a subsisting compact, binding the States ratifying it.

But, sir, I will not leave this point, all-important in establishing the true theory of our Government, on this argument, as demonstrative and conclusive as I hold it to be.

Another, not much less powerful, but of a different character, may be drawn from the tenth amended article, which provides that "the powers not delegated to the United States by the Constitution, nor prohibited by it to the States, are reserved to the States respectively or to the people." The article of ratification, which I have just cited, informs us that the Constitution, which delegates powers, was ratified by the States, and is binding between them. This informs us to whom the powers are delegated, — a most important fact in determining the point immediately at issue between the Senator and myself. According to his views, the Constitution created a union between individuals, if the solecism may be allowed, and that it formed, at least to the extent of the powers delegated, one people, and not a Federal Union of the States, as I contend; or, to express the same idea differently, that the delegation of powers was to the American people in the aggregate (for it is only by such delegation that they could be constituted one people), and not to the *United States,* — directly contrary to the article just cited, which declares that the powers are delegated to the United States. And here it is worthy of notice that the Senator cannot shelter himself under the ambiguous phrase, "to the people of the United States," under which he would certainly have taken refuge had the Constitution so expressed it; but fortunately for the cause of truth and the great principles of constitutional liberty for which I am contending, "people" is omitted: thus making the delegation of power clear and unequivocal to the *United States,* as distinct political communities, and conclusively proving that all the powers delegated are reciprocally delegated by the States to each other, as distinct political communities.

So much for the delegated powers. Now, as all admit, and as it is expressly provided for in the Constitution, the *reserved* powers are reserved "to the States *respectively*, or to the people." None will pretend that, as far as they are concerned, we are one people, though the argument to prove it, however absurd, would be far more plausible than that which goes to show that we are one people to the extent of the delegated powers. This reservation "to the people" might, in the hands of subtle and trained logicians, be a peg to hang a doubt upon; and had the expression "to the people" been connected, as fortunately it is not, with the delegated instead of the reserved powers, we should not have heard of this in the present discussion.

I have now established, I hope, beyond the power of controversy, every allegation contained in the first resolution — that the Constitution is a compact formed by the people of the several States, as distinct political communities, and subsisting and binding between the States in the same character; which brings me to the consideration of the consequences which may be fairly deduced, in reference to the character of our political system, from these established facts.

The first, and most important is, they conclusively establish that ours is a federal system — a system of States arranged in a Federal Union, each retaining its distinct existence and sovereignty. It is founded on compact; it is formed by sovereign communities, and is binding between them in their sovereign capacity. . . .

If we compare our present system with the old Confederation, which all acknowledge to have been *federal* in its character, we shall find that it possesses all the attributes which belong to that form of government as fully and completely as that did. In fact, *in this particular*, there is but a single difference, and that not essential, as regards the point immediately under consideration, though very important in other respects. The Confederation was the act of the State Government, and formed a union of Governments. The present Constitution is the act of the States themselves, or, which is the same thing, of the people of the several States, and forms a union of them as sovereign communities. The States, previous to the adoption of the Constitution, were as separate and distinct political bodies as the Governments which represent them, and there is nothing in the nature of things to prevent them from uniting under a compact, in a federal union, without being blended in one mass, any more than uniting the Governments themselves, in like manner, without merging them in a single Government. To illustrate what I have stated by reference to ordinary transactions, the Confederation was a contract between agents — the present Constitution a contract between the principals themselves; or, to take a more analogous case, one is a league made by ambassadors; the other, a league made by sovereigns — the latter no more tending to unite the parties into a single sovereignty than the former. The only difference is in the solemnity of the act and the force of the obligation.

There, indeed, results a most important difference, under our theory of government, as to the nature and character of the act itself, whether executed by the States themselves or by their Governments; but as a result, as I have already stated, not at all affecting the question under consideration, but which will throw much light on a subject, in relation to which I must think the Senator from Massachusetts has formed very confused conceptions.

The Senator dwelt much on the point that the present system is a constitution and a government, in contradistinction to the old Confederation, with a view of proving that the Constitution was not a compact. Now, I concede to the Senator that our present system is a constitution and a government; and that the former, the old Confederation, was not a constitution or government: not, however, for the reason which he assigned, that the former was a compact, and the latter not, but from the difference of the origin from which the two compacts are derived. According to our American conception, the people alone can form constitutions or governments, and not their agents. It is this difference, and this alone, which makes the distinction. Had the old Confederation been the act of the people of the several States, and not of their Governments, that instrument, imperfect as it was, would have been a constitution, and the agency which it created to execute its powers, a government. This is the true cause of the difference between the two acts, and not that, in regard to which the Senator seems to be bewildered.

There is another point on which this difference throws important light, and which has been frequently referred to in debate on this and former occasions. I refer to the expression in the preamble of the Constitution, which speaks of "forming a more perfect union," and in the letter of General Washington, laying the draft of the Convention before the old Congress, in which he speaks of "consolidating the Union"; both of which I conceive to refer simply to the fact that the present Union, as already stated, is a union between the States themselves, and not a union like that which had existed between the Governments of the States.

We will now proceed to consider some of the conclusions which necessarily follow from the facts and positions already established. They enable us to decide a question of vital importance under our system: Where does sovereignty reside? If I have succeeded in establishing the fact that ours is a federal system, as I conceive I conclusively have, that fact of itself determines the question which I have proposed. It is of the very essence of such a system that the sovereignty is in the parts, and not in the whole; or, to use the language of Mr. Palgrave, the parts are the units in such a system, and the whole the multiple; and not the whole the unit and the parts the fraction. Ours, then, is a government of twenty-four sovereignties, united by a constitutional compact, for the purpose of exercising certain powers through a common government as their joint agent, and not a union of the twenty-four sovereignties into one, which, according to the language of the Virginia Resolutions, already cited, would form a consolidation. And here I must express my surprise that the Senator from Virginia should avow himself the advocate of these very resolutions, when he distinctly maintained the idea of the union of the States in one sovereignty, which is expressly condemned by those resolutions as the essence of a consolidated government.

Another consequence is equally clear, that, whatever modifications were made in the condition of the States under the present Constitution, they extended only to the exercise of their powers by compact, and not to the sovereignty itself, and are such as sovereigns are competent to make: it being a conceded point that it is competent to them to stipulate to exercise their powers in a particular manner, or to abstain altogether from their exercise, or to delegate them to agents, without in any degree impairing sovereignty itself. The plain state of the facts as regards our Government is, that these States have agreed by compact to exercise their sovereign powers jointly, as already stated; and that, for this purpose, they have ratified the compact in their sovereign capacity, thereby making it the Constitution of each State, in no wise distinguished from their own separate Constitutions, but in the superadded obligation of compact — of faith mutually pledged to each other. In this compact, they have stipulated, among other things, that it may be amended by three-fourths of the States: that

is, they have conceded to each other by compact the right
to add new powers or to subtract old, by the consent of that
proportion of the States, without requiring, as otherwise
would have been the case, the consent of all: a modification
no more inconsistent, as has been supposed, with their sovereignty, than any other contained in the compact. In fact,
the provision to which I allude furnishes strong evidence
that the sovereignty is, as I contend, in the States severally, as the amendments are effected, not by any one three-
fourths, but by any three-fourths of the States, indicating
that the sovereignty is in each of the States.

If these views be correct, it follows, as a matter of course,
that the allegiance of the people is to their several States,
and that treason consists in resistance to the joint authority
of the *States* united, not, as has been absurdly contended,
in resistance to the *Government* of the United States, which,
by the provisions of the Constitution, has only the right of
punishing. . . .

Having now said what I intended in relation to my
first resolution, both in reply to the Senator from Massachusetts, and in vindication of its correctness, I will
now proceed to consider the conclusion drawn from it
in the second resolution — that the General Government
is not the exclusive and final judge of the extent of the
powers delegated to it, but that the States, as parties
of the compact, have a right to judge, in the last resort, of
the infractions of the compact, and of the mode and measure of redress.

It can scarcely be necessary, before so enlightened a body,
to premise that our system comprehends two distinct governments, — the General and State Governments, — which,
properly considered, form but one; the former representing
the joint authority of the States in their confederate capacity, and the latter that of each State separately. I have

premised this fact simply with a view of presenting distinctly the answer to the argument offered by the Senator from Massachusetts to prove that the General Government has a final and exclusive right to judge, not only of its delegated powers, but also of those reserved to the States. That gentleman relies for his main argument on the assertion that a government — which he defines to be an organized body, endowed with both will, and power, and authority in *proprio vigore* to execute its purpose — has a right inherently to judge of its powers. It is not my intention to comment upon the definition of the Senator, though it would not be difficult to show that his ideas of government are not very American. My object is to deal with the conclusion, and not the definition. Admit, then, that the Government has the right of judging of its powers, for which he contends. How, then, will he withhold, upon his own principle, the right of judging from the State Governments, which he has attributed to the General Government? If it belongs to one, on his principle it belongs to both; and if to both, when they differ, the veto, so abhorred by the Senator, is the necessary result: as neither, if the right be possessed by both, can control the other.

The Senator felt the force of this argument, and, in order to sustain his main position, he fell back on that clause of the Constitution which provides that "this Constitution, and the laws made in pursuance thereof, shall be the supreme law of the land."

This is admitted — no one has ever denied that the Constitution, and the laws made in *pursuance* of it, are of paramount authority. But it is equally undeniable that laws *not* made in pursuance are not only not of paramount authority, but are of no authority whatever, being of themselves null and void; which presents the question, Who are to judge whether the laws be or be not pursuant to the

Constitution? And thus the difficulty, instead of being taken away, is removed but one step further back. This the Senator also felt, and has attempted to overcome, by setting up, on the part of Congress and the judiciary, the final and exclusive right of judging, both for the Federal Government and the States, as to the extent of their respective powers. That I may do full justice to the gentleman, I will give his doctrine in his own words. He states: —

That there is a supreme law, composed of the constitution, the laws passed in pursuance of it, and the treaties; but in cases coming before Congress, not assuming the shape of cases in law and equity, so as to be subjects of judicial discussion, Congress must interpret the constitution so often as it has occasion to pass laws; and in cases capable of assuming a judicial shape, the Supreme Court must be the final interpreter.

Now, passing over this vague and loose phraseology, I would ask the Senator upon what principle can he concede this extensive power to the legislative and judicial departments, and withhold it entirely from the Executive? If one has the right it cannot be withheld from the other. I would also ask him on what principle — if the departments of the General Government are to possess the right of judging, finally and conclusively, of their respective powers — on what principle can the same right be withheld from the State Governments, which, as well as the General Government, properly considered, are but departments of the same general system, and form together, properly speaking, but one government? This was a favorite idea of Mr. Macon, for whose wisdom I have a respect increasing with my experience, and who I have frequently heard say that most of the misconceptions and errors in relation to our system originated in forgetting that they were but parts of the same system. I would further tell the Senator that, if this right be withheld from the State Governments; if this restraining influence, by which the General Government is confined to its proper sphere, be withdrawn, then that department of the Government from which he has withheld the right of judging of its own powers (the Executive) will, so far from being excluded, become the *sole* interpreter of the powers of the Government. It is the *armed* interpreter, with powers to execute its own construction, and without the aid of which the construction of the other departments will be impotent.

But I contend that the States have a far clearer right to the sole construction of their powers than any of the departments of the Federal Government can have. This power is expressly reserved, as I have stated on another occasion, not only against the several departments of the General Government, but against the United States themselves. I will not repeat the arguments which I then offered on this point, and which remain unanswered, but I must be permitted to offer strong additional proof of the views then taken, and which, if I am not mistaken, are conclusive on this point. It is drawn from the ratification of the Constitution by Virginia, and is in the following words: —

We, the delegates of the people of Virginia, duly elected in pursuance of a recommendation from the General Assembly, and now met in Convention, having fully and freely investigated and discussed the proceedings of the Federal Convention, and being prepared, as well as the most mature deliberation hath enabled us, to decide thereon, do, in the name and in behalf of the people of Virginia, declare and make known that the powers granted under the Constitution, being derived from the people of the United States, may be resumed by them whensoever the same shall be perverted to their injury or oppression, and that every power not granted thereby remains with them, and at their will; that, therefore, no right of any denomination can be cancelled, abridged, restrained, or modified by the Congress, by the Senate or House of Representatives, acting in any capacity, by the President or any department or officer of the United States, except in those in-

stances in which power is given by the Constitution for those purposes; and that, among other essential rights, the liberty of conscience and of the press cannot be cancelled, abridged, restrained,
or modified by any authority of the United States. With these
impressions, with a solemn appeal to the searcher of all hearts for
the purity of our intentions, and under the conviction that whatsoever imperfections may exist in the Constitution ought rather
to be examined in the mode prescribed therein, than to bring the
Union in danger by a delay, with the hope of obtaining amendments previous to the ratification — we, the said delegates, in the
name and in the behalf of the people of Virginia, do by these presents, assent to and ratify the Constitution recommended on the
17th day of September, 1787, by the Federal Convention, for the
government of the United States, hereby announcing to all those
whom it may concern, that the said Constitution is binding upon
the said people, according to an authentic copy hereto annexed,
in the words following, etc.

It thus appears that this sagacious State (I fear, however, that her sagacity is not so sharp-sighted now as formerly) ratified the Constitution, with an explanation as to
her reserved powers; that they were powers subject to her
own will, and reserved against every department of the
General Government — legislative, executive, and judicial
— as if she had a prophetic knowledge of the attempts
now made to impair and destroy them: which explanation
can be considered in no other light than as containing a condition on which she ratified, and, in fact, making part of
the Constitution of the United States — extending as well
to the other States as herself. I am no lawyer and it may
appear to be presumption in me to lay down the rule of
law which governs in such cases, in a controversy with so
distinguished an advocate as the Senator from Massachusetts. But I shall venture to lay it down as a rule in such
cases, which I have no fear that the gentleman will contradict, that, in case of a contract between several partners,
if the entrance of one on condition be admitted, the condi-

tion enures to the benefit of all the partners. But I do not rest the argument simply upon this view: Virginia proposed the tenth amended article, the one in question, and her ratification must be at least received as the highest evidence of its true meaning and interpretation. . . .

I have now, I trust, shown satisfactorily that there is no provision in the Constitution to authorize the General Government, through any of its departments, to control the action of a State within the sphere of its reserved powers, and that, of course, according to the principle laid down by the Senator from Massachusetts himself, the Government of the States, as well as the General Government, has the right to determine the extent of their respective powers, without the right on the part of either to control the other. The necessary result is the veto, to which he so much objects; and to get clear of which, he informs us, was the object for which the present Constitution was formed. I know not whence he has derived his information, but my impression is very different as to the immediate motives which led to the formation of that instrument. I have always understood that the principle was, to give to Congress the power to regulate commerce, to lay impost duties, and to raise a revenue for the payment of the public debt and the expenses of the Government; and to subject the action of the citizens individually to the operation of the laws, as a substitute for force. If the object had been to get clear of the veto of the States, as the Senator states, the Convention certainly performed their work in a most bungling manner. There was unquestionably a large party in that body, headed by men of distinguished talents and influence, who commenced early and worked earnestly to the last, to deprive the States — not directly, for that would have been too bold an attempt — but indirectly — of the veto. The good sense of the Convention, however, put down every effort, however disguised and perseveringly made. I do not deem it necessary to give, from the journals, the history of these various and unsuccessful attempts — though it would afford a very instructive lesson. It is sufficient to say that it was attempted by proposing to give Congress power to annul the acts of the States which they might deem inconsistent with the Constitution; to give to the President the power of appointing the governors of the States, with a view of vetoing state laws through his authority; and, finally, to give to the judiciary the power to decide controversies between the States and the General Government: all of which failed — fortunately for the liberty of the country — utterly and entirely failed; and in their failure we have the strongest evidence that it was not the intention of the Convention to deprive the States of the veto power. Had the attempt to deprive them of this power been directly made, and failed, every one would have seen and felt that it would furnish conclusive evidence in favor of its existence. Now, I would ask, What possible difference can it make in what form this attempt was made? whether by attempting to confer on the General Government a power incompatible with the exercise of the veto on the part of the States, or by attempting directly to deprive them of the right to exercise it? We have thus direct and strong proof that, in the opinion of the Convention, the States, unless deprived of it, possess the veto power — or, what is another name for the same thing, the right of nullification. I know that there is a diversity of opinion among the friends of State Rights in regard to this power, which I regret, as I cannot but consider it as a power essential to the protection of the minor and local interests of the community, and the liberty and the union of the country. It is the very shield of State Rights, and the only power by which that system of injustice against which we have contended for more than thirteen years can be arrested: a system of hostile legislation — of plundering by law, which must necessarily lead to a conflict of arms if not prevented.

But I rest the right of a State to judge of the extent of its reserved powers, in the last resort, on higher grounds — that the Constitution is a compact, to which the States are parties in their sovereign capacity; and that, as in all other cases of compact between parties having no common umpire, each has a right to judge for itself. To the truth of this proposition the Senator from Massachusetts has himself assented, if the Constitution itself be a compact — and that it is, I have shown, I trust, beyond the possibility of a doubt. Having established this point, I now claim, as I stated I would do in the course of the discussion, the admissions of the Senator, and, among them, the right of secession and nullification, which he conceded would necessarily follow if the Constitution be indeed a compact.

SECOND INAUGURAL ADDRESS [1]

ABRAHAM LINCOLN

FELLOW-COUNTRYMEN, At this second appearance to take the oath of the Presidential office, there is less occasion for an extended address than there was at the first. Then a statement, somewhat in detail, of a course to be pursued, seemed fitting and proper. Now, at the expiration of four years, during which public declarations have been constantly called forth on every point and phase of the great contest which still absorbs the attention and engrosses the energies of the nation, little that is new could be presented. The progress of our arms, upon which all else chiefly depends, is as well known to the public as to myself; and it is, I trust, reasonably satisfactory and encouraging to all. With high hope for the future, no prediction in regard to it is ventured.

On the occasion corresponding to this four years ago, all thoughts were anxiously directed to an impending civil war. All dreaded it — all sought to avert it. While the inaugural address was being delivered from this place, devoted altogether to saving the Union without war, insurgent agents were in the city seeking to destroy it without war — seeking to dissolve the Union, and divide effects, by negotiation. Both parties deprecated war; but one of them would make war rather than let the nation survive; and the other would accept war rather than let it perish. And the war came.

One-eighth of the whole population were colored slaves, not distributed generally over the Union, but localized in the Southern part of it. These slaves constituted a peculiar

[1] Delivered at the Capitol, March 4, 1865.

and powerful interest. All knew that this interest was, some-how, the cause of the war. To strengthen, perpetuate, and extend this interest was the object for which the insurgents would rend the Union, even by war; while the Government claimed no right to do more than to restrict the territorial enlargement of it.

Neither party expected for the war the magnitude or the duration which it has already attained. Neither anticipated that the cause of the conflict might cease with, or even before, the conflict itself should cease. Each looked for an easier triumph, and a result less fundamental and astounding. Both read the same Bible, and pray to the same God; and each invokes his aid against the other. It may seem strange that any men should dare to ask a just God's assistance in wringing their bread from the sweat of other men's faces; but let us judge not, that we be not judged. The prayers of both could not be answered — that of neither has been answered fully.

The Almighty has his own purposes. "Woe unto the world because of offenses! for it must needs be that offenses come; but woe to that man by whom the offense cometh." If we shall suppose that American slavery is one of those offenses which, in the Providence of God, must needs come, but which, having continued through his appointed time, he now wills to remove, and that he gives to both North and South this terrible war, as the woe due to those by whom the offense came, shall we discern therein any departure from those divine attributes which the believers in a living God always ascribe to him? Fondly do we hope — fervently do we pray — that this mighty scourge of war may speedily pass away. Yet, if God wills that it continue until all the wealth piled by the bondman's two hundred and fifty years of unrequited toil shall be sunk, and until every drop of blood drawn with the lash shall be paid by another drawn with the sword, as was said three thousand years ago, so still it must be said, "The judgments of the Lord are true and righteous altogether."

With malice toward none; with charity for all; with firmness in the right, as God gives us to see the right, let us strive on to finish the work we are in; to bind up the nation's wounds; to care for him who shall have borne the battle, and for his widow, and his orphan — to do all which may achieve and cherish a just and lasting peace among ourselves, and with all nations.

HOW TO PRESERVE THE LOCAL SELF-GOVERNMENT OF THE STATES [1]

ELIHU ROOT

This gathering peculiarly represents two ancient Commonwealths, each looking back to a century and a half of colonial history before the formation of the American Union, each possessed of strong individuality, derived from the long practice of self-government, and both conspicuous among all the States for leadership in population and wealth, for commerce and manufacture, for art and science, and for the priceless traditions of great citizens in former generations. It seems appropriate to make here some observations upon a subject which is much in the minds of thoughtful Americans in these days.

What is to be the future of the States of the Union under our dual system of constitutional government?

The conditions under which the clauses of the Constitution distributing powers to the National and State Governments are now and henceforth to be applied, are widely different from the conditions which were or could have been within the contemplation of the framers of the Constitution, and widely different from those which obtained during the early years of the Republic. When the authors of *The Federalist* argued and expounded the reasons for union and the utility of the provisions contained in the Constitution, each separate colony transformed into a State was complete in

[1] A speech at the dinner of the Pennsylvania Society in New York, December 12, 1906. Reprinted, through the generous permission of the Harvard University Press, from *Addresses on Government and Citizenship.* (1916.)

itself and sufficient to itself, except as to a few exceedingly
simple external relations of State to State and to foreign
nations; from the origin of production to the final consumption of the product, from the birth of a citizen to his death,
the business, the social and the political life of each separate
community began and ended, for the most part, within the
limits of the State itself; the long time required for travel
and communications between the different centers of population, the difficulties and hardships of long and laborious
journeys, the slowness of the mails, and the enormous cost of
transporting goods, kept the people of each State tributary
to their own separate colonial center of trade and influence,
and kept their activities within the ample and sufficient
jurisdiction of the local laws of their State. The fear of the
fathers of the Republic was that these separate and self-
sufficient communities would fall apart, that the Union
would resolve into its constituent elements, or that, as it
grew in population and area, it would split up into a number
of separate confederacies. Few of the men of 1787 would
have deemed it possible that the Union they were forming
could be maintained among eighty-five millions of people,
spread over the vast expanse from the Atlantic to the Pacific
and from the Lakes to the Gulf.

Three principal causes have made this possible.

One cause has been the growth of a National sentiment,
which was at first almost imperceptible. The very difficulties and hardships to which our Nation was subjected in its
early years, the injuries to our commerce, and the insults
and indignities to our flag on the part of both of the con-
testants in the great Napoleonic wars, served to keep the
Nation and National interests and National dignity constantly before the minds and in the feelings of the people.
As the tide of emigration swept westward, new States were
formed of citizens who looked back to the older States as the

homes of their childhood and their affection and the origin of their laws and customs, and who never had the peculiar and special, separate political life of the colonies. The Civil War settled the supremacy of the Nation throughout the territory of the Union, and its sacrifices sanctified and made enduring that National sentiment. Our country as a whole, the noble and beloved land of every citizen of every State, has become the object of pride and devotion among all our people, North and South, within the limits of the proud old colonial Commonwealths, throughout the vast region where Burr once dreamed of a separate empire dominating the valley of the Mississippi, and upon the far-distant shores of the Pacific; and by the side of this strong and glowing loyalty to the Nation, sentiment for the separate States has become dim and faint in comparison.

The second great influence has been the knitting together, in ties of common interest, of the people forming the once separate communities through the working of free trade among the States. Never was a concession, dictated by enlightened judgment for the common benefit, more richly repaid than that by which the States surrendered in the Federal Constitution the right to lay imposts or duties on imports or exports without the consent of Congress. To it we owe the domestic market for the products of our farms and forests and mines and factories without a parallel in history, and an internal trade which already exceeds the entire foreign trade of all the rest of the world; and to it we owe in a high degree the constant drawing together of all parts of our vast and diversified country in the bonds of common interest and in the improving good understanding and kindly feeling of frequent intercourse.

The third great cause of change is the marvelous development of facilities for travel and communication produced by the inventions and discoveries of the past century. The

swift trains that pass over our two hundred and twenty
thousand miles of railroad, the seventy millions of messages
that flash over the more than fourteen hundred thousand
miles of telegraph wires, the conversations across the vast
spaces through our more than four million four hundred
thousand telephone instruments, take no note of State
lines; they have broken down the barriers between the separate communities and they have led to a reorganization of
the business and social life of the people of the United States
along lines which, for the most part, altogether ignore the
boundaries of the States. I left the borders of Virginia this
afternoon and traversed Maryland, Delaware, Pennsylvania, and New Jersey to the State of New York, and, bar-
ring accident, I shall breakfast to-morrow morning again
on the shore of the Potomac. The time required for this
journey would hardly have sufficed for an ordinary carriage
drive from the adjoining County of Westchester a hundred
years ago. Any one of us can go now into a neighboring room
in this hotel and talk with a friend in Boston or Chicago and
recognize his voice and transact business which formerly
would have required months to accomplish, if it could have
been done at all. The lines of trade, of financial operation,
of social intercourse, of thought and opinion that radiate
from the great centers of life in our country such as Boston
and New York, and Philadelphia and Baltimore, and Chicago and St. Louis, and New Orleans and San Francisco,
and many another great city, are perfectly regardless of
State distinctions. Our whole life has swung away from the
old State centers and is crystallizing about National centers;
the farmer harvests his grain and fattens his cattle, not as
formerly, with reference to the wants of his own home community, but for markets thousands of miles away; the manufacturer operates his mills and his factories to meet the
needs of far-distant consumers; the merchant has his cus-

tomers in many States; all — the farmer, the manufacturer, the merchant, the laborer — look for the supplies of their food and clothing, not to the resources of the home farm, or village, but to the resources of the whole continent. The people move in great throngs to and fro from State to State and across States; the important news of each community is read at every breakfast-table throughout the country; the interchange of thought and sentiment and information is universal; in the wide range of daily life and activity and interest the old lines between the States and the old barriers which kept the States as separate communities are completely lost from sight. The growth of National habits in the daily life of a homogeneous people keeps pace with the growth of National sentiment.

Such changes in the life of the people cannot fail to produce corresponding political changes. Some of those changes can be plainly seen now in progress. It is plainly to be seen that the people of the country are coming to the conclusion that in certain important respects the local laws of the separate States, which were adequate for the due and just regulation and control of the business which was transacted, and the activity which began and ended within the limits of the several States, are inadequate for the due and just control of the business and activities which extend throughout all the States, and that such power of regulation and control is gradually passing into the hands of the National Government. Sometimes by an assertion of the interstate commerce power, sometimes by an assertion of the taxing power, the National Government is taking up the performance of duties which under the changed conditions the separate States are no longer capable of adequately performing. The Federal Anti-Trust Law, the Anti-Rebate Law, the Railroad Rate Law, the Meat-Inspection Law, the Oleomargarine Law, the Pure-Food Law, are examples of the purpose of the people of the United States to do through the agency of the National Government the things which the separate State Governments formerly did adequately but no longer do adequately. The end is not yet. The process that interweaves the life and action of the people in every section of our country with the people in every other section, continues and will continue with increasing force and effect; we are urging forward in a development of business and social life which tends more and more to the obliteration of State lines and the decrease of State power as compared with National power; the relations of the business over which the Federal Government is assuming control, of interstate transportation with State transportation, of interstate commerce with State commerce, are so intimate and the separation of the two is so impracticable, that the tendency is plainly toward the practical control of the National Government over both. New projects of National control are mooted; control of insurance, uniform divorce laws, child-labor laws, and many others affecting matters formerly entirely within the cognizance of the States are proposed.

With these changes and tendencies, in what way can the power of the States be preserved?

I submit to your judgment, and I desire to press upon you with all the earnestness I possess, that there is but one way in which the States of the Union can maintain their power and authority under the conditions which are now before us, and that way is by an awakening on the part of the States to a realization of their own duties to the country at large. Under the conditions which now exist, no State can live unto itself alone, and regulate its affairs with sole reference to its own treasury, its own convenience, its own special interests. Every State is bound to frame its legislation and its administration with reference not only to its own special affairs, but with reference to the effect upon all its sister States, as every individual is found to regulate his conduct with some reference to its effect upon his neighbors. The more populous the community and the closer individuals are brought together, the more imperative becomes the necessity which constrains and limits individual conduct. If any State is maintaining laws which afford opportunity and authority for practices condemned by the public sense of the whole country, or laws which, through the operation of our modern system of communications and business, are injurious to the interests of the whole country, that State is violating the conditions upon which alone its power can be preserved. If any State maintains laws which promote and foster the enormous overcapitalization of corporations condemned by the people of the country generally; if any State maintains laws designed to make easy the formation of trusts and the creation of monopolies; if any State maintains laws which permit conditions of child labor revolting to the sense of mankind; if any State maintains laws of marriage and divorce so far inconsistent with the general standard of the Nation as violently to derange the domestic relations, which the majority of the States desire to preserve, that State is promoting the tendency of the people of the country to seek relief through the National Government and to press forward the movement for National Control and the extinction of local control. The intervention of the National Government in many of the matters which it has recently undertaken would have been wholly unnecessary if the States themselves had been alive to their duty toward the general body of the country.

It is useless for the advocates of State rights to inveigh against the supremacy of the constitutional laws of the United States or against the extension of National authority in the fields of necessary control where the States themselves fail in the performance of their duty. The instinct for self-government among the people of the United States is too strong to permit them long to respect any one's right to exercise a power which he fails to exercise. The governmental control which they deem just and necessary they will have. It may be that such control would better be exercised in particular instances by the Governments of the States, but the people will have the control they need, either from the States or from the National Government; and if the States fail to furnish it in due measure, sooner or later constructions of the Constitution will be found to vest the power where it will be exercised — in the National Government. The true and only way to preserve State authority is to be found in the awakened conscience of the States, their broadened views and higher standard of responsibility to the general public; in effective legislation by the States in conformity to the general moral sense of the country; and in the vigorous exercise for the general public good of that State authority which is to be preserved.

III
AMERICAN DEMOCRACY

FIRST INAUGURAL ADDRESS[1]

THOMAS JEFFERSON

FRIENDS AND FELLOW-CITIZENS: Called upon to undertake the duties of the first executive office of our country, I
avail myself of the presence of that portion of my fellow-
citizens which is here assembled to express my grateful
thanks for the favor with which they have been pleased to
look toward me, to declare a sincere consciousness that the
task is above my talents, and that I approach it with those
anxious and awful presentiments which the greatness of the
charge and the weakness of my powers so justly inspire. A
rising nation, spread over a wide and fruitful land, travers-
ing all the seas with the rich productions of their industry,
engaged in commerce with nations who feel power and forget right, advancing rapidly to destinies beyond the reach
of mortal eye — when I contemplate these transcendent objects, and see the honor, the happiness, and the hopes of this
beloved country committed to the issue and the auspices of
this day, I shrink from the contemplation, and humble myself before the magnitude of the undertaking. Utterly, indeed, should I despair did not the presence of many whom I
here see remind me that in the other high authorities provided by our Constitution I shall find resources of wisdom,
of virtue, and of zeal on which to rely under all difficulties.
To you, then, gentlemen, who are charged with the sovereign
functions of legislation, and to those associated with you,
I look with encouragement for that guidance and support
which may enable us to steer with safety the vessel in which

1 Delivered at Washington, D.C., March 4, 1801.

we are all embarked amidst the conflicting elements of a troubled world.

During the contest of opinion through which we have passed, the animation of discussion and of exertions has sometimes worn an aspect which might impose on strangers unused to think freely and to speak and to write what they think; but this being now decided by the voice of the nation, announced according to the rules of the Constitution, all will, of course, arrange themselves under the will of the law, and unite in common efforts for the common good. All, too, will bear in mind this sacred principle, that though the will of the majority is in all cases to prevail, that will, to be rightful, must be reasonable; that the minority possess their equal rights, which equal law must protect, and to violate which would be oppression. Let us, then, fellow-citizens, unite with one heart and one mind. Let us restore to social intercourse that harmony and affection without which liberty and even life itself are but dreary things. And let us reflect that, having banished from our land that religious intolerance under which mankind so long bled and suffered, we have yet gained little if we countenance a political intolerance as despotic, as wicked, and capable of as bitter and bloody persecutions. During the throes and convulsions of the ancient world, during the agonizing spasms of infuriated man seeking through blood and slaughter his long-lost liberty, it was not wonderful that the agitation of the billows should reach even this distant and peaceful shore; that this should be more felt and feared by some and less by others, and should divide opinions as to measures of safety. But every difference of opinion is not a difference of principle. We have called by different names brethren of the same principle. We are all Republicans, we are all Federalists. If there be any among us who would wish to dissolve this Union or to change its republican form, let them stand undisturbed as monuments of the safety with which error of opinion may be tolerated where reason is left free to combat it. I know, indeed, that some honest men fear that a republican government cannot be strong, that this Government is not strong enough; but would the honest patriot, in the full tide of successful experiment, abandon a government which has so far kept us free and firm, on the theoretic and visionary fear that this Government, the world's best hope, may by possibility want energy to preserve itself? I trust not. I believe this, on the contrary, the strongest Government on earth. I believe it the only one where every man, at the call of the law, would fly to the standard of the law, and would meet invasions of the public order as his own personal concern. Sometimes it is said that man cannot be trusted with the government of himself. Can he, then, be trusted with the government of others? Or have we found angels in the forms of kings to govern him? Let history answer this question.

Let us, then, with courage and confidence pursue our own Federal and Republican principles, our attachment to union and representative government. Kindly separated by nature and a wide ocean from the exterminating havoc of one quarter of the globe; too high-minded to endure the degradations of the others; possessing a chosen country, with room enough for our descendants to the thousandth and thousandth generation; entertaining a due sense of our equal right to the use of our own faculties, to the acquisitions of our own industry, to honor and confidence from our fellow-citizens, resulting not from birth, but from our actions and their sense of them; enlightened by a benign religion, professed, indeed, and practiced in various forms, yet all of them inculcating honesty, truth, temperance, gratitude, and the love of man; acknowledging and adoring an overruling Providence, which by all its dispensations proves

that it delights in the happiness of man here and his greater
happiness hereafter — with all these blessings, what more
is necessary to make us a happy and a prosperous people?
Still one thing more, fellow-citizens — a wise and frugal
Government, which shall restrain men from injuring one
another, shall leave them otherwise free to regulate their
own pursuits of industry and improvement, and shall not
take from the mouth of labor the bread it has earned. This
is the sum of good government, and this is necessary to
close the circle of our felicities.

About to enter, fellow-citizens, on the exercise of duties
which comprehend everything dear and valuable to you, it is
proper that you should understand what I deem the essential
principle of our Government, and consequently those which
ought to shape its Administration. I will compress them
within the narrowest compass they will bear, stating the
general principle, but not all its limitations. Equal and
exact justice to all men, of whatever state or persuasion,
religious or political; peace, commerce, and honest friendship with all nations, entangling alliances with none; the
support of the State governments in all their rights, as the
most competent administrations for our domestic concerns
and the surest bulwarks against anti-republican tendencies;
the preservation of the Central Government in its whole
constitutional vigor, as the sheet anchor of our peace at
home and safety abroad; a jealous care of the right of election by the people — a mild and safe corrective of abuses
which are lopped by the sword of revolution where peaceable
remedies are unprovided; absolute acquiescence in the decisions of the majority, the vital principle of republics, from
which is no appeal but to force, the vital principle and immediate parent of despotism; a well-disciplined militia, our
best reliance in peace and for the first moments of war, till
regulars may relieve them; the supremacy of the civil over

the military authority; economy in the public expense, that labor may be lightly burthened; the honest payment of our debts and sacred preservation of the public faith; encouragement of agriculture, and of commerce as its handmaid; the diffusion of information and the arraignment of all abuses at the bar of the public reason; freedom of religion; freedom of the press, and freedom of person under the protection of the habeas corpus; and trial by juries impartially selected. These principles form the bright constellation which has gone before us and guided our steps through an age of revolution and reformation. The wisdom of our sages and blood of our heroes have been devoted to their attainment. They should be the creed of our political faith, the text of civic instruction, the touchstone by which to try the services of those we trust; and should we wander from them in moments of error or of alarm, let us hasten to retrace our steps and to regain the road which alone leads to peace, liberty, and safety.

I repair, then, fellow-citizens, to the post you have assigned me. With experience enough in subordinate offices to have seen the difficulties of this, the greatest of all, I have learnt to expect that it will rarely fall to the lot of imperfect man to retire from this station with the reputation and the favor which bring him into it. Without pretensions to that high confidence you reposed in our first and greatest revolutionary character, whose preëminent services had entitled him to the first place in his country's love and destined for him the fairest page in the volume of faithful history, I ask so much confidence only as may give firmness and effect to the legal administration of your affairs. I shall often go wrong through defect of judgment. When right, I shall often be thought wrong by those whose positions will not command a view of the whole ground. I ask your indulgence for my own errors, which will never be intentional, and your support against the errors of others, who may condemn what they would not if seen in all its parts. The approbation implied by your suffrage is a great consolation to me for the past, and my future solicitude will be to retain the good opinion of those who have bestowed it in advance, to conciliate that of others by doing them all the good in my power, and to be instrumental to the happiness and freedom of all.

Relying, then, on the patronage of your good-will, I advance with obedience to the work, ready to retire from it whenever you become sensible how much better choice it is in your power to make. And may that Infinite Power which rules the destinies of the universe lead our councils to what is best, and give them a favorable issue for your peace and prosperity.

GETTYSBURG ADDRESS [1]

ABRAHAM LINCOLN

FOURSCORE and seven years ago our fathers brought forth on this continent a new nation, conceived in liberty, and dedicated to the proposition that all men are created equal. Now we are engaged in a great civil war, testing whether that nation, or any nation so conceived and so dedicated, can long endure. We are met on a great battle-field of that war. We have come to dedicate a portion of that field as a final resting-place for those who here gave their lives that that nation might live. It is altogether fitting and proper that we should do this.

But, in a larger sense we cannot dedicate — we cannot consecrate — we cannot hallow — this ground. The brave men, living and dead, who struggled here, have consecrated it far above our poor power to add or detract. The world will little note nor long remember what we say here, but it can never forget what they did here. It is for us, the living, rather, to be dedicated here to the unfinished work which they who fought here have thus far so nobly advanced. It is rather for us to be here dedicated to the great task remaining before us — that from these honored dead we take increased devotion to that cause for which they gave the last full measure of devotion; that we here highly resolve that these dead shall not have died in vain; that this nation, under God, shall have a new birth of freedom; and that government of the people, by the people, for the people, shall not perish from the earth.

[1] Delivered at Gettysburg, Pennsylvania, November 19, 1863.

ABRAHAM LINCOLN [1]

RALPH WALDO EMERSON

WE meet under the gloom of a calamity which darkens
down over the minds of good men in all civil society, as the
fearful tidings travel over sea, over land, from country to
country, like the shadow of an uncalculated eclipse over the
planet. Old as history is, and manifold as are its tragedies,
I doubt if any death has caused so much pain to mankind
as this has caused, or will cause, on its announcement; and
this, not so much because nations are by modern arts brought
so closely together, as because of the mysterious hopes and
fears which, in the present day, are connected with the name
and institutions of America.

In this country, on Saturday, every one was struck dumb,
and saw at first only deep below deep, as he meditated on
the ghastly blow. And perhaps, at this hour, when the coffin
which contains the dust of the President sets forward on its
long march through mourning States, on its way to his home
in Illinois, we might well be silent, and suffer the awful voices
of the time to thunder to us. Yes, but that first despair was
brief: the man was not so to be mourned. He was the most
active and hopeful of men; and his work had not perished:
but acclamations of praise for the task he had accomplished
burst out into a song of triumph, which even tears for his
death cannot keep down.

The President stood before us as a man of the people. He
was thoroughly American, had never crossed the sea, had
never been spoiled by English insularity or French dissipa-

[1] Spoken at the funeral services held in Concord, April 19, 1865.

tion; a quite native, aboriginal man, as an acorn from the oak; no aping of foreigners, no frivolous accomplishments, Kentuckian born, working on a farm,' a flatboatman, a captain in the Black Hawk War, a country lawyer, a representative in the rural Legislature of Illinois; — on such modest foundations the broad structure of his fame was laid. How slowly, and yet by happily prepared steps, he came to his place. All of us remember — it is only a history of five or six years — the surprise and the disappointment of the country at his first nomination by the Convention at Chicago. Mr. Seward, then in the culmination of his good fame, was the favorite of the Eastern States. And when the new and comparatively unknown name of Lincoln was announced (notwithstanding the report of the acclamations of that Convention), we heard the result coldly and sadly. It seemed too rash, on a purely local reputation, to build so grave a trust in such anxious times; and men naturally talked of the chances in politics as incalculable. But it turned out not to be chance. The profound good opinion which the people of Illinois and of the West had conceived of him, and which they had imparted to their colleagues that they also might justify themselves to their constituents at home, was not rash, though they did not begin to know the riches of his worth.

A plain man of the people, an extraordinary fortune attended him. He offered no shining qualities at the first encounter; he did not offend by superiority. He had a face and manner which disarmed suspicion, which inspired confidence, which confirmed good-will. He was a man without vices. He had a strong sense of duty, which it was very easy for him to obey. Then, he had what farmers call a long head; was excellent in working out the sum for himself; in arguing his case and convincing you fairly and firmly. Then, it turned out that he was a great worker; had prodigious faculty of performance; worked easily. A good worker is so rare; everybody has some disabling quality. In a host of young men that start together and promise so many brilliant leaders for the next age, each fails on trial; one by bad health, one by conceit, or by love of pleasure, or lethargy, or an ugly temper, — each has some disqualifying fault that throws him out of the career. But this man was sound to the core, cheerful, persistent, all right for labor, and liked nothing so well.

Then, he had a vast good-nature, which made him tolerant and accessible to all; fair-minded, leaning to the claim of the petitioner; affable, and not sensible to the affliction which the innumerable visits paid to him when President would have brought to any one else. And how this good-nature became a noble humanity, in many a tragic case which the events of the war brought to him, every one will remember; and with what increasing tenderness he dealt when a whole race was thrown on his compassion. The poor negro said of him, on an impressive occasion, "Massa Linkum am eberywhere."

Then his broad good-humor, running easily into jocular talk, in which he delighted and in which he excelled, was a rich gift to this wise man. It enabled him to keep his secret; to meet every kind of man and every rank in society; to take off the edge of the severest decisions; to mask his own purpose and sound his companion; and to catch with true instinct the temper of every company he addressed. And, more than all, it is to a man of severe labor, in anxious and exhausting crises, the natural restorative, good as sleep, and is the protection of the overdriven brain against rancor and insanity.

He is the author of a multitude of good sayings, so disguised as pleasantries that it is certain they had no reputation at first but as jests; and only later, by the very acceptance and adoption they find in the mouths of millions, turn out to be the wisdom of the hour. I am sure if this man had ruled in a period of less facility of printing, he would have become mythological in a very few years, like Æsop or Pilpay, or one of the Seven Wise Masters, by his fables and proverbs. But the weight and penetration of many passages in his letters, messages and speeches, hidden now by the very closeness of their application to the moment, are destined hereafter to wide fame. What pregnant definitions; what unerring common sense; what foresight; and, on great occasion, what lofty, and more than national, what humane tone! His brief speech at Gettysburg will not easily be surpassed by words on any recorded occasion. This, and one other American speech, that of John Brown to the court that tried him, and a part of Kossuth's speech at Birmingham, can only be compared with each other, and with no fourth.

His occupying the chair of State was a triumph of the good sense of mankind, and of the public conscience. This middle-class country had got a middle-class President, at last. Yes, in manners and sympathies, but not in powers, for his powers were superior. This man grew according to the need. His mind mastered the problem of the day; and, as the problem grew, so did his comprehension of it. Rarely was man so fitted to the event. In the midst of fears and jealousies, in the Babel of counsels and parties, this man wrought incessantly with all his might and all his honesty, laboring to find what the people wanted, and how to obtain that. It cannot be said there is any exaggeration of his worth. If ever a man was fairly tested, he was. There was no lack of resistance, nor of slander, nor of ridicule. The times have allowed no state secrets; the nation has been in such ferment, such multitudes had to be trusted, that no secret could be kept. Every door was ajar, and we know all that befell.

Then, what an occasion was the whirlwind of the war. Here was place for no holiday magistrate, no fair-weather sailor; the new pilot was hurried to the helm in a tornado. In four years, — four years of battle-days, — his endurance, his fertility of resources, his magnanimity, were sorely tried and never found wanting. There, by his courage, his justice, his even temper, his fertile counsel, his humanity, he stood a heroic figure in the centre of a heroic epoch. He is the true history of the American people in his time. Step by step he walked before them; slow with their slowness, quickening his march by theirs, the true representative of this continent; an entirely public man; father of his country, the pulse of twenty millions throbbing in his heart, the thought of their minds articulated by his tongue.

Adam Smith remarks that the axe, which in Houbraken's portraits of British kings and worthies is engraved under those who have suffered at the block, adds a certain lofty charm to the picture. And who does not see, even in this tragedy so recent, how fast the terror and ruin of the massacre are already burning into glory around the victim? Far happier this fate than to have lived to be wished away; to have watched the decay of his own faculties; to have seen, — perhaps even he, — the proverbial ingratitude of statesmen; to have seen mean men preferred. Had he not lived long enough to keep the greatest promise that ever man made to his fellow-men, — the practical abolition of slavery? He had seen Tennessee, Missouri and Maryland emancipate their slaves. He had seen Savannah, Charleston and Richmond surrendered; had seen the main army of the rebellion lay down its arms. He had conquered the public opinion of Canada, England and France. Only Washington can compare with him in fortune.

And what if it should turn out, in the unfolding of the web, that he had reached the term; that this heroic deliverer could no longer serve us; that the rebellion had touched its natural conclusion, and what remained to be done required new and uncommitted hands, — a new spirit born out of the ashes of the war; and that Heaven, wishing to show the world a completed benefactor, shall make him serve his country even more by his death than by his life? Nations, like kings, are not good by facility and complaisance. "The kindness of kings consists in justice and strength." Easy good-nature has been the dangerous foible of the Republic, and it was necessary that its enemies should outrage it, and drive us to unwonted firmness, to secure the salvation of this country in the next ages.

The ancients believed in a serene and beautiful Genius which ruled in the affairs of nations; which, with a slow but stern justice, carried forward the fortunes of certain chosen houses, weeding out single offenders or offending families, and securing at last the firm prosperity of the favorites of Heaven. It was too narrow a view of the Eternal Nemesis. There is a serene Providence which rules the fate of nations, which makes little account of time, little of one generation or race, makes no account of disasters, conquers alike by what is called defeat or by what is called victory, thrusts aside enemy and obstruction, crushes everything immoral as inhuman, and obtains the ultimate triumph of the best race by the sacrifice of everything which resists the moral laws of the world. It makes its own instruments, creates the man for the time, trains him in poverty, inspires his genius, and arms him for his task. It has given every race its own talent, and ordains that only that race which combines perfectly with the virtues of all shall endure.

CONTRIBUTIONS OF THE WEST TO AMERICAN DEMOCRACY [1]

FREDERICK J. TURNER

POLITICAL thought in the period of the French Revolution
tended to treat democracy as an absolute system applicable
to all times and to all peoples, a system that was to be created by the act of the people themselves on philosophical
principles. Ever since that era there has been an inclination
on the part of writers on democracy to emphasize the ana-
lytical and theoretical treatment to the neglect of the underlying factors of historical development.

If, however, we consider the underlying conditions and
forces that create the democratic type of government, and
at times contradict the external forms to which the name
democracy is applied, we shall find that under this name
there have appeared a multitude of political types radically
unlike in fact. The careful student of history must, therefore, seek the explanation of the forms and changes of political institutions in the social and economic forces that determine them. To know that at any one time a Nation may
be called a democracy, an aristocracy, or a monarchy, is not
so important as to know what are the social and economic
tendencies of the State. These are the vital forces that
work beneath the surface and dominate the external form.
It is to changes in the economic and social life of a people
that we must look for the forces that ultimately create and
modify organs of political action. For the time, adaptation

[1] *Atlantic Monthly*, January, 1903. Reprinted through the generous
permission of the author and of the Atlantic Monthly Company.

of political structure may be incomplete or concealed. Old organs will be utilized to express new forces, and so gradual and subtle will be the change that it may hardly be recognized. The pseudo-democracies under the Medici at Florence and under Augustus at Rome are familiar examples of this type. Or again, if the political structure be rigid, incapable of responding to the changes demanded by growth, the expansive forces of social and economic transformation may rend it in some catastrophe like that of the French Revolution. In all these changes both conscious ideals and unconscious social reorganization are at work.

These facts are familiar to the student, and yet it is doubtful if they have been fully considered in connection with American democracy. For a century at least, in conventional expression, Americans have referred to a "glorious Constitution" in explaining the stability and prosperity of their democracy. We have believed as a Nation that other peoples had only to will our democratic institutions in order to repeat our own career.

In dealing with Western contributions to democracy, it is essential that the considerations which have just been mentioned shall be kept in mind. Whatever these contributions may have been, we find ourselves at the present time in an era of such profound economic and social transformation as to raise the question of the effect of these changes upon the democratic institutions of the United States. Within a decade four marked changes have occurred in our National development: taken together they constitute a revolution.

First, there is the exhaustion of the supply of free land and the closing of the movement of Western advance as an effective factor in American development. The Superintendent of the Census in 1890 announced the fact that a frontier line could no longer be traced in the population map of the United States, which decade after decade had represented the advance of settlement. The continent has been crossed. The first rough conquest of the wilderness is accomplished, and that great supply of free lands which year after year has served to reinforce the democratic influences in the United States is exhausted. It is true that vast tracts of Government land are still untaken, but they constitute the arid region, only a small fraction of them capable of conquest, and then only by the application of capital and combined effort. The free lands that made the American pioneer have gone.

In the second place, contemporaneously with this there has been such a concentration of capital in the control of fundamental industries as to make a new epoch in the economic development of the United States. The iron, the coal, and the cattle of the country have all fallen under the domination of a few great corporations with allied interests, and by the rapid combination of the important railroad systems and steamship lines, in concert with these same forces, even the breadstuffs and the manufactures of the Nation are to some degree controlled in a similar way. This is largely the work of the last decade. The development of the greatest iron mines of Lake Superior occurred in the early nineties, and in the same decade came the combination by which the coal and the coke of the country, and the transportation systems that connect them with the iron mines, have been brought under a few concentrated managements. Side by side with this concentration of capital has gone the combination of labor in the same vast industries. The one is in a certain sense the concomitant of the other, but the movement acquires an additional significance because of the fact that during the past fifteen years the labor class has been so recruited by a tide of foreign immigration that this class is now largely made up of persons of foreign parentage, and the lines of cleavage which begin to appear in this country between capital and labor have been accentuated by distinctions of nationality.

A third phenomenon connected with the two just mentioned is the expansion of the United States politically and commercially into lands beyond the seas. A cycle of American development has been completed. Up to the close of the War of 1812, this country was involved in the fortunes of the European state system. The first quarter of a century of our National existence was almost a continual struggle to prevent ourselves being drawn into the European wars. At the close of that era of conflict, the United States set its face toward the West. It began the settlement and improvement of the vast interior of the country. Here was the field of our colonization, here the field of our political activity. This process being completed, it is not strange that we find the United States again involved in world-politics. The revolution that occurred four years ago, when the United States struck down that ancient nation under whose auspices the New World was discovered, is hardly yet more than dimly understood. The insular wreckage of the Spanish War, Porto Rico and the Philippines, with the problems presented by the Hawaiian Islands, Cuba, the Isthmian Canal, and China, all are indications of the new direction of the ship of State, and while we thus turn our attention overseas, our concentrated industrial strength has given us a striking power against the commerce of Europe that is already producing consternation in the Old World. Having completed the conquest of the wilderness, and having consolidated our interests, we are beginning to consider the relations of democracy and empire.

And fourth, the political parties of the United States now tend to divide on issues that involve the question of Socialism. The rise of the Populist Party in the last decade, and the acceptance of so many of its principles by the Democratic Party under the leadership of Mr. Bryan, show in striking manner the birth of new political ideas, the reformation of the lines of political conflict.

It is doubtful if in any ten years of American history more significant factors in our growth have revealed themselves. The struggle of the pioneer farmers to subdue the arid lands of the Great Plains in the eighties was followed by the official announcement of the extinction of the frontier line in 1890. The dramatic outcome of the Chicago Convention of 1896 marked the rise into power of the representatives of Populistic change. Two years later came the battle of Manila, which broke down the old isolation of the Nation, and started it on a path the goal of which no man can foretell; and finally, but two years ago came that concentration of which the billion and a half dollar steel trust and the union of the Northern continental railways are stupendous examples. Is it not obvious, then, that the student who seeks for the explanation of democracy in the social and economic forces that underlie political forms must make inquiry into the conditions that have produced our democratic institutions, if he would estimate the effects of these vast changes? As a contribution to this inquiry, let us now turn to an examination of the part that the West has played in shaping our democracy.

From the beginning of the settlement of America, the frontier regions have exercised a steady influence toward democracy. In Virginia, to take an example, it can be traced as early as the period of Bacon's Rebellion, a hundred years before our Declaration of Independence. The small landholders, seeing that their powers were steadily passing into the hands of the wealthy planters who controlled Church and State and lands, rose in revolt. A generation later, in the governorship of Alexander Spotswood, we find a contest between the frontier settlers and the property-holding classes of the coast. The democracy with which Spotswood had to struggle, and of which he so bitterly complained, was a democracy made up of small landholders, of the newer immigrants, and of indented servants, who at the expiration of their time of servitude passed into the interior to take up lands and engage in pioneer farming. The "War of the Regulation" just on the eve of the American Revolution shows the steady persistence of this struggle between the classes of the interior and those of the coast. The Declaration of Grievances which the back counties of the Carolinas then drew up against the aristocracy that dominated the politics of those colonies exhibits the contest between the democracy of the frontier and the established classes who apportioned the Legislature in such fashion as to secure effective control of government. Indeed, in a period before the outbreak of the American Revolution, one can trace a distinct belt of democratic territory extending from the back country of New England down through western New York, Pennsylvania, and the South. In each colony this region was in conflict with the dominant classes of the coast. It constituted a quasi-revolutionary area before the days of the Revolution, and it formed the basis on which the Democratic Party was afterwards established. It was, therefore, in the West, as it was in the period before the Declaration of Independence, that the struggle for democratic development first revealed itself, and in that area the essential ideas of American democracy had already appeared. Through the period of the Revolution and of the Confederation a similar contest can be noted. On the frontier of New England, along the western border of Pennsylvania, Virginia, and the Carolinas, and in the communities beyond the Alleghany Mountains, there arose a demand of the frontier settlers for independent statehood based on democratic provisions. There is a strain of fierceness in their energetic petitions demanding self-government under the theory that every people have the right to establish their own political institutions in an area which they have won from the wilderness. Those revolutionary principles based on natural rights, for which the seaboard colonies were contending, were taken up with frontier energy in an attempt to apply them to the lands of the West. No one can read their petitions denouncing the control exercised by the wealthy landholders of the coast, appealing to the record of their conquest of the wilderness, and demanding the possession of the lands for which they have fought the Indians, and which they had reduced by their axe to civilization, without recognizing in these frontier communities the cradle of a belligerent Western democracy. "A fool can sometimes put on his coat better than a wise man can do it for him," — such is the philosophy of its petitions. In this period also came the contests of the interior agricultural portion of New England against the coastwise merchants and property-holders, of which Shays' Rebellion is the best known, although by no means an isolated instance. By the time of the constitutional convention, this struggle for democracy had effected a fairly well-defined division into parties. Although these parties did not at first recognize their interstate connections, there were similar issues on which they split in almost all the States. The demands for an issue of paper money, the stay of execution against debtors, and the relief against excessive taxation were found in every colony in the interior agricultural regions. The rise of this significant movement awakened the apprehensions of the men of means, and in the debates over the basis of suffrage for the House of Representatives in the Constitutional Convention of 1787 leaders of the conservative party did not hesitate to demand that safeguards to property should be furnished the coast against the interior. The outcome of the debate left the question of suffrage for the House of Representatives dependent upon the policy of the separate States. This was in effect imposing a property qualification throughout the Nation as a whole, and it was only as the interior of the country developed that these restrictions gradually gave way in the direction of manhood suffrage.

All of these scattered democratic tendencies Jefferson combined, in the period of Washington's Presidency, into the Democratic-Republican Party. Jefferson was the first prophet of American democracy, and when we analyze the essential features of his gospel, it is clear that the Western influence was the dominant element. Jefferson himself was born in the frontier region of Virginia, on the edge of the Blue Ridge, in the middle of the eighteenth century. His father was a pioneer. Jefferson's *Notes on Virginia* reveal clearly his conception that democracy should have an agricultural basis, and that manufacturing development and city life were dangerous to the purity of the body politic. Simplicity and economy in government, the right of revolution, the freedom of the individual, the belief that those who win the vacant lands are entitled to shape their own government in their own way, these are all parts of the platform of political principles to which he gave his adhesion, and they are all elements eminently characteristic of the Western democracy into which he was born. In the period of the Revolution he had brought in a series of measures which tended to throw the power of Virginia into the hands of the settlers in the interior rather than of the coastwise aristocracy. The repeal of the laws of entail and primogeniture would have destroyed the great estates on which the planting aristocracy based its power. The abolition of the Established Church would still further have diminished the influence of the coastwise party in favor of the dissenting sects of the interior. His scheme of general public education

reflected the same tendency, and his demand for the abolition of slavery was characteristic of a representative of the
West rather than of the old-time aristocracy of the coast.
His sympathy with the Western expansion culminated in
the Louisiana Purchase. In a word, the tendencies of Jefferson's legislation were to replace the dominance of the planting aristocracy by the dominance of the interior class, which
had sought in vain to achieve its liberties in the period of
Bacon's Rebellion.

Nevertheless, Thomas Jefferson was the John the Baptist
of democracy, not its Moses. Only with the slow setting of
the tide of settlement farther and farther toward the interior did the democratic influence grow strong enough to
take actual possession of the Government. The period from
1800 to 1820 saw a steady increase in these tendencies. The
established classes in New England and the South began to
take alarm. Perhaps no better illustration of the apprehensions of the old-time Federal conservative can be given than
these utterances of President Dwight, of Yale College, in the
book of travels which he published in that period: —

The class of pioneers cannot live in regular society. They are
too idle, too talkative, too passionate, too prodigal, and too shift-
less to acquire either property or character. They are impatient
of the restraints of law, religion, and morality, and grumble about
the taxes by which the Rulers, Ministers, and Schoolmasters are
supported. . . . After exposing the injustice of the community in
neglecting to invest persons of such superior merit in public offices,
in many an eloquent harangue uttered by many a kitchen fire, in
every blacksmith shop, in every corner of the streets, and finding
all their efforts vain, they become at length discouraged, and under
the pressure of poverty, the fear of the gaol, and consciousness of
public contempt, leave their native places and betake themselves
to the wilderness.

Such was a conservative's impression of that pioneer
movement of New England colonists who had spread up the

valley of the Connecticut into New Hampshire, Vermont, and western New York in the period of which he wrote, and who afterwards went on to possess the Northwest. New England Federalism looked with a shudder at the democratic ideas of those who refused to recognize the established order. But in that period there came into the Union a sisterhood of frontier States — Ohio, Indiana, Illinois, Missouri — with provisions for the franchise that brought in complete democracy. Even the newly created States of the Southwest showed the same tendency. The wind of democracy blew so strongly from the West, that even in the older States of New York, Massachusetts, Connecticut, and Virginia, conventions were called, which liberalized their constitutions by strengthening the democratic basis of the State. In the same time the labor population of the cities began to assert its power and its determination to share in government. Of this frontier democracy which now took possession of the Nation, Andrew Jackson was the very personification. He was born in the backwoods of the Carolinas in the midst of the turbulent democracy that preceded the Revolution, and he grew up in the frontier State of Tennessee. In the midst of this region of personal feuds and frontier ideals of law, he quickly rose to leadership. The appearance of this frontiersman on the floor of Congress was an omen full of significance. He reached Philadelphia at the close of Washington's Administration, having ridden on horseback nearly eight hundred miles to his destination. Gallatin, himself a Western man, describes Jackson as he entered the halls of Congress: "A tall, lank, uncouth-looking personage, with long locks of hair hanging over his face and a cue down his back tied in an eel-skin; his dress singular; his manners those of a rough backwoodsman." And Jefferson testified: "When I was President of the Senate he was a Senator, and he could never speak on account of the rashness of his feelings. I have seen

him attempt it repeatedly and as often choke with rage."
At last the frontier in the person of its typical man had found
a place in the Government. This six-foot backwoodsman,
with blue eyes that could blaze on occasion, this choleric,
impetuous, self-willed Scotch-Irish leader of men, this expert duelist, and ready fighter, this embodiment of the tenacious, vehement, personal West, was in politics to stay. The
frontier democracy of that time had the instincts of the
clansman in the days of Scotch border warfare. Vehement
and tenacious as the democracy was, strenuously as each
man contended with his neighbor for the spoils of the new
country that opened before them, they all had respect for
the man who best expressed their aspirations and their ideas.
Every community had its hero. In the War of 1812 and the
subsequent Indian fighting Jackson made good his claim, not
only to the loyalty of the people of Tennessee, but of the
whole West, and even of the Nation. He had the essential
traits of the Kentucky and Tennessee frontier. It was a
frontier free from the influence of European ideas and institutions. The men of the "Western World" turned their
backs upon the Atlantic Ocean, and with a grim energy
and self-reliance began to build up a society free from the
dominance of ancient forms.

The Westerner defended himself and resented governmental restrictions. The duel and the blood-feud found con-
genial soil in Kentucky and Tennessee. The idea of the
personality of law was often dominant over the organized
machinery of justice. That method was best which was
most direct and effective. The backwoodsman was intolerant of men who split hairs, or scrupled over the method of
reaching the right. In a word, the unchecked development
of the individual was the significant product of this frontier
democracy. It sought rather to express itself by choosing
a man of the people, than by the formation of elaborate

governmental institutions. It was because Andrew Jackson personified these essential Western traits that in his Presidency he became the idol and the mouthpiece of the popular will. In his assaults upon the Bank as an engine of aristocracy, and in his denunciation of Nullification, he went directly to his object with the ruthless energy of a frontiersman. For formal law and the subleties of State sovereignty he had the contempt of a backwoodsman. Nor is it without significance that this typical man of the new democracy will always be associated with the triumph of the spoils system in National politics. To the new democracy of the West, office was an opportunity to exercise natural rights as an equal citizen of the community. Rotation in office served not simply to allow the successful man to punish his enemies and reward his friends, but it also furnished the training in the actual conduct of political affairs which every American claimed as his birthright. Only in a primitive democracy of the type of the United States in 1830 could such a system have existed without the ruin of the State. National government in that period was no complex and nicely adjusted machine, and the evils of the system were long in making themselves fully apparent.

The triumph of Andrew Jackson marked the end of an old era of trained statesmen for the Presidency. With him began the era of the popular hero. Even Martin Van Buren, whom we think of in connection with the East, was born in a log house under conditions that were not unlike parts of the older West. Harrison was the hero of the Northwest, as Jackson had been of the Southwest. Polk was a typical Tennesseean, eager to expand the Nation, and Zachary Taylor was what Webster called a "frontier colonel." During the period that followed Jackson, power passed from the region of Kentucky and Tennessee to the border of the Mississippi. The natural democratic tendencies that had earlier shown themselves in the Gulf States were destroyed, however, by the spread of cotton culture, and the development of great plantations in that region. What had been typical of the democracy of the Revolutionary frontier and of the frontier of Andrew Jackson was now to be seen in the States between the Ohio and the Mississippi. As Andrew Jackson is the typical democrat of the former region, so Abraham Lincoln is the very embodiment of the pioneer period of the old Northwest. Indeed, he is the embodiment of the democracy of the West. How can one speak of him except in the words of Lowell's great "Commemoration Ode": —

> "For him her Old-World moulds aside she threw,
> And, choosing sweet clay from the breast
>   Of the unexhausted West,
> With stuff untainted shaped a hero new,
> Wise, steadfast in the strength of God, and true.
>
> .   .   .   .
>
> His was no lonely mountain-peak of mind,
> Thrusting to thin air o'er our cloudy bars,
> A sea-mark now, now lost in vapors blind;
> Broad prairie rather, genial, level-lined,
> Fruitful and friendly for all human kind,
> Yet also nigh to heaven and loved of loftiest stars.
>   Nothing of Europe here,
>
> .   .   .   .
>
> New birth of our new soil, the first American."

The pioneer life from which Lincoln came differed in important respects from the frontier democracy typified by Andrew Jackson. Jackson's democracy was contentious, individualistic, and it sought the ideal of local self-government and expansion. Lincoln represents rather the pioneer folk who entered the forest of the great Northwest to chop out a home, to build up their fortunes in the midst of a continually ascending industrial movement. In the democracy of the Southwest, industrial development and city life were only minor factors, but to the democracy of the Northwest they were its very life. To widen the area of this clearing, to contend with one another for the mastery of the industrial resources of the rich provinces, to struggle for a place in the ascending movement of society, to transmit to one's offspring the chance for education, for industrial betterment, for the rise in life which the hardships of the pioneer existence denied to the pioneer himself, these were some of the ideals of the region to which Lincoln came. The men were commonwealth builders, industry builders. Whereas the type of hero in the Southwest was militant, in the Northwest he was industrial. It was in the midst of these "plain people," as he loved to call them, that Lincoln grew to manhood. As Emerson says: "He is the true history of the American people in his time." The years of his early life were the years when the democracy of the Northwest came into struggle with the institution of slavery that threatened to forbid the expansion of the democratic pioneer life in the West. In President Eliot's essay on *Five American Contributions to Civilization*, he instances as one of the supreme tests of American democracy its attitude upon the question of slavery. But if democracy chose wisely and worked effectively toward the solution of this problem, it must be remembered that Western democracy took the lead. The rail-splitter himself became the Nation's President in that fierce time of struggle, and the armies of the woodsmen and pioneer farmers recruited in the old Northwest, under the leadership of Sherman and Grant, made free the Father of the Waters, marched through Georgia, and helped to force the struggle to a conclusion at Appomattox. The free pioneer democracy struck down slaveholding aristocracy on its march to the West.

The last chapter in the development of Western democracy is the one that deals with its conquest over the vast spaces of the new West. At each new stage of Western development, the people have had to grapple with larger areas, with vaster combinations. The little colony of Massachusetts veterans that settled at Marietta received a land grant as large as the State of Rhode Island. The band of Connecticut pioneers that followed Moses Cleaveland to the Connecticut Reserve occupied a region as large as the parent State. The area which settlers of New England stock occupied on the prairies of northern Illinois surpassed the combined area of Massachusetts, Connecticut, and Rhode Island. Men who had become accustomed to the narrow valleys and the little towns of the East found themselves out on the boundless spaces of the West dealing with units of such magnitude as dwarfed their former experience. The Great Lakes, the prairies, the Great Plains, the Rocky Mountains, the Mississippi and the Missouri, furnished new standards of measurement for the achievement of this industrial democracy. Individualism began to give way to coöperation and to governmental activity. Even in the earlier days of the democratic conquest of the wilderness, demands had been made upon the Government for support in internal improvements, but this new West showed a growing tendency to call to its assistance the powerful arm of National authority. In the period since the Civil War, the vast public domain has been donated to the individual farmer, to States for education, to railroads for the construction of transportation lines. Moreover, with the advent of democracy in the last fifteen years upon the Great Plains, new physical conditions have presented themselves which have accelerated the social tendency of Western democracy. The pioneer farmer of the days of Lincoln could place his family on the flatboat, strike into the wilderness, cut out his clearing, and with little or no capital go on to the achievement of industrial independence. Even the homesteader on the Western prairies found it impossible to work out a similar independent destiny, although the factor of transportation made a

serious and increasing impediment to the free working-out
of his individual career. But when the arid lands and the
mineral resources of the Far West were reached, no conquest was possible by the old individual pioneer methods.
Here expensive irrigation works must be constructed, co-
operative activity was demanded in utilization of the water-
supply, capital beyond the reach of the small farmer was
required. In a word, the physiographic province itself decreed that the destiny of this new frontier should be social
rather than individual.

Magnitude of social achievement is the watchword of the
democracy since the Civil War. From petty towns built in the
marshes, cities arose whose greatness and industrial power
are the wonder of our time. The conditions were ideal for
the production of captains of industry. The old democratic
admiration for the self-made man, its old deference to the
rights of competitive individual development, together with
the stupendous natural resources that opened to the conquest
of the keenest and the strongest, gave such conditions of
mobility as enabled the development of the vast industries
which in our own decade have marked the West.

Thus, in brief, have been outlined the large phases of the
development of Western democracy in the different areas
which it has conquered. There has been a steady development of the industrial ideal, and a steady increase of the
social tendency, in this later movement of Western democracy. While the individualism of the frontier, so prominent
in the earliest days of the Western advance, has been preserved as an ideal, more and more these individuals struggling each with the other, dealing with vaster and vaster
areas, with larger and larger problems, have found it necessary to combine under the leadership of the strongest. This
is the explanation of the rise of those preëminent captains of
industry whose genius has concentrated capital to control

the fundamental resources of the Nation. If now in the way of recapitulation, we try to pick out from the influences that have gone to the making of Western democracy the factors which constitute the net result of this movement, we shall have to mention at least the following: —

Most important of all has been the fact that an area of free land has continually lain on the western border of the settled area of the United States. Whenever social conditions tended to crystallize in the East, whenever capital tended to press upon labor or political restraints to impede the freedom of the mass, there was this gate of escape to the free conditions of the frontier. These free lands promoted individualism, economic equality, freedom to rise, democracy. Men would not accept inferior wages and a permanent position of social subordination when this promised land of freedom and equality was theirs for the taking. Who would rest content under oppressive legislative conditions when with a slight effort he might reach a land wherein to become a co-worker in the building of free cities and free States on the lines of his own ideal? In a word, then, free lands meant free opportunities. Their existence has differentiated the American democracy from the democracies which have preceded it, because ever, as democracy in the East took the form of a highly specialized and complicated industrial society, in the West it kept in touch with primitive conditions, and by action and reaction these two forces have shaped our history.

In the next place, these free lands and this treasury of industrial resources have existed over such vast spaces that they have demanded of democracy increasing spaciousness of design and power of execution. Western democracy is contrasted with the democracy of all other times in the largeness of the tasks to which it has set its hand, and in the vast achievements which it has wrought out in the control of nature and of politics. Upon the region of the Middle West alone could be set down all of the great countries of central Europe, — France, Germany, Italy, and Austro-Hungary, — and there would still be a liberal margin. It would be difficult to over-emphasize the importance of this training upon democracy. Never before in the history of the world has a democracy existed on so vast an area and handled things in the gross with such success, with such largeness of design, and such grasp upon the means of execution. In short, democracy has learned in the West of the United States how to deal with the problem of magnitude. The old historic democracies were but little States with primitive economic conditions.

But the very task of dealing with vast resources, over vast areas, under the conditions of free competition furnished by the West, has produced the rise of those captains of industry whose success in consolidating economic power now raises the question as to whether democracy under such conditions can survive. For the old military type of Western leaders like George Rogers Clark, Andrew Jackson, and William Henry Harrison have been substituted such industrial leaders as James Hill, John D. Rockefeller, and Andrew Carnegie.

The question is imperative, then, What ideals persist from this democratic experience of the West; and have they acquired sufficient momentum to sustain themselves under conditions so radically unlike those in the days of their origin? In other words, the question put at the beginning of this discussion becomes pertinent. Under the forms of the American democracy is there in reality evolving such a concentration of economic and social power in the hands of a comparatively few men as may make political democracy an appearance rather than a reality? The free lands are gone. The material forces that gave vitality to Western democracy are passing away. It is to the realm of the spirit, to the domain of ideals and legislation, that we must look for Western influence upon democracy in our own days.

Western democracy has been from the time of its birth idealistic. The very fact of the wilderness appealed to men as a fair, blank page on which to write a new chapter in the story of man's struggle for a higher type of society. The Western wilds, from the Alleghanies to the Pacific, constituted the richest free gift that was ever spread out before civilized man. To the peasant and artisan of the Old World, bound by the chains of social class, as old as custom and as inevitable as fate, the West offered an exit into a free life and greater well-being among the bounties of nature, into the midst of resources that demanded manly exertion, and that gave in return the chance for indefinite ascent in the scale of social advance. "To each she offered gifts after his will." Never again can such an opportunity come to the sons of men. It was unique, and the thing is so near us, so much a part of our lives, that we do not even yet comprehend its vast significance. The existence of this land of opportunity has made America the goal of idealists from the days of the Pilgrim Fathers. With all the materialism of the pioneer movements, this idealistic conception of the vacant lands as an opportunity for a new order of things is unmistakably present. Kipling's "Song of the English" has given it expression: —

"We were dreamers, dreaming greatly, in the man-stifled town;
We yearned beyond the sky-line where the strange roads go down.
Came the Whisper, came the Vision, came the Power with the Need,
Till the Soul that is not man's soul was lent us to lead.
As the deer breaks — as the steer breaks — from the herd where they
    graze,
In the faith of little children we went on our ways.
Then the wood failed — then the food failed — then the last water dried —
In the faith of little children we lay down and died.

"On the sand-drift — on the veldt-side — in the fern-scrub we lay,
That our sons might follow after by the bones on the way.
Follow after — follow after! We have watered the root
And the bud has come to blossom that ripens for fruit!
Follow after — we are waiting by the trails that we lost
For the sound of many footsteps, for the tread of a host.

"Follow after — follow after — for the harvest is sown:
By the bones about the wayside ye shall come to your own!"

This was the vision that called to Roger Williams, — that "prophetic soul ravished of truth disembodied," "unable to enter into treaty with its environment," and forced to seek the wilderness. "Oh, how sweet," wrote William Penn, from his forest refuge, "is the quiet of these parts, freed from the troubles and perplexities of woeful Europe." And here he projected what he called his "Holy Experiment in Government."

If the later West offers few such striking illustrations of the relation of the wilderness to idealistic schemes, and if some of the designs were fantastic and abortive, none the less the influence is a fact. Hardly a Western State but has been the Mecca of some sect or band of social reformers, anxious to put into practice their ideals, in vacant land, far removed from the checks of a settled form of social organization. Consider the Dunkards, the Icarians, the Fourierists, the Mormons, and similar idealists who sought our Western wilds. But the idealistic influence is not limited to the dreamers' conception of a new State. It gave to the pioneer farmer and city builder a restless energy, a quick capacity for judgment and action, a belief in liberty, freedom of opportunity, and a resistance to the domination of class which infused a vitality and power into the individual atoms of this democratic mass. Even as he dwelt among the stumps of his newly cut clearing, the pioneer had the creative vision of a new order of society. In imagination he pushed back the forest boundary to the confines of a mighty Commonwealth; he willed that log cabins should become the lofty buildings of great cities. He decreed that his children should enter into a heritage of education, comfort, and social welfare, and for this ideal he bore the scars of the wilderness. Possessed with this idea he ennobled his task and laid deep foundations for a democratic State. Nor was this idealism by any means limited to the American pioneer.

To the old native democratic stock has been added a vast army of recruits from the Old World. There are in the Middle West alone four million persons of German parentage out of a total of seven millions in the country. Over a million persons of Scandinavian parentage live in the same region. This immigration culminated in the early eighties, and although there have been fluctuations since, it long continued a most extraordinary phenomenon. The democracy of the newer West is deeply affected by the ideals brought by these immigrants from the Old World. To them America was not simply a new home; it was a land of opportunity, of freedom, of democracy. It meant to them, as to the American pioneer that preceded them, the opportunity to destroy the bonds of social caste that bound them in their older home, to hew out for themselves in a new country a destiny proportioned to the powers that God had given them, a chance to place their families under better conditions and to win a larger life than the life that they had left behind. He who believes that even the hordes of recent immigrants from southern Italy are drawn to these shores by nothing more than a dull and blind materialism has not penetrated into the heart of the problem. The idealism and expectation of these children of the Old World, the hopes which they have formed for a newer and freer life across the seas, are almost pathetic when one considers how far they are from the possibility of fruition. He who would take stock of American

CONTRIBUTIONS OF WEST TO DEMOCRACY 93

democracy must not forget the accumulation of human purposes and ideals which immigration has added to the American populace.

In this connection it must also be remembered that these democratic ideals have existed at each stage of the advance of the frontier, and have left behind them deep and enduring effects on the thinking of the whole country. Long after the frontier period of a particular region of the United States has passed away, the conception of society, the ideals and aspirations which it produced, persist in the minds of the people. So recent has been the transition of the greater portion of the United States from frontier conditions to conditions of settled life, that we are, over the larger portion of the United States, hardly a generation removed from the primitive conditions of the West. If, indeed, we ourselves were not pioneers, our fathers were, and the inherited ways of looking at things, the fundamental assumptions of the American people, have all been shaped by this experience of democracy on its westward march. This experience has been wrought into the very warp and woof of American thought. Even those masters of industry and capital who have risen to power by the conquest of Western resources came from the midst of this society and still profess its principles. John D. Rockefeller was born on a New York farm, and began his career as a young business man in St. Louis. Marcus Hanna was a Cleveland grocer's clerk at the age of twenty. Claus Spreckles, the sugar king, came from Germany as a steerage passenger to the United States in 1848. Marshal Field was a farmer boy in Conway, Massachusetts, until he left to grow up with the young Chicago. Andrew Carnegie came as a ten-year-old boy from Scotland to Pittsburgh, then a distinctively Western town. He built up his fortunes through successive grades until he became the dominating factor in the great iron industries, and paved the way for that colossal achievement, the Steel Trust. Whatever may be the tendencies of this corporation, there can be little doubt of the democratic ideals of Mr. Carnegie himself. With lavish hand he has strewn millions through the United States for the promotion of libraries. The effect of this library movement in perpetuating the democracy that comes from an intelligent and self-respecting people can hardly be measured. In his *Triumphant Democracy*, published in 1886, Mr. Carnegie, the ironmaster, said, in reference to the mineral wealth of the United States: "Thank God, these treasures are in the hands of an intelligent people, the Democracy, to be used for the general good of the masses, and not made the spoils of monarchs, courts, and aristocracy, to be turned to the base and selfish ends of a privileged hereditary class." It would be hard to find a more rigorous assertion of democratic doctrine than the celebrated utterance, attributed to the same man, that he should feel it a disgrace to die rich.

In enumerating the services of American democracy, President Eliot includes the corporation as one of its achievements, declaring that "freedom of incorporation, though no longer exclusively a democratic agency, has given a strong support to democratic institutions." In one sense this is doubtless true, since the corporation has been one of the means by which small properties can be aggregated into an effective working body. Socialistic writers have long been fond of pointing out also that these various concentrations pave the way for and make possible social control. From this point of view it is possible that the masters of industry may prove to be not so much an incipient aristocracy as the pathfinders for democracy in reducing the industrial world to systematic consolidation suited to democratic control. The great geniuses that have built up the modern industrial concentration were trained in the midst of democratic society. They were the product of these democratic conditions. Freedom to rise was the very condition of their existence. Whether they will be followed by successors who will adopt the exploitation of the masses, and who will be capable of retaining under efficient control these vast resources, is one of the questions which we shall have to face.

This, at least, is clear: American democracy is fundamentally the outcome of the experiences of the American people in dealing with the West. Western democracy through the whole of its earlier period tended to the production of a society of which the most distinctive fact was the freedom of the individual to rise under conditions of social mobility, and whose ambition was the liberty and well-being of the masses. This conception has vitalized all American democracy, and has brought it into sharp contrasts with the democracies of history, and with those modern efforts of Europe to create an artificial democratic order by legislation. The problem of the United States is not to create democracy, but to conserve democratic institutions and ideals. In the later period of its development, Western democracy has been gaining experience in the problem of social control. It has steadily enlarged the sphere of its action and the instruments for its perpetuation. By its system of public schools, from the grades to the graduate work of the great universities, the West has created a larger single body of intelligent plain people than can be found elsewhere in the world. Its educational forces are more democratic than those of the East, and counting the common schools and colleges together, the Middle West alone has twice as many students as New England and the Middle States combined. Its political tendencies, whether we consider Democracy, Populism, or Republicanism, are distinctly in the direction of greater social control and the conservation of the old democratic ideals. To these ideals the West as a whole adheres with even a passionate determination. If, in working out its mastery of the resources of the interior, it has produced a type of industrial leader so powerful as to be the wonder of the world, nevertheless, it is still to be determined whether these men constitute a menace to democratic institutions, or the most efficient factor for adjusting democratic control to the new conditions.

Whatever shall be the outcome of the rush of this huge industrial modern United States to its place among the nations of the earth, the formation of its Western democracy will always remain one of the wonderful chapters in the history of the human race. Into this vast shaggy continent of ours poured the first feeble tide of European settlement. European men, institutions, and ideas were lodged in the American wilderness, and this great American West took them to her bosom, taught them a new way of looking upon the destiny of the common man, trained them in adaptation to the conditions of the New World, to the creation of new institutions to meet new needs, and ever as society on her eastern border grew to resemble the Old World in its social forms and its industry, ever, as it began to lose faith in the ideals of democracy, she opened new provinces, and dowered new democracies in her most distant domains with her material treasures and with the ennobling influence that the fierce love of freedom, the strength that came from hewing out a home, making a school and a church, and creating a higher future for his family, furnished to the pioneer. She gave to the world such types as the farmer Thomas Jefferson, with his Declaration of Independence, his statute for religious toleration, and his purchase of Louisiana. She gave us Andrew Jackson, that fierce Tennessee spirit who broke down the traditions of conservative rule, swept away the privacies and privileges of officialdom, and, like a Gothic leader, opened the temple of the Nation to the populace.

She gave us Abraham Lincoln, whose gaunt frontier form and gnarled, massive hand told of the conflict with the forest, whose grasp of the axe-handle of the pioneer was no firmer than his grasp of the helm of the ship of State as it breasted the seas of civil war. She gave us the tragedy of the pioneer farmer as he marched daringly on to the conquest of the arid lands, and met his first defeat by forces too strong to be dealt with under the old conditions. She has furnished to this new democracy her stores of mineral wealth, that dwarf those of the Old World, and her provinces that in themselves are vaster and more productive than most of the nations of Europe. Out of her bounty has come a Nation whose industrial competition alarms the Old World, and the masters of whose resources wield wealth and power vaster than the wealth and power of kings. Best of all, the West gave, not only to the American, but to the unhappy and oppressed of all lands, a vision of hope, and assurance that the world held a place where were to be found high faith in man and the will and power to furnish him the opportunity to grow to the full measure of his own capacity. Great and powerful as are the new sons of her loins, the Republic is greater than they. The paths of the pioneer have widened into broad highways. The forest clearing has expanded into affluent Commonwealths. Let us see to it that the ideals of the pioneer in his log cabin shall enlarge into the spiritual life of a democracy where civic power shall dominate and utilize individual achievement for the common good.

THE PRESENT CRISIS [1]

JAMES RUSSELL LOWELL

WHEN a deed is done for Freedom, through the broad earth's
    aching breast
Runs a thrill of joy prophetic, trembling on from east to
    west,
And the slave, where'er he cowers, feels the soul within him
    climb
To the awful verge of manhood, as the energy sublime
Of a century bursts full-blossomed on the thorny stem of
    Time.

Through the walls of hut and palace shoots the instantane-
    ous throe,
When the travail of the Ages wrings earth's systems to and
    fro;
At the birth of each new Era, with a recognizing start,
Nation wildly looks at nation, standing with mute lips apart,
And glad Truth's yet mightier man-child leaps beneath the
    Future's heart.

So the Evil's triumph sendeth, with a terror and a chill,
Under continent to continent, the sense of coming ill,
And the slave, where'er he cowers, feels his sympathies with
    God
In hot tear-drops ebbing earthward, to be drunk up by the
    sod,
Till a corpse crawls round unburied, delving in the nobler
    clod.

[1] Written in December, 1844.

For mankind are one in spirit, and an instinct bears along,
Round the earth's electric circle, the swift flash of right or
    wrong;
Whether conscious or unconscious, yet Humanity's vast
    frame
Through its ocean-sundered fibres feels the gush of joy or
    shame; —
In the gain or loss of one race all the rest have equal claim.

Once to every man and nation comes the moment to decide,
In the strife of Truth with Falsehood, for the good or evil
    side;
Some great cause, God's new Messiah, offering each the
    bloom or blight,
Parts the goats upon the left hand, and the sheep upon the
    right,
And the choice goes by forever 'twixt that darkness and that
    light.

Hast thou chosen, O my people, on whose party thou shalt
    stand,
Ere the Doom from its worn sandals shakes the dust against
    our land?
Though the cause of Evil prosper, yet 't is Truth alone is
    strong,
And, albeit she wander outcast now, I see around her throng
Troops of beautiful, tall angels, to enshield her from all
    wrong.

Backward look across the ages and the beacon-moments
    see,
That, like peaks of some sunk continent, jut through
    Oblivion's sea;
Not an ear in court or market for the low foreboding cry

Of those Crises, God's stern winnowers, from whose feet
    earth's chaff must fly;
Never shows the choice momentous till the judgment hath
    passed by.

Careless seems the great Avenger; history's pages but re-
    cord
One death-grapple in the darkness 'twixt old systems and
    the Word;
Truth forever on the scaffold, Wrong forever on the
    throne, —
Yet that scaffold sways the future, and, behind the dim un-
    known,
Standeth God within the shadow, keeping watch above his
    own.

We see dimly in the Present what is small and what is
    great,
Slow of faith how weak an arm may turn the iron helm of
    fate,
But the soul is still oracular; amid the market's din,
List the ominous stern whisper from the Delphic cave
    within, —
"They enslave their children's children who make compro-
    mise with sin."

Slavery, the earth-born Cyclops, fellest of the giant brood,
Sons of brutish Force and Darkness, who have drenched
    the earth with blood,
Famished in his self-made desert, blinded by our purer
    day,
Gropes in yet unblasted regions for his miserable prey; —
Shall we guide his gory fingers where our helpless children
    play?

Then to side with Truth is noble when we share her wretched
    crust,
Ere her cause bring fame and profit, and 't is prosperous to
    be just;
Then it is the brave man chooses, while the coward stands
    aside,
Doubting in his abject spirit, till his Lord is crucified,
And the multitude make virtue of the faith they had denied.

Count me o'er earth's chosen heroes, — they were souls that
    stood alone,
While the men they agonized for hurled the contumelious
    stone,
Stood serene, and down the future saw the golden beam in-
    cline
To the side of perfect justice, mastered by their faith
    divine,
By one man's plain truth to manhood and to God's supreme
    design.

By the light of burning heretics Christ's bleeding feet I
    track,
Toiling up new Calvaries ever with the cross that turns not
    back,
And these mounts of anguish number how each generation
    learned
One new word of that grand *Credo* which in prophet-hearts
    hath burned
Since the first man stood God-conquered with his face to
    heaven upturned.

For Humanity sweeps onward: where to-day the martyr
    stands,
On the morrow crouches Judas with the silver in his hands;

Far in front the cross stands ready and the crackling fagots
　　burn,
While the hooting mob of yesterday in silent awe return
To glean up the scattered ashes into History's golden urn.

'T is as easy to be heroes as to sit the idle slaves
Of a legendary virtue carved upon our fathers' graves,
Worshippers of light ancestral make the present light a
　　crime; —
Was the Mayflower launched by cowards, steered by men
　　behind their time?
Turn those tracks toward Past or Future, that make Ply-
　　mouth Rock sublime?

They were men of present valor, stalwart old iconoclasts,
Unconvinced by axe or gibbet that all virtue was the
　　Past's;
But we make their truth our falsehood, thinking that hath
　　made us free,
Hoarding it in mouldy parchments, while our tender spirits
　　flee
The rude grasp of that great Impulse which drove them
　　across the sea.

They have rights who dare maintain them; we are traitors
　　to our sires,
Smothering in their holy ashes Freedom's new-lit altar-
　　fires;
Shall we make their creed our jailer? Shall we, in our haste
　　to slay,
From the tombs of the old prophets steal the funeral lamps
　　away
To light up the martyr-fagots round the prophets of to-
　　day?

New occasions teach new duties; Time makes ancient good
    uncouth;
They must upward still, and onward, who would keep
    abreast of Truth;
Lo, before us gleam her camp-fires! we ourselves must Pil-
    grims be,
Launch our Mayflower, and steer boldly through the desper-
    ate winter sea,
Nor attempt the Future's portal with the Past's blood-
    rusted key.

RISE, O DAYS, FROM YOUR FATHOMLESS DEEPS [1]

WALT WHITMAN

1

RISE, O days, from your fathomless deeps, till you loftier, fiercer sweep!

Long for my soul, hungering gymnastic, I devour'd what the earth gave me;

Long I roam'd the woods of the north — long I watch'd Niagara pouring;

I travel'd the prairies over, and slept on their breast — I cross'd the Nevadas, I cross'd the plateaus;

I ascended the towering rocks along the Pacific, I sail'd out to sea;

I sail'd through the storm, I was refresh'd by the storm;

I watch'd with joy the threatening maws of the waves;

I mark'd the white combs where they career'd so high, curling over;

I heard the wind piping, I saw the black clouds;

Saw from below what arose and mounted (O superb! O wild as my heart, and powerful!),

Heard the continuous thunder, as it bellow'd after the lightning;

Noted the slender and jagged threads of lightning, as sudden and fast amid the din they chased each other across the sky;

[1] Included in "Drum-Taps," *Leaves of Grass*. Reprinted through the generous permission of Mr. Horace Traubel.

— These, and such as these, I, elate, saw — saw with won-
    der, yet pensive and masterful;
All the menacing might of the globe uprisen around me;.
Yet there with my soul I fed — I fed content, supercilious.

2

'T was well, O soul! 't was a good preparation you gave me!
Now we advance our latent and ampler hunger to fill;
Now we go forth to receive what the earth and the sea never
    gave us;
Not through the mighty woods we go, but through the
    mightier cities;
Something for us is pouring now, more than Niagara pouring;
Torrents of men (sources and rills of the Northwest, are
    you indeed inexhaustible?),
What, to pavements and homesteads here — what were
    those storms of the mountains and sea?
What, to passions I witness around me to-day? Was the
    sea risen?
Was the wind piping the pipe of death under the black
    clouds?
Lo! from deeps more unfathomable, something more deadly
    and savage;
Manhattan, rising, advancing with menacing front —
    Cincinnati, Chicago, unchain'd;
— What was that swell I saw on the ocean? behold what
    comes here!
How it climbs with daring feet and hands! how it dashes!
How the true thunder bellows after the lightning! how
    bright the flashes of lightning!
How DEMOCRACY, with desperate vengeful part strides
    on, shown through the dark by those flashes of light-
    ning!

(Yet a mournful wail and low sob I fancied I heard through
        the dark,
In a lull of the deafening confusion.)

3

Thunder on! stride on, Democracy! strike with vengeful
        stroke!
And do you rise higher than ever yet, O days, O cities!
Crash heavier, heavier yet, O storms! you have done me good;
My soul, prepared in the mountains, absorbs your immortal
        strong nutriment;
— Long had I walk'd my cities, my country roads, through
        farms, only half-satisfied;
One doubt, nauseous, undulating like a snake, crawl'd on
        the ground before me,
Continually preceding my steps, turning upon me oft, iron-
        ically hissing low;
— The cities I loved so well, I abandon'd and left — I sped
        to the certainties suitable to me;
Hungering, hungering, hungering, for primal energies, and
        Nature's dauntlessness.
I refresh'd myself with it only, I could relish it only;
I waited the bursting forth of the pent fire — on the water
        and air I waited long;
— But now I no longer wait — I am fully satisfied — I am
        glutted;
I have witness'd the true lightning — I have witness'd my
        cities electric;
I have lived to behold man burst forth, and warlike America
        rise;
Hence I will seek no more the food of the northern solitary
        wilds,
No more the mountains roam, or sail the stormy sea.

THOU MOTHER WITH THY EQUAL BROOD[1]

WALT WHITMAN

1

Thou Mother with thy equal brood,
Thou varied chain of different States, yet one identity only,
A special song before I go I'd sing o'er all the rest,
For thee, the future.

I'd sow a seed for thee of endless Nationality,
I'd fashion thy ensemble including body and soul,
I'd show away ahead thy real Union, and how it may be
    accomplish'd.

The paths to the house I seek to make,
But leave to those to come the house itself.

Belief I sing and preparation;
As Life and Nature are not great with reference to the pres-
    ent only,
But greater still from what is yet to come,
Out of that formula for thee I sing.

2

As a strong bird on pinions free,
Joyous, the amplest spaces heavenward cleaving,
Such be the thought I'd think of thee America,
Such be the recitative I'd bring for thee.

[1] Reprinted from *Leaves of Grass* through the generous permission of
Mr. Horace Traubel.

The conceits of the poets of other lands I'd bring thee
    not,
Nor the compliments that have served their turn so long,
Nor rhyme, nor the classics, nor perfume of foreign court or
    indoor library;
But an odor I'd bring as from forests of pine in Maine, or
    breath of an Illinois prairie,
With open airs of Virginia or Georgia or Tennessee, or from
    Texas uplands, or Florida's glades,
Or the Saguenay's black stream, or the wide blue spread of
    Huron,
With presentment of Yellowstone's scenes, or Yosemite,
And murmuring under, pervading all, I'd bring the rustling
    sea-sound,
That endlessly sounds from the two Great Seas of the world.

And for thy subtler sense subtler refrains dread Mother,
Preludes of intellect tallying these and thee, mind-formulas
    fitted for thee, real and sane and large as these and
    thee,
Thou! mounting higher, diving deeper than we knew, thou
    transcendental Union!
By thee fact to be justified, blended with thought,
Thought of man justified, blended with God,
Through they idea, lo, the immortal reality!
Through thy reality, lo, the immortal idea!

3

Brain of the New World, what a task is thine,
To formulate the Modern — out of the peerless grandeur of
    the modern,
Out of thyself, comprising science, to recast poems, churches,
    art,

(Recast, may-be discard them, end them — may-be their
    work is done, who knows?)
By vision, hand, conception, on the background of the
    mighty past, the dead,
To limn with absolute faith the mighty living present.

And yet thou living present brain, heir of the dead, the Old
    World brain,
Thou that lay folded like an unborn babe within its folds so
    long,
Thou carefully prepared by it so long — haply thou but un-
    foldest it, only maturest it,
It to eventuate in thee — the essence of the by-gone time
    contain'd in thee,
Its poems, churches, arts, unwitting to themselves, destined
    with reference to thee;
Thou but the apples, long, long, long a-growing,
The fruit of all the Old repining to-day in thee.

4

Sail, sail thy best, ship of Democracy,
Of value is thy freight, 't is not the Present only,
The Past is also stored in thee,
Thou holdest not the venture of thyself alone, not of the
    Western continent alone,
Earth's *résumé* entire floats on thy keel O ship, is steadied by
    thy spars,
With thee Time voyages in trust, the antecedent nations
    sink or swim with thee.
With all their ancient struggles, martyrs, heroes, epics, wars,
    thou bear'st the other continents,
Theirs, theirs as much as thine, the destination-port tri-
    umphant;

Steer then with good strong hand and wary eye O helms-
  man, thou carriest great companions,
Venerable priestly Asia sails this day with thee,
And royal feudal Europe sails with thee.

5

Beautiful world of new superber birth that rises to my eyes,
Like a limitless golden cloud filling the western sky,
Emblem of general maternity lifted above all,
Sacred shape of the bearer of daughters and sons,
Out of thy teeming womb thy giant babes in ceaseless pro-
  cession issuing,
Acceding from such gestation, taking and giving continual
  strength and life,
World of the real — world of the twain in one,
World of the soul, born by the world of the real alone, led
  to identity, body, by it alone,
Yet in beginning only, incalculable masses of composite
  precious materials,
By history's cycles forwarded, by every nation, language,
  hither sent,
Ready, collected here, a freer, vast, electric world, to be
  constructed here,
(The true New World, the world of orbic science, morals,
  literatures to come,)
Thou wonder world yet undefined, unform'd, neither do I
  define thee,
How can I pierce the impenetrable blank of the future?
I feel thy ominous greatness evil as well as good,
I watch thee advancing, absorbing the present, transcend-
  ing the past,
I see thy light lighting, and thy shadow shadowing, as if the
  entire globe,

But I do not undertake to define thee, hardly to compre-
    hend thee,
I but thee name, thee prophesy, as now,
I merely thee ejaculate!

Thee in thy future,
Thee in thy only permanent life, career, thy own unloosen'd
    mind, thy soaring spirit,
Thee as another equally needed sun, radiant, ablaze, swift-
    moving, fructifying all,
Thee risen in potent cheerfulness and joy, in endless great
    hilarity,
Scattering for good the cloud that hung so long, that
    weigh'd so long upon the mind of man,
The doubt, suspicion, dread, of gradual, certain decadence
    of man;
Thee in thy larger, saner brood of female, male — thee in thy
    athletes, moral, spiritual, South, North, West, East,
(To thy immortal breasts, Mother of All, thy every daugh-
    ter, son, endear'd alike, forever equal,)
Thee in thy own musicians, singers, artists, unborn yet, but
    certain,
Thee in thy moral wealth and civilization, (until which thy
    proudest material civilization must remain in vain,)
Thee in thy all-supplying, all-enclosing worship — thee in
    no single bible, saviour, merely,
Thy saviours countless, latent within thyself, thy bibles
    incessant within thyself, equal to any, divine as any,
(Thy soaring course thee formulating, not in thy two great
    wars, nor in thy century's visible growth,
But far more in these leaves and chants, thy chants, great
    Mother!)
Thee in an education grown of thee, in teachers, studies,
    students, born of thee,

Thee in thy democratic fêtes en-masse, thy high original
   festivals, operas, lecturers, preachers,
Thee in thy ultimata, (the preparations only now completed,
   the edifice on sure foundations tied,)
Thee in thy pinnacles, intellect, thought, thy topmost rational joys, thy love and godlike aspiration,
In thy resplendent coming literati, thy full-lung'd orators,
   thy sacerdotal bards, kosmic savans,
These! these in thee, (certain to come,) to-day I prophesy.

6

Land tolerating all, accepting all, not for the good alone, all
   good for thee,
Land in the realms of God to be a realm unto thyself,
Under the rule of God to be a rule unto thyself.

(Lo, where arise three peerless stars,
To be thy natal stars my country, Ensemble, Evolution,
   Freedom,
Set in the sky of Law.)

Land of unprecedented faith, God's faith,
Thy soil, thy very subsoil, all upheav'd,
The general inner earth so long, so sedulously draped over,
   now hence for what it is boldly laid bare,
Open'd by thee to heaven's light for benefit or bale.

Not for success alone,
Not to fair-sail unintermitted always,
The storm shall dash thy face, the murk of war and worse
   than war shall cover thee all over,
(Wert capable of war, its tug and trials? be capable of peace,
   its trials,

For the tug and moral strain of nations came at last in pros-
    perous peace, not war;)
In many a smiling mask death shall appro⸝ ⸝ beguiling
    thee, thou in disease shalt swelter,
The livid cancer spread its hideous claws, clinging upon thy
    breasts, seeking to strike thee deep within,
Consumption of the worst, moral consumption, shall rouge
    thy face with hectic,
But thou shalt face thy fortunes, thy diseases, and surmount
    them all,
Whatever they are to-day and whatever through time they
    may be,
They each and all shall lift and pass away and cease from
    thee,
While thou, Time's spirals rounding, out of thyself, thyself
    still extricating, fusing,
Equable, natural, mystical Union thou, (the mortal with
    immortal blent,)
Shalt soar toward the fulfilment of the future, the spirit of
    the body and the mind,
The soul, its destinies.

The soul, its destinies, the real real,
(Purport of all these apparitions of the real;)
In thee America, the soul, its destinies,
Thou globe of globes! thou wonder nebulous!
By many a throe of heat and cold convuls'd, (by these thy-
    self solidifying,)
Thou mental, moral orb — thou New, indeed new, Spiritual
    World!
The Present holds thee not — for such vast growth as thine,
For such unparallel'd flight as thine, such brood as thine,
The FUTURE only holds thee and can hold thee.

A CHARTER OF DEMOCRACY [1]

THEODORE ROOSEVELT

Mr. President, and Members of the Ohio Constitutional
Convention: —

I am profoundly sensible of the honor you have done me
in asking me to address you. You are engaged in the fundamental work of self-government; you are engaged in framing a Constitution under and in accordance with which the
people are to get and to do justice and absolutely to rule
themselves. No representative body can have a higher task.
To carry it through successfully there is need to combine
practical common sense of the most hard-headed kind with
a spirit of lofty idealism. Without idealism your work will
be but a sordid makeshift; and without the hard-headed
common sense the idealism will be either wasted or worse
than wasted.

I shall not try to speak to you of matters of detail. Each
of our Commonwealths has its own local needs, local customs, and habits of thought, different from those of other
Commonwealths; and each must therefore apply in its own
fashion the great principles of our political life. But these
principles themselves are in their essence applicable everywhere, and of some of them I shall speak to you. I cannot
touch upon them all; the subject is too vast and the time too
limited; if any one of you cares to know my views of these
matters which I do not to-day discuss, I will gladly send him

[1] An address delivered before the Ohio Constitutional Convention,
Columbus, Ohio, February, 1912. Reprinted (entire, save for the passage
on the recall of judges) through the generous permission of the author and
of the Outlook Publishing Company.

a copy of the speeches I made in 1910, which I think cover most of the ground.

I believe in pure democracy. With Lincoln, I hold that "this country, with its institutions, belongs to the people who inhabit it. Whenever they shall grow weary of the existing Government, they can exercise their constitutional right of amending it." We Progressives believe that the people have the right, the power, and the duty to protect themselves and their own welfare; that human rights are supreme over all other rights; that wealth should be the servant, not the master, of the people. We believe that unless representative government does absolutely represent the people it is not representative government at all. We test the worth of all men and all measures by asking how they contribute to the welfare of the men, women, and children of whom this Nation is composed. We are engaged in one of the great battles of the age-long contest waged against privilege on behalf of the common welfare. We hold it a prime duty of the people to free our Government from the control of money in politics. For this purpose we advocate, not as ends in themselves, but as weapons in the hands of the people, all governmental devices which will make the representatives of the people more easily and certainly responsible to the people's will.

This country, as Lincoln said, belongs to the people. So do the natural resources which make it rich. They supply the basis of our prosperity now and hereafter. In preserving them, which is a National duty, we must not forget that monopoly is based on the control of natural resources and natural advantages, and that it will help the people little to conserve our natural wealth unless the benefits which it can yield are secured to the people. Let us remember, also, that Conservation does not stop with the natural resources, but that the principle of making the best use of all we have requires with equal or greater insistence that we shall stop the

waste of human life in industry and prevent the waste of
human welfare which flows from the unfair use of concentrated power and wealth in the hands of men whose
eagerness for profit blinds them to the cost of what they do.
We have no higher duty than to promote the efficiency of
the individual. There is no surer road to the efficiency of
the Nation.

I am emphatically a believer in constitutionalism, and
because of this fact I no less emphatically protest against
any theory that would make of the Constitution a means of
thwarting instead of securing the absolute right of the people
to rule themselves and to provide for their own social and
industrial well-being. All constitutions, those of the States
no less than that of the Nation, are designed, and must be
interpreted and administered, so as to fit human rights. Lincoln so interpreted and administered the National Constitution. Buchanan attempted the reverse, attempted to fit
human rights to, and limit them by, the Constitution. It
was Buchanan who treated the courts as a fetish, who pro-
tested against and condemned all criticism of the judges for
unjust and unrighteous decisions, and upheld the Constitution as an instrument for the protection of privilege and of
vested wrong. It was Lincoln who appealed to the people
against the judges when the judges went wrong, who ad-
vocated and secured what was practically the recall of
the Dred Scott decision, and who treated the Constitution as a living force for righteousness. We stand for applying the Constitution to the issues of to-day as Lincoln
applied it to the issues of his day; Lincoln, mind you, and
not Buchanan, was the real upholder and preserver of the
Constitution, for the true progressive, the progressive of
the Lincoln stamp, is the only true constitutionalist, the
only real conservative. The object of every American Constitution worth calling such must be what it is set forth

to be in the preamble to the National Constitution, "to establish justice," that is, to secure justice as between man and man by means of genuine popular self-government. If the Constitution is successfully invoked to nullify the effort to remedy injustice, it is proof positive either that the Constitution needs immediate amendment or else that it is being wrongfully and improperly construed. I therefore very earnestly ask you clearly to provide in this Constitution means which will enable the people readily to amend it if at any point it works injustice, and also means which will permit the people themselves by popular vote, after due deliberation and discussion, but finally and without appeal, to settle what the proper construction of any constitutional point is. It is often said that ours is a government of checks and balances. But this should only mean that these checks and balances obtain as among the several different kinds of representatives of the people — judicial, executive, and legislative — to whom the people have delegated certain portions of their power. It does not mean that the people have parted with their power or cannot resume it. The "division of powers" is merely the division among the representatives of the powers delegated to them; the term must not be held to mean that the people have divided their power with their delegates. The power is the people's, and only the people's. It is right and proper that provision should be made rendering it necessary for the people to take ample time to make up their minds on any point; but there should also be complete provision to have their decision put into immediate and living effect when it has thus been deliberately and definitely reached.

I hold it to be the duty of every public servant, and of every man who in public or in private life holds a position of leadership in thought or action, to endeavor honestly and fearlessly to guide his fellow-countrymen to right decisions;

but I emphatically dissent from the view that it is either wise or necessary to try to devise methods which under the Constitution will automatically prevent the people from deciding for themselves what governmental action they deem just and proper. It is impossible to invent constitutional devices which will prevent the popular will from being effective for wrong without also preventing it from being effective for right. The only safe course to follow in this great American democracy is to provide for making the popular judgment really effective. When this is done, then it is our duty to see that the people, having the full power, realize their heavy responsibility for exercising that power aright. But it is a false constitutionalism, a false statesmanship, to endeavor by the exercise of a perverted ingenuity to seem to give the people full power and at the same time to trick them out of it. Yet that is precisely what is done in every case where the State permits its representatives, whether on the bench or in the Legislature or in executive office, to declare that it has not the power to right grave social wrongs, or that any of the officers created by the people, and rightfully the servants of the people, can set themselves up to be the masters of the people. Constitution-makers should make it clear beyond shadow of doubt that the people in their legislative capacity have the power to enact into law any measure they deem necessary for the betterment of social and industrial conditions. The wisdom of framing any particular law of this kind is a proper subject of debate; but the power of the people to enact the law should not be subject to debate. To hold the contrary view is to be false to the cause of the people, to the cause of American Democracy.

Lincoln, with his clear vision, his ingrained sense of justice, and his spirit of kindly friendliness to all, forecast our present struggle and saw the way out. What he said

should be pondered by capitalist and workingman alike.
He spoke as follows (I condense): —

I hold that while man exists it is his duty to improve not only
his condition but to assist in ameliorating mankind. Labor is prior
to and independent of capital. Labor is the superior of capital, and
deserves much the higher consideration. Capital has its rights,
which are as worthy of protection as any other rights. Nor should
this lead to a war upon property. Property is the fruit of labor.
Property is desirable, is a positive good in the world. Let not him
who is houseless pull down the house of another, but let him work
diligently and build one for himself, thus by example assuring that
his own shall be safe from violence when built.

This last sentence characteristically shows Lincoln's
homely, kindly common sense. His is the attitude that we
ought to take. He showed the proper sense of proportion in
his relative estimates of capital and labor, of human rights
and the rights of wealth. Above all, in what he thus said, as
on so many other occasions, he taught the indispensable
lesson of the need of wise kindliness and charity, of sanity
and moderation, in the dealings of men one with another.

We should discriminate between two purposes we have in
view. The first is the effort to provide what are themselves
the ends of good government; the second is the effort to
provide proper machinery for the achievement of these ends.

The ends of good government in our democracy are to
secure by genuine popular rule a high average of moral and
material well-being among our citizens. It has been well
said that in the past we have paid attention only to the
accumulation of prosperity, and that from henceforth we
must pay equal attention to the proper distribution of prosperity. This is true. The only prosperity worth having is
that which affects the mass of the people. We are bound to
strive for the fair distribution of prosperity. But it behooves
us to remember that there is no use in devising methods for

the proper distribution of prosperity unless the prosperity is there to distribute. I hold it to be our duty to see that the wage-worker, the small producer, the ordinary consumer, shall get their fair share of the benefit of business prosperity. But it either is or ought to be evident to every one that business has to prosper before anybody can get any benefit from it. Therefore I hold that he is the real progressive, that he is the genuine champion of the people, who endeavors to shape the policy alike of the Nation and of the several States so as to encourage legitimate and honest business at the same time that he wars against all crookedness and injustice and unfairness and tyranny in the business world (for of course we can only get business put on a basis of permanent prosperity when the element of injustice is taken out of it). This is the reason why I have for so many years insisted, as regards our National Government, that it is both futile and mischievous to endeavor to correct the evils of big business by an attempt to restore business conditions as they were in the middle of the last century, before railways and telegraphs had rendered larger business organizations both inevitable and desirable. The effort to restore such conditions, and to trust for justice solely to such proposed restoration, is as foolish as if we should attempt to arm our troops with the flintlocks of Washington's Continentals instead of with modern weapons of precision. Flintlock legislation, of the kind that seeks to prohibit all combinations, good or bad, is bound to fail, and the effort, in so far as it accomplishes anything at all, merely means that some of the worst combinations are not checked, and that honest business is checked. What is needed is, first, the recognition that modern business conditions have come to stay, in so far at least as these conditions mean that business must be done in larger units, and then the cool-headed and resolute determination to introduce an effective method of regulating big corporations so as to help legitimate business as an incident to thoroughly and completely safeguarding the interests of the people as a whole. We are a business people. The tillers of the soil, the wage-workers, the business men — these are the three big and vitally important divisions of our population. The welfare of each division is vitally necessary to the welfare of the people as a whole. The great mass of business is of course done by men whose business is either small or of moderate size. The middle-sized business men form an element of strength which is of literally incalculable value to the Nation. Taken as a class, they are among our best citizens. They have not been seekers after enormous fortunes; they have been moderately and justly prosperous, by reason of dealing fairly with their customers, competitors, and employees. They are satisfied with a legitimate profit that will pay their expenses of living and lay by something for those who come after, and the additional amount necessary for the betterment and improvement of their plant. The average business man of this type is, as a rule, a leading citizen of his community, foremost in everything that tells for its betterment, a man whom his neighbors look up to and respect; he is in no sense dangerous to his community, just because he is an integral part of his community, bone of its bone and flesh of its flesh. His life fibers are intertwined with the life fibers of his fellow-citizens. Yet nowadays many men of this kind, when they come to make necessary trade agreements with one another, find themselves in danger of becoming unwitting transgressors of the law, and are at a loss to know what the law forbids and what it permits. This is all wrong. There should be a fixed governmental policy, a policy which shall clearly define and punish wrongdoing, and shall give in advance full information to any man as to just what he can and just what he cannot legally and properly do. It is absurd and wicked to treat the deliberate lawbreaker as on an exact par with the man eager to obey the law, whose only desire is to find out from some competent governmental authority what the law is and then live up to it. It is absurd to endeavor to regulate business in the interest of the public by means of longdrawn lawsuits without any accompaniment of administrative control and regulation, and without any attempt to discriminate between the honest man who has succeeded in business because of rendering a service to the public and the dishonest man who has succeeded in business by cheating the public.

So much for the small business man and the middle-sized business man. Now for big business. It is imperative to exercise over big business a control and supervision which is unnecessary as regards small business. All business must be conducted under the law, and all business men, big or little, must act justly. But a wicked big interest is necessarily more dangerous to the community than a wicked little interest. "Big business" in the past has been responsible for much of the special privilege which must be unsparingly cut out of our National life. I do not believe in making mere size of and by itself criminal. The mere fact of size, however, does unquestionably carry the potentiality of such grave wrong-doing that there should be by law provision made for the strict supervision and regulation of these great industrial concerns doing an inter-State business, much as we now regulate the transportation agencies which are engaged in inter-State business. The anti-trust law does good in so far as it can be invoked against combinations which really are monopolies or which restrict production or which artificially raise prices. But in so far as its workings are uncertain, or as it threatens corporations which have not been guilty of anti-social conduct, it does harm. Moreover, it cannot by itself accomplish more than a trifling part of the governmental regulation of big business which is needed. The Nation and the States must coöperate in this matter. Among the States that have entered this field Wisconsin has taken a leading place. Following Senator La Follette, a number of practical workers and thinkers in Wisconsin have turned that State into an experimental laboratory of wise governmental action in aid of social and industrial justice. They have initiated the kind of progressive government which means not merely the preservation of true democracy, but the extension of the principle of true democracy into industrialism as well as into politics. One prime reason why the State has been so successful in this policy lies in the fact that it has done justice to corporations precisely as it has exacted justice from them. Its Public Utilities Commission in a recent report answered certain critics as follows: —

To be generous to the people of the State at the expense of justice to the carriers would be a species of official brigandage that ought to hold the perpetrators up to the execration of all honest men. Indeed, we have no idea that the people of Wisconsin have the remotest desire to deprive the railroads of the State of aught that, in equality and good conscience, belongs to them, and if any of them have, their wishes cannot be gratified by this Commission.

This is precisely the attitude we should take towards big business. It is the practical application of the principle of the square deal. Not only as a matter of justice, but in our own interest, we should scrupulously respect the rights of honest and decent business and should encourage it where its activities make, as they often do make, for the common good. It is for the advantage of all of us when business prospers. It is for the advantage of all of us to have the United States become the leading nation in international trade, and we should not deprive this Nation, we should not deprive this people, of the instruments best adapted to secure such international commercial supremacy. In other words, our demand is that big business give the people a square deal and that the people give a square deal to any man engaged in big business who honestly endeavors to do what is right and proper.

On the other hand, any corporation, big or little, which has gained its position by unfair methods and by interference with the rights of others, which has raised prices or limited output in improper fashion and been guilty of demoralizing and corrupt practices, should not only be broken up, but it should be made the business of some competent governmental body by constant supervision to see that it does not come together again, save under such strict control as to insure the community against all danger of a repetition of the bad conduct. The chief trouble with big business has arisen from the fact that big business has so often refused to abide by the principle of the square deal; the opposition which I personally have encountered from big business has in every case arisen not because I did not give a square deal but because I did.

All business into which the element of monopoly in any way or degree enters, and where it proves in practice impossible totally to eliminate this element of monopoly, should be carefully supervised, regulated, and controlled by governmental authority; and such control should be exercised by administrative, rather than by judicial, officers. No effort should be made to destroy a big corporation merely because it is big, merely because it has shown itself a peculiarly efficient business instrument. But we should not fear, if necessary, to bring the regulation of big corporations to the point of controlling conditions so that the wage-worker shall have a wage more than sufficient to cover the bare cost of living, and hours of labor not so excessive as to wreck his strength by the strain of unending toil and leave him unfit to do his duty as a good citizen in the community.

Where regulation by competition (which is, of course, preferable) proves insufficient, we should not shrink from bringing governmental regulation to the point of control of monopoly prices if it should ever become necessary to do so, just as in exceptional cases railway rates are now regulated.

In emphasizing the part of the administrative department in regulating combinations and checking absolute monopoly, I do not, of course, overlook the obvious fact that the legislature and the judiciary must do their part. The legislature should make it more clear exactly what methods are illegal, and then the judiciary will be in a better position to punish adequately and relentlessly those who insist on defying the clear legislative decrees. I do not believe any absolute private monopoly is justified, but if our great combinations are properly supervised, so that immoral practices are prevented, absolute monopoly will not come to pass, as the laws of competition and efficiency are against it.

The important thing is this: that, under such government recognition as we may give to that which is beneficent and wholesome in large business organizations, we shall be most vigilant never to allow them to crystallize into a condition which shall make private initiative difficult. It is of the utmost importance that in the future we shall keep the broad path of opportunity just as open and easy for our children as it was for our fathers during the period which has been the glory of America's industrial history — that it shall be not only possible but easy for an ambitious man, whose character has so impressed itself upon his neighbors that they are willing to give him capital and credit, to start in business for himself, and, if his superior efficiency deserves it, to triumph over the biggest organization that may happen to exist in his particular field. Whatever practices upon the part of large combinations may threaten to discourage such a man, or deny to him that which in the judgment of the community is a square deal, should be specifically defined by the statutes as crimes. And in every case the individual corporation officer responsible for such unfair dealing should be punished.

We grudge no man a fortune which represents his own power and sagacity exercised with entire regard to the welfare of his fellows. We have only praise for the business man whose business success comes as an incident to doing good work for his fellows. But we should so shape conditions that a fortune shall be obtained only in honorable fashion, in such fashion that its gaining represents benefit to the community.

In a word, then, our fundamental purpose must be to secure genuine equality of opportunity. No man should receive a dollar unless that dollar has been fairly earned. Every dollar received should represent a dollar's worth of service rendered. No watering of stocks should be permitted; and it can be prevented only by close governmental supervision of all stock issues, so as to prevent overcapitalization.

We stand for the rights of property, but we stand even more for the rights of man. We will protect the rights of the wealthy man, but we maintain that he holds his wealth subject to the general right of the community to regulate its business use as the public welfare requires.

We also maintain that the Nation and the several States have the right to regulate the terms and conditions of labor, which is the chief element of wealth, directly in the interest of the common good. It is our prime duty to shape the industrial and social forces so that they may tell for the material and moral upbuilding of the farmer and the wageworker, just as they should do in the case of the business man. You, framers of this Constitution, be careful so to frame it that under it the people shall leave themselves free to do whatever is necessary in order to help the farmers of the State to get for themselves and their wives and children not only the benefits of better farming but also those of better business methods and better conditions of life on the farm.

Moreover, shape your constitutional action so that the people will be able through their legislative bodies, or, failing that, by direct popular vote, to provide workmen's compensation acts, to regulate the hours of labor for children and for women, to provide for their safety while at work, and to prevent overwork or work under unhygienic or unsafe conditions. See to it that no restrictions are placed upon legislative powers that will prevent the enactment of laws under which your people can promote the general welfare, the common good. Thus only will the "general welfare" clause of our Constitution become a vital force for progress, instead of remaining a mere phrase. This also applies to the police powers of the Government. Make it perfectly clear that on every point of this kind it is your intention that the people shall decide for themselves how far the laws to achieve their purposes shall go, and that their decision shall be binding upon every citizen in the State, official or non-official, unless, of course, the Supreme Court of the Nation in any given case decides otherwise.

So much for the ends of government; and I have, of course, merely sketched in outline what the ends should be. Now for the machinery by which these ends are to be achieved; and here again remember I only sketch in outline and do not for a moment pretend to work out in detail the methods of achieving your purposes. Let me at the outset urge upon you to remember that, while machinery is important, it is easy to overestimate its importance; and, moreover, that each community has the absolute right to determine for itself what that machinery shall be, subject only to the fundamental law of the Nation as expressed in the Constitution of the United States. Massachusetts has the right to have

appointive judges who serve during good behavior, subject
to removal, not by impeachment, but by simple majority
vote of the two houses of the Legislature whenever the representatives of the people feel that the needs of the people
require such removal. New York has the right to have a long-
term elective judiciary. Ohio has the right to have a short-
term elective judiciary without the recall. California, Ore-
gon, and Arizona have each and every one of them the
right to have a short-term elective judiciary with the recall.
Personally, of the four systems I prefer the Massachusetts
one, if addition be made to it as I hereinafter indicate; but
that is merely my preference; and neither I nor any one else
within or without public life has the right to impose his
preference upon any community when the question is as to
how that community chooses to arrange for its executive,
legislative, or judicial functions. But as you have invited
me to address you here, I will give you my views as to the
kind of governmental machinery which at this time and
under existing social and industrial conditions it seems to me
that, as a people, we need.

In the first place, I believe in the short ballot. You cannot get good service from the public servant if you cannot
see him, and there is no more effective way of hiding him
than by mixing him up with a multitude of others so that
they are none of them important enough to catch the eye of
the average, workaday citizen. The crook in public life is
not ordinarily the man whom the people themselves elect
directly to a highly important and responsible position. The
type of boss who has made the name of politician odious
rarely himself runs for high elective office; and if he does and
is elected, the people have only themselves to blame. The
professional politician and the professional lobbyist thrive
most rankly under a system which provides a multitude of
elective officers, of such divided responsibility and of such

obscurity that the public knows, and can know, but little as
to their duties and the way they perform them. The people
have nothing whatever to fear from giving any public servant power so long as they retain their own power to hold
him accountable for his use of the power they have delegated
to him. You will get best service where you elect only a few
men, and where each man has his definite duties and responsibilities, and is obliged to work in the open, so that the
people know who he is and what he is doing, and have the
information that will enable them to hold him to account
for his stewardship.

I believe in providing for direct nominations by the people,
including therein direct preferential primaries for the election
of delegates to the National nominating conventions. Not
as a matter of theory, but as a matter of plain and proved
experience, we find that the convention system, while it often
records the popular will, is also often used by adroit politicians as a method of thwarting the popular will. In other
words, the existing machinery for nominations is cumbrous,
and is not designed to secure the real expression of the popular desire. Now as good citizens we are all of us willing to
acquiesce cheerfully in a nomination secured by the expression of a majority of the people, but we do not like to acquiesce in a nomination secured by adroit political management in defeating the wish of the majority of the people.

I believe in the election of United States Senators by direct
vote. Just as actual experience convinced our people that
Presidents should be elected (as they now are in practice,
although not in theory) by direct vote of the people instead
of by indirect vote through an untrammeled electoral college,
so actual experience has convinced us that Senators should
be elected by direct vote of the people instead of indirectly
through the various Legislatures.

I believe in the initiative and the referendum, which

should be used not to destroy representative government, but to correct it whenever it becomes misrepresentative. Here again I am concerned not with theories but with actual facts. If in any State the people are themselves satisfied with their present representative system, then it is of course their right to keep that system unchanged; and it is nobody's business but theirs. But in actual practice it has been found in very many States that legislative bodies have not been responsive to the popular will. Therefore I believe that the State should provide for the possibility of direct popular action in order to make good such legislative failure. The power to invoke such direct action, both by initiative and by referendum, should be provided in such fashion as to prevent its being wantonly or too frequently used. I do not believe that it should be made the easy or ordinary way of taking action. In the great majority of cases it is far better that action on legislative matters should be taken by those specially delegated to perform the task; in other words, that the work should be done by the experts chosen to perform it. But where the men thus delegated fail to perform their duty, then it should be in the power of the people themselves to perform the duty. In a recent speech Governor McGovern, of Wisconsin, has described the plan which has been there adopted. Under this plan the effort to obtain the law is first to be made through the Legislature, the bill being pushed as far as it will go; so that the details of the proposed measure may be threshed over in actual legislative debate. This gives opportunity to perfect it in form and invites public scrutiny. Then, if the Legislature fails to enact it, it can be enacted by the people on their own initiative, taken at least four months before election. Moreover, where possible, the question actually to be voted on by the people should be made as simple as possible. In short, I believe that the initiative and referendum should be used, not as substitutes for representative government, but as methods of making such government really representative. Action by the initiative or referendum ought not to be the normal way of legislation; but the power to take it should be provided in the Constitution, so that if the representatives fail truly to represent the people on some matter of sufficient importance to rouse popular interest, then the people shall have in their hands the facilities to make good the failure. And I urge you not to try to put constitutional fetters on the Legislature, as so many constitution-makers have recently done. Such action on your part would invite the courts to render nugatory every legislative act to better social conditions. Give the Legislature an entirely free hand; and then provide by the initiative and referendum that the people shall have power to reverse or supplement the work of the Legislature should it ever become necessary.

As to the recall, I do not believe that there is any great necessity for it as regards short-term elective officers. On abstract grounds I was originally inclined to be hostile to it. I know of one case where it was actually used with mischievous results. On the other hand, in three cases in municipalities on the Pacific Coast which have come to my knowledge it was used with excellent results. I believe it should be generally provided, but with such restrictions as will make it available only when there is a widespread and genuine public feeling among a majority of the voters.

There remains the question of the recall of judges. . . .

Now, gentlemen, in closing, and in thanking you for your courtesy, let me add one word. Keep clearly in view what are the fundamental ends of government. Remember that methods are merely the machinery by which these ends are to be achieved. I hope that not only you and I but all our people may ever remember that while good laws are necessary, while it is necessary to have the right kind of governmental machinery, yet that the all-important matter is to have the right kind of man behind the law. A State cannot rise without proper laws, but the best laws that the wit of man can devise will amount to nothing if the State does not contain the right kind of man, the right kind of woman. A good Constitution, and good laws under the Constitution, and fearless and upright officials to administer the laws — all these are necessary; but the prime requisite in our National life is, and must always be, the possession by the average citizen of the right kind of character. Our aim must be the moralization of the individual, of the government, of the people as a whole. We desire the moralization not only of political conditions but of industrial conditions, so that every force in the community, individual and collective, may be directed towards securing for the average man, and average woman, a higher and better and fuller life, in the things of the body no less than those of the mind and the soul.

THE AMERICAN SCHOLAR [1]

RALPH WALDO EMERSON

MR. PRESIDENT AND GENTLEMEN, — I greet you on the recommencement of our literary year. Our anniversary is one of hope, and, perhaps, not enough of labor. We do not meet for games of strength or skill, for the recitation of histories, tragedies, and odes, like the ancient Greeks; for parliaments of love and poesy, like the Troubadours; nor for the advancement of science, like our contemporaries in the British and European capitals. Thus far, our holiday has been simply a friendly sign of the survival of the love of letters amongst a people too busy to give to letters any more. As such it is precious as the sign of an indestructible instinct. Perhaps the time is already come when it ought to be, and will be, something else; when the sluggard intellect of this continent will look from under its iron lids and fill the postponed expectation of the world with something better than the exertions of mechanical skill. Our day of dependence, our long apprenticeship to the learning of other lands, draws to a close. The millions that around us are rushing into life, cannot always be fed on the sere remains of foreign harvests. Events, actions arise, that must be sung, that will sing themselves. Who can doubt that poetry will revive and lead in a new age, as the star in the constellation Harp, which now flames in our zenith, astronomers announce, shall one day be the pole-star for a thousand years?

---

[1] Our "Intellectual Declaration of Independence," as Oliver Wendell Holmes called it, was delivered before the Phi Beta Kappa Society, in Cambridge, Massachusetts, August 31, 1837.

In this hope I accept the topic which not only usage but the nature of our association seem to prescribe to this day, — the AMERICAN SCHOLAR. Year by year we come up hither to read one more chapter of his biography. Let us inquire what light new days and events have thrown on his char-)cter and his hopes.

It is one of those fables which out of an unknown an- tiquity convey an unlooked-for wisdom, that the gods, in the beginning, divided Man into men, that he might be more helpful to himself; just as the hand was divided into fingers, the better to answer its end.

The old fable covers a doctrine ever new and sublime; that there is One Man, — present to all particular men only partially, or through one faculty; and that you must take the whole society to find the whole man. Man is not a farmer, or a professor, or an engineer, but he is all. Man is priest, and scholar, and statesman, and producer, and soldier. In the *divided* or social state these functions are parcelled out to individuals, each of whom aims to do his stint of the joint work, whilst each other performs his. The fable implies that the individual, to possess himself, must sometimes return from his own labor to embrace all the other laborers. But, unfortunately, this original unit, this fountain of power, has been so distributed to multitudes, has been so minutely subdivided and peddled out, that it is spilled into drops, and cannot be gathered. The state of society is one in which the members have suffered amputation from the trunk, and strut about so many walking monsters, — a good finger, a neck, a stomach, an elbow, but never a man.

Man is thus metamorphosed into a thing, into many things. The planter, who is Man sent out into the field to gather food, is seldom cheered by any idea of the true dig- nity of his ministry. He sees his bushel and his cart, and nothing beyond, and sinks into the farmer, instead of Man on the farm. The tradesman scarcely ever gives an ideal worth to his work, but is ridden by the routine of his craft, and the soul is subject to dollars. The priest becomes a form; the attorney a statute-book; the mechanic a machine; the sailor a rope of the ship.

In this distribution of functions the scholar is the delegated intellect. In the right state he is *Man Thinking*. In the degenerate state, when the victim of society, he tends to become a mere thinker, or still worse, the parrot of other men's thinking.

In this view of him, as Man Thinking, the theory of his office is contained. Him Nature solicits with all her placid, all her monitory pictures; him the past instructs; him the future invites. Is not indeed every man a student, and do not all things exist for the student's behoof? And, finally, is not the true scholar the only true master? But the old oracle said, "All things have two handles: beware of the wrong one." In life, too often, the scholar errs with mankind and forfeits his privilege. Let us see him in his school, and consider him in reference to the main influences he receives.

I. The first in time and the first in importance of the influences upon the mind is that of nature. Every day, the sun; and, after sunset, Night and her stars. Ever the winds blow; ever the grass grows. Every day, men and women, conversing, beholding and beholden. The scholar is he of all men whom this spectacle most engages. He must settle its value in his mind. What is nature to him? There is never a beginning, there is never an end, to the inexplicable continuity of this web of God, but always circular power returning into itself. Therein it resembles his own spirit, whose beginning, whose ending, he never can find, — so entire, so boundless. Far too as her splendors shine, system on system shooting like rays, upward, downward, without centre, without circumference, — in the mass and in the particle, Nature hastens to render account of herself to the mind. Classification begins. To the young mind everything is individual, stands by itself. By and by, it finds how to join two things and see in them one nature; then three, then three thousand; and so, tyrannized over by its own unifying instinct, it goes on tying things together, diminishing anomalies, discovering roots running under ground whereby contrary and remote things cohere and flower out from one stem. It presently learns that since the dawn of history there has been a constant accumulation and classifying of facts. But what is classification but the perceiving that these objects are not chaotic, and are not foreign, but have a law which is also a law of the human mind? The astronomer discovers that geometry, a pure abstraction of the human mind, is the measure of planetary motion. The chemist finds proportions and intelligible method throughout matter; and science is nothing but the finding of analogy, identity, in the most remote parts. The ambitious soul sits down before each refractory fact; one after another reduces all strange constitutions, all new powers, to their class and their law, and goes on forever to animate the last fibre of organization, the outskirts of nature, by insight.

Thus to him, to this school-boy under the bending dome of day, is suggested that he and it proceed from one root; one is leaf and one is flower; relation, sympathy, stirring in every vein. And what is that root? Is not that the soul of his soul? A thought too bold; a dream too wild. Yet when this spiritual light shall have revealed the law of more earthly natures, — when he has learned to worship the soul, and to see that the natural philosophy that now is, is only the first gropings of its gigantic hand, he shall look forward to an ever expanding knowledge as to a becoming creator. He shall see that nature is the opposite of the soul, answering to it part for part. One is seal and one is print. Its beauty is the beauty of his own mind. Its laws are the laws of his own mind. Nature then becomes to him the measure of his attainments. So much of nature as he is ignorant of, so much of his own mind does he not yet possess. And, in fine, the ancient precept, "Know thyself," and the modern precept, "Study nature," become at last one maxim.

II. The next great influence into the spirit of the scholar is the mind of the Past, — in whatever form, whether of literature, of art, of institutions, that mind is inscribed. Books are the best type of the influence of the past, and perhaps we shall get at the truth, — learn the amount of this influence more conveniently, — by considering their value alone.

The theory of books is noble. The scholar of the first age received into him the world around; brooded thereon; gave it the new arrangement of his own mind, and uttered it again. It came into him life; it went out from him truth. It came to him short-lived actions; it went out from him immortal thoughts. It came to him business; it went from him poetry. It was dead fact; now, it is quick thought. It can stand, and it can go. It now endures, it now flies, it now inspires. Precisely in proportion to the depth of mind from which it issued, so high does it soar, so long does it sing.

Or, I might say, it depends on how far the process had gone, of transmuting life into truth. In proportion to the completeness of the distillation, so will the purity and imperishableness of the product be. But none is quite perfect. As no air-pump can by any means make a perfect vacuum, so neither can any artist entirely exclude the conventional, the local, the perishable from his book, or write a book of pure thought, that shall be as efficient, in all respects, to a remote posterity, as to contemporaries, or rather to the second age. Each age, it is found, must write its own books;

or rather, each generation for the next succeeding. The books of an older period will not fit this.

Yet hence arises a grave mischief. The sacredness which attaches to the act of creation, the act of thought, is transferred to the record. The poet chanting was felt to be a divine man: henceforth the chant is divine also. The writer was a just and wise spirit: henceforward it is settled the book is perfect; as love of the hero corrupts into worship of his statue. Instantly the book becomes noxious: the guide is a tyrant. The sluggish and perverted mind of the multitude, slow to open to the incursions of Reason, having once so opened, having once received this book, stands upon it, and makes an outcry if it is disparaged. Colleges are built on it. Books are written on it by thinkers, not by Man Thinking; by men of talent, that is, who start wrong, who set out from accepted dogmas, not from their own sight of principles. Meek young men grow up in libraries, believing it their duty to accept the views which Cicero, which Locke, which Bacon, have given; forgetful that Cicero, Locke, and Bacon were only young men in libraries when they wrote these books.

Hence, instead of Man Thinking, we have the bookworm. Hence the book-learned class, who value books, as such; not as related to nature and the human constitution, but as making a sort of Third Estate with the world and the soul. Hence the restorers of readings, the emendators, the bibliomaniacs of all degrees.

Books are the best of things, well used; abused, among the worst. What is the right use? What is the one end which all means go to effect? They are for nothing but to inspire. I had better never see a book than to be warped by its attraction clean out of my own orbit, and made a satellite instead of a system. The one thing in the world, of value, is the active soul. This every man is entitled to; this every man contains within him, although in almost all men obstructed, and as yet unborn. The soul active sees absolute truth and utters truth, or creates. In this action it is genius; not the privilege of here and there a favorite, but the sound estate of every man. In its essence it is progressive. The book, the college, the school of art, the institution of any kind, stop with some past utterance of genius. This is good, say they, — let us hold by this. They pin me down. They look backward and not forward. But genius looks forward: the eyes of man are set in his forehead, not in his hindhead: man hopes: genius creates. Whatever talents may be, if the man create not, the pure efflux of the Deity is not his; — cinders and smoke there may be, but not yet flame. There are creative manners, there are creative actions, and creative words; manners, actions, words, that is, indicative of no custom or authority, but springing spontaneous from the mind's own sense of good and fair.

On the other part, instead of being its own seer, let it receive from another mind its truth, though it were in torrents of light, without periods of solitude, inquest, and self-recovery, and a fatal disservice is done. Genius is always sufficiently the enemy of genius by over-influence. The literature of every nation bears me witness. The English dramatic poets have Shakspearized now for two hundred years.

Undoubtedly there is a right way of reading, so it be sternly subordinated. Man Thinking must not be subdued by his instruments. Books are for the scholar's idle times. When he can read God directly, the hour is too precious to be wasted in other men's transcripts of their readings. But when the intervals of darkness come, as come they must, — when the sun is hid and the stars withdraw their shining, — we repair to the lamps which were kindled by their ray, to guide our steps to the East again, where the dawn is. We hear, that we may speak. The Arabian proverb says, "A fig tree, looking on a fig tree, becometh fruitful."

It is remarkable, the character of the pleasure we derive from the best books. They impress us with the conviction that one nature wrote and the same reads. We read the verses of one of the great English poets, of Chaucer, of Marvell, of Dryden, with the most modern joy, — with a pleasure, I mean, which is in great part caused by the abstraction of all *time* from their verses. There is some awe mixed with the joy of our surprise, when this poet, who lived in some past world, two or three hundred years ago, says that which lies close to my own soul, that which I also had well-nigh thought and said. But for the evidence thence afforded to the philosophical doctrine of the identity of all minds, we should suppose some preëstablished harmony, some foresight of souls that were to be, and some preparation of stores for their future wants, like the fact observed in insects, who lay up food before death for the young grub they shall never see.

I would not be hurried by any love of system, by any exaggeration of instincts, to underrate the Book. We all know, that as the human body can be nourished on any food, though it were boiled grass and the broth of shoes, so the human mind can be fed by any knowledge. And great and heroic men have existed who had almost no other information than by the printed page. I only would say that it needs a strong head to bear that diet. One must be an inventor to read well. As the proverb says, "He that would bring home the wealth of the Indies, must carry out the wealth of the Indies." There is then creative reading as well as creative writing. When the mind is braced by labor and invention, the page of whatever book we read becomes luminous with manifold allusion. Every sentence is doubly significant, and the sense of our author is as broad as the world.

We then see, what is always true, that as the seer's hour of vision is short and rare among heavy days and months, so is its record, perchance, the least part of his volume. The discerning will read, in his Plato or Shakspeare, only that least part, — only the authentic utterances of the oracle; — all the rest he rejects, were it never so many times Plato's and Shakespeare's.

Of course there is a portion of reading quite indispensable to a wise man. History and exact science he must learn by laborious reading. Colleges, in like manner, have their indispensable office, — to teach elements. But they can only highly serve us when they aim not to drill, but to create; when they gather from far every ray of various genius to their hospitable halls, and by the concentrated fires, set the hearts of their youth on flame. Thought and knowledge are natures in which apparatus and pretension avail nothing. Gowns and pecuniary foundations, though of towns of gold, can never countervail the least sentence or syllable of wit. Forget this, and our American colleges will recede in their public importance, whilst they grow richer every year.

III. There goes in the world a notion that the scholar should be a recluse, a valetudinarian, — as unfit for any handiwork or public labor as a penknife for an axe. The so-called "practical men" sneer at speculative men, as if, because they speculate or *see*, they could do nothing. I have heard it said that the clergy, — who are always more universally than any other class, the scholars of their day, — are addressed as women; that the rough, spontaneous conversation of men they do not hear, but only a mincing and diluted speech. They are often virtually disfranchised; and indeed there are advocates for their celibacy. As far as this is true of the studious classes, it is not just and wise. Action is with the scholar subordinate, but it is essential. Without it he is not yet man. Without it thought can never ripen into truth. Whilst the world hangs before the eye as a cloud of beauty, we cannot even see its beauty. Inaction is cowardice, but there can be no scholar without the heroic mind. The preamble of thought, the transition through which it passes from the unconscious to the conscious, is action. Only so much do I know, as I have lived. Instantly we know whose words are loaded with life, and whose not.

The world, — this shadow of the soul, or *other me*, lies wide around. Its attractions are the keys which unlock my thoughts and make me acquainted with myself. I run eagerly into this resounding tumult. I grasp the hands of those next me, and take my place in the ring to suffer and to work, taught by an instinct that so shall the dumb abyss be vocal with speech. I pierce its order; I dissipate its fear; I dispose of it within the circuit of my expanding life. So much only of life as I know by experience, so much of the wilderness have I vanquished and planted, or so far have I extended my being, my dominion. I do not see how any man can afford, for the sake of his nerves and his nap, to spare any action in which he can partake. It is pearls and rubies to his discourse. Drudgery, calamity, exasperation, want, are instructors in eloquence and wisdom. The true scholar grudges every opportunity of action past by, as a loss of power.

It is the raw material out of which the intellect moulds her splendid products. A strange process too, this by which experience is converted into thought, as a mulberry leaf is converted into satin. The manufacture goes forward at all hours.

The actions and events of our childhood and youth are now matters of calmest observation. They lie like fair pictures in the air. Not so with our recent actions, — with the business which we now have in hand. On this we are quite unable to speculate. Our affections as yet circulate through it. We no more feel or know it than we feel the feet, or the hand, or the brain of our body. The new deed is yet a part of life, — remains for a time immersed in our unconscious life. In some contemplative hour it detaches itself from the life like a ripe fruit, to become a thought of the mind. Instantly it is raised, transfigured; the corruptible has put on incorruption. Henceforth it is an object of beauty, however base its origin and neighborhood. Observe too the impossibility of antedating this act. In its grub state, it cannot fly, it cannot shine, it is a dull grub. But suddenly, without observation, the selfsame thing unfurls beautiful wings, and is an angel of wisdom. So is there no fact, no event, in our private history, which shall not, sooner or later, lose its adhesive, inert form, and astonish us by soaring from our body into the empyrean. Cradle and infancy, school and playground, the fear of boys, and dogs, and ferules, the love of little maids and berries, and many another fact that once filled the whole sky, are gone already; friend and relative, profession and party, town and country, nation and world, must also soar and sing.

Of course, he who has put forth his total strength in fit actions has the richest return of wisdom. I will not shut myself out of this globe of action, and transplant an oak into a flower-pot, there to hunger and pine; nor trust the revenue of some single faculty, and exhaust one vein of thought, much like those Savoyards, who, getting their livelihood by carving shepherds, shepherdesses, and smoking Dutchmen, for all Europe, went out one day to the mountain to find stock, and discovered that they had whittled up the last of their pine-trees. Authors we have, in numbers, who have written out their vein, and who, moved by a commendable prudence, sail for Greece or Palestine, follow the trapper into the prairie, or ramble round Algiers, to replenish their merchantable stock.

If it were only for a vocabulary, the scholar would be covetous of action. Life is our dictionary. Years are well spent in country labors; in town; in the insight into trades and manufactures; in frank intercourse with many men and women; in science; in art; to the one end of mastering in all their facts a language by which to illustrate and embody our perceptions. I learn immediately from any speaker how much he has already lived, through the poverty or the splendor of his speech. Life lies behind us as the quarry from whence we get tiles and copestones for the masonry of to-day. This is the way to learn grammar. Colleges and books only copy the language which the field and the work-yard made.

But the final value of action, like that of books, and better than books, is that it is a resource. That great principle of Undulation in nature, that shows itself in the inspiring and expiring of the breath; in desire and satiety; in the ebb and flow of the sea; in day and night; in heat and cold; and, as yet more deeply ingrained in every atom and every fluid, is known to us under the name of Polarity, — these "fits of easy transmission and reflection," as Newton called them,— are the law of nature because they are the law of spirit.

The mind now thinks, now acts, and each fit reproduces the other. When the artist has exhausted his materials, when the fancy no longer paints, when thoughts are no longer apprehended and books are a weariness, — he has always the resource *to live*. Character is higher than intellect. Thinking is the function. Living is the functionary. The stream retreats to its source. A great soul will be strong to live, as well as strong to think. Does he lack organ or medium to impart his truth? He can still fall back on this elemental force of living them. This is a total act. Thinking is a partial act. Let the grandeur of justice shine in his affairs. Let the beauty of affection cheer his lowly roof. Those "far from fame," who dwell and act with him, will feel the force of his constitution in the doings and passages of the day better than it can be measured by any public and designed display. Time shall teach him that the scholar loses no hour which the man lives. Herein he unfolds the sacred germ of his instinct, screened from influence. What is lost in seemliness is gained in strength. Not out of those on whom systems of education have exhausted their culture, comes the helpful giant to destroy the old or to build the new, but out of unhandselled savage nature; out of terrible Druids and Berserkers come at last Alfred and Shakspeare.

I hear therefore with joy whatever is beginning to be said of the dignity and necessity of labor to every citizen. There is virtue yet in the hoe and the spade, for learned as well as for unlearned hands. And labor is everywhere welcome; always we are invited to work; only be this limitation observed, that a man shall not for the sake of wider activity sacrifice any opinion to the popular judgments and modes of action.

I have now spoken of the education of the scholar by nature, by books, and by action. It remains to say somewhat of his duties.

They are such as become Man Thinking. They may all be comprised in self-trust. The office of the scholar is to cheer, to raise, and to guide men by showing them facts amidst appearances. He plies the slow, unhonored, and unpaid task of observation. Flamsteed and Herschel, in their glazed observatories, may catalogue the stars with the praise of all men, and the results being splendid and useful, honor is sure. But he, in his private observatory, cataloguing obscure and nebulous stars of the human mind, which as yet no man has thought of as such, — watching days and months sometimes for a few facts; correcting still his old records; —

must relinquish display and immediate fame. In the long
period of his preparation he must betray often an ignorance
and shiftlessness in popular arts, incurring the disdain of the
able who shoulder him aside. Long he must stammer in
his speech; often forego the living for the dead. Worse yet,
he must accept, — how often! poverty and solitude. For
the ease and pleasure of treading the old road, accepting the
fashions, the education, the religion of society, he takes the
cross of making his own, and, of course, the self-accusation,
the faint heart, the frequent uncertainty and loss of time,
which are the nettles and tangling vines in the way of the
self-relying and self-directed; and the state of virtual hostility in which he seems to stand to society, and especially
to educated society. For all this loss and scorn what offset?
He is to find consolation in exercising the highest functions
of human nature. He is one who raises himself from private
considerations and breathes and lives on public and illustrious thoughts. He is the world's eye. He is the world's heart.
He is to resist the vulgar prosperity that retrogrades ever to
barbarism, by preserving and communicating heroic sentiments, noble biographies, melodious verse, and the conclusions of history. Whatsoever oracles the human heart, in
all emergencies, in all solemn hours, has uttered as its com-
mentary on the world of actions, — these he shall receive
and impart. And whatsoever new verdict Reason from her
inviolable seat pronounces on the passing men and events
of to-day, — this he shall hear and promulgate.

These being his functions, it becomes him to feel all confidence in himself, and to defer never to the popular cry. He
and he only knows the world. The world of any moment is
the merest appearance. Some great decorum, some fetish of
a government, some ephemeral trade, or war, or man, is
cried up by half mankind and cried down by the other half,
as if all depended on this particular up or down. The odds

are that the whole question is not worth the poorest thought which the scholar has lost in listening to the controversy. Let him not quit his belief that a popgun is a popgun, though the ancient and honorable of the earth affirm it to be the crack of doom. In silence, in steadiness, in severe abstraction, let him hold by himself; add observation to observation, patient of neglect, patient of reproach, and bide his own time, — happy enough if he can satisfy himself alone that this day he has seen something truly. Success treads on every right step. For the instinct is sure, that prompts him to tell his brother what he thinks. He then learns that in going down into the secrets of his own mind he has descended into the secrets of all minds. He learns that he who has mastered any law in his private thoughts, is master to that extent of all men whose language he speaks, and of all into whose language his own can be translated. The poet, in utter solitude remembering his spontaneous thoughts and recording them, is found to have recorded that which men in crowded cities find true for them also. The orator distrusts at first the fitness of his frank confessions, his want of knowledge of the persons he addresses, until he finds that he is the complement of his hearers; — that they drink his words because he fulfils for them their own nature; the deeper he dives into his privatest, secretest presentiment, to his wonder he finds this is the most acceptable, most public, and universally true. The people delight in it; the better part of every man feels, This is my music; this is myself.

In self-trust all the virtues are comprehended. Free should the scholar be, — free and brave. Free even to the definition of freedom, "without any hindrance that does not arise out of his own constitution." Brave; for fear is a thing which a scholar by his very function puts behind him. Fear always springs from ignorance. It is a shame to

him if his tranquillity, amid dangerous times, arise from the
presumption that like children and women his is a protected
class; or if he seek a temporary peace by the diversion of
his thoughts from politics or vexed questions, hiding his
head like an ostrich in the flowering bushes, peeping into
microscopes, and turning rhymes, as a boy whistles to keep
his courage up. So is the danger a danger still; so is the fear
worse. Manlike let him turn and face it. Let him look into
its eye and search its nature, inspect its origin, — see the
whelping of this lion, — which lies no great way back; he
will then find in himself a perfect comprehension of its nature
and extent; he will have made his hands meet on the other
side, and can henceforth defy it and pass on superior. The
world is his who can see through its pretension. What deaf-
ness, what stone-blind custom, what overgrown error you
behold is there only by sufferance, — by your sufferance.
See it to be a lie, and you have already dealt it its mortal
blow.

Yes, we are the cowed, — we the trustless. It is a mischievous notion that we are come late into nature; that the
world was finished a long time ago. As the world was plastic
and fluid in the hands of God, so it is ever to so much of his
attributes as we bring to it. To ignorance and sin, it is flint.
They adapt themselves to it as they may; but in proportion
as a man has any thing in him divine, the firmament flows
before him and takes his signet and form. Not he is great
who can alter matter, but he who can alter my state of mind.
They are the kings of the world who give the color of their
present thought to all nature and all art, and persuade men
by the cheerful serenity of their carrying the matter, that
this thing which they do is the apple which the ages have
desired to pluck, now at last ripe, and inviting nations to the
harvest. The great man makes the great thing. Wherever
Macdonald sits, there is the head of the table. Linnæus

makes botany the most alluring of studies, and wins it from the farmer and the herb-woman; Davy, chemistry; and Cuvier, fossils. The day is always his who works in it with serenity and great aims. The unstable estimates of men crowd to him whose mind is filled with a truth, as the heaped waves of the Atlantic follow the moon.

For this self-trust, the reason is deeper than can be fathomed, — darker than can be enlightened. I might not carry with me the feeling of my audience in stating my own belief. But I have already shown the ground of my hope, in adverting to the doctrine that man is one. I believe man has been wronged; he has wronged himself. He has almost lost the light that can lead him back to his prerogatives. Men are become of no account. Men in history, men in the world of to-day, are bugs, are spawn, and called "the mass" and "the herd." In a century, in a millennium, one or two men; that is to say, one or two approximations to the right state of every man. All the rest behold in the hero or the poet their own green and crude being, — ripened; yes, and are content to be less, so *that* may attain to its full stature. What a testimony, full of grandeur, full of pity, is borne to the demands of his own nature, by the poor clansman, the poor partisan, who rejoices in the glory of his chief. The poor and the low find some amends to their immense moral capacity, for their acquiescence in a political and social inferiority. They are content to be brushed like flies from the path of a great person, so that justice shall be done by him to that common nature which it is the dearest desire of all to see enlarged and glorified. They sun themselves in the great man's light, and feel it to be their own element. They cast the dignity of man from their downtrod selves upon the shoulders of a hero, and will perish to add one drop of blood to make that great heart beat, those giant sinews combat and conquer. He lives for us, and we live in him.

Men such as they are, very naturally seek money or power; and power because it is as good as money, — the "spoils," so called, "of office." And why not? for they aspire to the highest, and this, in their sleep-walking, they dream is highest. Wake them and they shall quit the false good and leap to the true, and leave governments to clerks and desks. This revolution is to be wrought by the gradual domestication of the idea of Culture. The main enterprise of the world for splendor, for extent, is the upbuilding of a man. Here are the materials strewn along the ground. The private life of one man shall be a more illustrious monarchy, more formidable to its enemy, more sweet and serene in its influence to its friend, than any kingdom in history. For a man, rightly viewed, comprehendeth the particular natures of all men. Each philosopher, each bard, each actor has only done for me, as by a delegate, what one day I can do for myself. The books which once we valued more than the apple of the eye, we have quite exhausted. What is that but saying that we have come up with the point of view which the universal mind took through the eyes of one scribe; we have been that man, and have passed on. First, one, then another, we drain all cisterns, and waxing greater by all these supplies, we crave a better and more abundant food. The man has never lived that can feed us ever. The human mind cannot be enshrined in a person who shall set a barrier on any one side to this unbounded, unboundable empire. It is one central fire, which, flaming now out of the lips of Etna, lightens the capes of Sicily, and now out of the throat of Vesuvius, illuminates the towers and vineyards of Naples. It is one light which beams out of a thousand stars. It is one soul which animates all men.

But I have dwelt perhaps tediously upon this abstraction of the Scholar. I ought not to delay longer to add what I have to say of nearer reference to the time and to this country.

Historically, there is thought to be a difference in the ideas which predominate over successive epochs, and there are data for marking the genius of the Classic, of the Romantic, and now of the Reflective or Philosophical age. With the views I have intimated of the oneness or the identity of the mind through all individuals, I do not much dwell on these differences. In fact, I believe each individual passes through all three. The boy is a Greek; the youth, romantic; the adult, reflective. I deny not, however, that a revolution in the leading idea may be distinctly enough traced.

Our age is bewailed as the age of Introversion. Must that needs be evil? We, it seems, are critical; we are embarrassed with second thoughts; we cannot enjoy any thing for hankering to know whereof the pleasure consists; we are lined with eyes; we see with our feet; the time is infected with Hamlet's unhappiness, —

"Sicklied o'er with the pale cast of thought."

It is so bad then? Sight is the last thing to be pitied. Would we be blind? Do we fear lest we should outsee nature and God, and drink truth dry? I look upon the discontent of the literary class as a mere announcement of the fact that they find themselves not in the state of mind of their fathers, and regret the coming state as untried; as a boy dreads the water before he has learned that he can swim. If there is any period one would desire to be born in, is it not the age of Revolution; when the old and the new stand side by side and admit of being compared; when the energies of all men are searched by fear and by hope; when the historic glories of the old can be compensated by the rich possibilities of the new era? This time, like all times, is a very good one, if we but know what to do with it.

I read with some joy of the auspicious signs of the coming days, as they glimmer already through poetry and art, through philosophy and science, through church and state.

One of these signs is the fact that the same movement which affected the elevation of what was called the lowest class in the state, assumed in literature a very marked and as benign an aspect. Instead of the sublime and beautiful, the near, the low, the common, was explored and poetized. That which had been negligently trodden under foot by those who were harnessing and provisioning themselves for long journeys into far countries, is suddenly found to be richer than all foreign parts. The literature of the poor, the feelings of the child, the philosophy of the street, the meaning of household life, are the topics of the time. It is a great stride. It is a sign, — is it not? of new vigor when the extremities are made active, when currents of warm life run into the hands and the feet. I ask not for the great, the remote, the romantic; what is doing in Italy or Arabia; what is Greek art, or Provençal minstrelsy; I embrace the common, I explore and sit at the feet of the familiar, the low. Give me insight into to-day, and you may have the antique and future worlds. What would we really know the meaning of? The meal in the firkin; the milk in the pan; the ballad in the street; the news of the boat; the glance of the eye; the form and the gait of the body; — show me the ultimate reason of these matters; show me the sublime presence of the highest spiritual cause lurking, as always it does lurk, in these suburbs and extremities of nature; let me see every trifle bristling with the polarity that ranges it instantly on an eternal law; and the shop, the plough, and the ledger referred to the like cause by which light undulates and poets sing; — and the world lies no longer a dull miscellany and lumber-room, but has form and order; there is no trifle, there is no puzzle, but one design unites and animates the farthest pinnacle and the lowest trench.

This idea has inspired the genius of Goldsmith, Burns, Cowper, and, in a newer time, of Goethe, Wordsworth, and Carlyle. This idea they have differently followed and with various success. In contrast with their writing, the style of Pope, of Johnson, of Gibbon, looks cold and pedantic. This writing is blood-warm. Man is surprised to find that things near are not less beautiful and wondrous than things remote. The near explains the far. The drop is a small ocean. A man is related to all nature. This perception of the worth of the vulgar is fruitful in discoveries. Goethe, in this very thing the most modern of the moderns, has shown us, as none ever did, the genius of the ancients.

There is one man of genius who has done much for this philosophy of life, whose literary value has never yet been rightly estimated; — I mean Emanuel Swedenborg. The most imaginative of men, yet writing with the precision of a mathematician, he endeavored to engraft a purely philo-sophical Ethics on the popular Christianity of his time. Such an attempt of course must have difficulty which no genius could surmount. But he saw and showed the connection between nature and the affections of the soul. He pierced the emblematic or spiritual character of the visible, audible, tangible world. Especially did his shade-loving muse hover over and interpret the lower parts of nature; he showed the mysterious bond that allies moral evil to the foul material forms, and has given in epical parables a theory of insanity, of beasts, of unclean and fearful things.

Another sign of our times, also marked by an analogous political movement, is the new importance given to the single person. Every thing that tends to insulate the indi-vidual, — to surround him with barriers of natural respect, so that each man shall feel the world is his, and man shall treat with man as a sovereign state with a sovereign state, — tends to true union as well as greatness. "I learned," said the melancholy Pestalozzi, "that no man in God's wide earth is either willing or able to help any other man." Help must come from the bosom alone. The scholar is that man who must take up into himself all the ability of the time, all the contributions of the past, all the hopes of the future. He must be an university of knowledges. If there be one lesson more than another which should pierce his ear, it is, The world is nothing, the man is all; in yourself is the law of all nature, and you know not yet how a globule of sap ascends; in yourself slumbers the whole of Reason; it is for you to know all; it is for you to dare all. Mr. President and Gentlemen, this confidence in the unsearched might of man belongs, by all motives, by all prophecy, by all preparation, to the American Scholar. We have listened too long to the courtly muses of Europe. The spirit of the American free-man is already suspected to be timid, imitative, tame. Public and private avarice make the air we breathe thick and fat. The scholar is decent, indolent, complaisant. See already the tragic consequence. The mind of this country, taught to aim at low objects, eats upon itself. There is no work for any but the decorous and the complaisant. Young men of the fairest promise, who begin life upon our shores, inflated by the mountain winds, shined upon by all the stars of God, find the earth below not in unison with these, but are hindered from action by the disgust which the principles on which business is managed inspire, and turn drudges, or die of disgust, some of them suicides. What is the remedy? They did not yet see, and thousands of young men as hopeful now crowding to the barriers for the career do not yet see, that if the single man plant himself indomitably on his instincts, and there abide, the huge world will come round to him. Patience, — patience; with the shades of all the good and great for company; and for solace the perspective of your own infinite life; and for work the study and the communication of principles, the making those instincts prevalent, the conversion of the world. Is it not the chief disgrace in the world, not to be an unit; — not to be reckoned one character; — not to yield that peculiar fruit which each man was created to bear, but to be reckoned in the gross, in the hundred, or the thousand, of the party, the section, to which we belong; and our opinion predicted geographically, as the north, or the south? Not so, brothers and friends, — please God, ours shall not be so. We will walk on our own feet; we will work with our own hands; we will speak our own minds. The study of letters shall be no longer a name for pity, for doubt, and for sensual indulgence. The dread of man and the love of man shall be a wall of defence and a wreath of joy around all. A nation of men will for the first time exist, because each believes himself inspired by the Divine Soul which also inspires all men.

DEMOCRACY IN EDUCATION [1]

PHILANDER P. CLAXTON

A STUDY of the chapters of the portion of the report submitted herewith and of certain other chapters which were not ready in time to be included in this report shows that within the year there has been in this country an increase in tendency toward democracy in education, toward giving to every child of whatever condition a full and equal opportunity with all other children for that degree and kind of education, that quantity and quality of education, which will develop in the fullest measure its manhood or womanhood, its human qualities, prepare it for the duties and responsibilities of democratic citizenship, for participation in civic and social life, and for making an honest living, contributing its part to the Commonwealth, and serving humanity by some useful occupation, followed intelligently and skillfully with good-will and strong purpose. In a larger degree than ever before are we beginning to understand that, next to the right to live, this is the most important right of every child. If democracy has any valuable and ultimate meaning it is equality of opportunity. But there can be no equality of opportunity without equality of opportunity in education. If to any child this is denied and it is permitted to grow to manhood or womanhood without that education which prepares it for good living, for the duties and responsibilities of citizenship, and for making an honest living by some intelligent, useful occupation, then there is nothing

[1] From the Report of the United States Commissioner of Education (1915), vol. I, p. xvi.

which individual or society can do, nothing which man or God can do, to make good the loss. More than ever before are we beginning to understand that material progress, social purity, civic righteousness, political stability and strength, and the possibilities of culture and the attainment of higher ideals, all depend on the right education of all the people. If any man or woman follows his or her trade or profession with less intelligence and skill than he or she might, the total amount of wealth produced is less than it might be. If any lack knowledge of fundamental principles of government and institutional life necessary for intelligent citizenship in our democracy, the civic and political life of city, State, and Nation is affected thereby. If the health, the culture, or the moral education of any has been neglected, all society and each of its members must suffer as a result. If any, through wrong education or the inculcation of false ideals, work at occupations for which they are not fitted or in which they may not serve themselves and society as well as they might in other ways, their own lives and the lives of us all are less full and satisfactory than they might otherwise be. We are bound up in the sheaf of life together, and our interests from the lowest to the highest and from the highest to the lowest are inextricably interwoven. Therefore the liberal use of public funds for the support of schools and other agencies of education is more and more clearly recognized as good business, and careful thinking and planning for the fullest and best education of all the children of all the people as the highest duty of citizenship.

CAN DEMOCRACY BE ORGANIZED?[1]

EDWIN A. ALDERMAN

THE United States of America is one of the oldest Governments on earth. England and Russia alone, among the nations of Europe, equal it in age, and even England has undergone such radical changes in the past century, as compared with the United States, as to constitute us, with our unchanged Government since 1789, the most stable of modern nations. Our nearness to the perspective and our absorption in our own life have blinded us to the inspiring National panorama, as it has unfolded itself before the world. First, a group of rustic communities, making common cause in behalf of ancient guarantees of English freedom; then suspicious colonies, unused to the ways of democracies, striving after some bond amid the clash of jealous interests; then a wonderful paper-writing, compact of high sense and human foresight and tragic compromise; then a young Republic, lacking the instinct of unity, but virile, unlovely, raw, wayward, in its confident young strength. Some confused decades of sad, earnest effort to pluck out an evil growth planted in its life by the hard necessities of compromise by the fathers, but which needs must blossom into the flower of civil war before it could be plucked out and thrown to the void. Then young manhood, nursing its youth, whole and undivisible, proven by trial of fire and dark days, opening its eye upon a new world of steam and force, and seizing

[1] Spoken before the North Carolina Literary and Historical Society, November 9, 1915, by the president of the University of Virginia. Reprinted from the Proceedings of the Society with the generous permission of the author.

greedily and selfishly every coign of vantage; and to-day the most venerable Republic, the richest of nations, the champion and exemplar of World Democracy.

No nation, I venture to assert, was ever born grounded on so definite and fixed a principle and with so conscious a purpose. Such a wealth of hope for humanity never before gathered about a mere political experiment, and such a mass of pure idealism never before suffused itself into the framework of a State. How can such a Nation so begun, so advanced, so beset, be so guided, that all of its citizens shall indeed become free men, entering continually into the possession of intellectual, material, and moral benefits? How can a people devoted to individualism and freedom retain that individualism which guarantees freedom and yet engraft upon their social order that genius for coöperation which alone insures power and progress? These are the final interrogatories of democracy as a sane vision glimpses it, robbed of its earlier illusions. The fathers of this Republic did not understand the present mould of democracy. The very word was obnoxious to them. Their ideal was a State the citizens of which chose their leaders and then trusted them. They did not foresee the socialized State. They did not envisage a minute and paternal organization of society which may be achieved alike by Prussian absolutism or mere socialism, which is chronologically, if not logically, the child of democracy. The fear that tugged at their hearts was the fear of tyranny, the dread of kings, the denial of self-direction, which prevented a man from speaking his opinion or going his way as he willed. Their democracy was a working government which should give effect to the will of the people and at the same time provide sufficient safeguard for individual liberty. The emphasis of the time was everywhere upon the rights of the individual rather more than upon the duties of the citizen. When their theories, as

Mr. Hadley points out, seemed likely to secure this result, the fathers published them boldly; when they seemed likely to interfere, they ignored them. The creed, then, which had a religious sanction in an age of moral imagination to men of superb human enthusiasm like Washington, Franklin, Jefferson, and Adams, was the belief that democracy, considered as individual freedom, was the final form of human society. It is idle to deny that a century of trial has somewhat dulled the halo about this ancient concept of democracy, but in my judgment only to men of little faith. It is quite true that our democracy of to-day is not what Rousseau thought it would be, nor Lord Byron, nor Shelley, nor Karl Marx. But as we meditate about it and conclude that it has not realized all of its hopes, we ought to try to settle first what it has done and then place that to its credit. Here are some things that I think democracy has done, or helped to do. It has abated sectarian fury. Sectarian fury is ridiculous in this age; it was not always so. It has abolished slavery. It has protected and enlarged manhood suffrage and has gone far toward womanhood suffrage. It has mitigated much social injustice. It has developed a touching and almost sublime faith in the power of education, illustrating it by expending six hundred million dollars a year in the most daring thing that democracy has ever tried to do; namely, to fit for citizenship every human being born within its borders. It has increased kindness and gentleness, and thus diminished the fury of partisanship. It has preserved the form of the Union through the storm of a civil war, and yet has had power to touch with healing unity and forgiveness its passions and tragedies. It has conquered and civilized a vast continent. It has developed great agencies of culture and has somehow made itself a symbol of individual prosperity. It has developed a common consciousness and a volunteer statesmanship among its free citizens as manifested more strikingly than elsewhere in the world in great educational, religious, scientific and philanthropic societies, which profoundly influence and mould society. Out of what other State could have issued as a volunteer movement so efficient an agency as the Commission for the Relief of Belgium or the Rockefeller Sanitary Commission? It has permitted and fostered the growth of a public press of gigantic power reflecting the crudities and impulses of a vast and varied population, but charged with a fierce idealism and staunch patriotism that have almost given it a place among the coördinate branches of our organized Government. It has stimulated inventive genius and business enterprise to a point never before reached in human annals. It has brought to American-mindedness millions of men of all races, creeds and ideals. I do not, therefore, think that democracy as it has evolved among us has failed. What autocracy on earth has done as much? It has justified itself of the sufferings and sacrifices and the dreams of the men who established it in this new land. But it has also without doubt, by the very trust that it places in men, developed new shapes of temptations and wrong-doing. Democracy, like a man's character, is never clear out of danger. The moral life of men, said Froude, is like the flight of a bird in the air; he is sustained only by effort, and when he ceases to exert himself he falls. And the same, it seems to me, is impressively true of institutional and governmental life.

Patriotism — which is hard to define and new with every age — and public spirit — which is hard to define and new with every age — must constantly redefine themselves. Patriotism meant manhood's rights when Washington took it to his heart. It somehow spelled culture, refinement and distinction of mind when Emerson in his Phi Beta Kappa address besought the sluggish intellect of his country to look up from under its iron lids. It signified National ideals and theories of government to the soldiers of Lee and to the soldiers of Grant. It meant industrial greatness and a splendid desire to annex nature to man's uses when the great business leaders of this generation and of the last generation built up their great businesses and tied the Union together in a unity of steel and steam more completely than all the wars could do, and did it with a patriotism and a statesmanship and an imagination that no man can deny. The honest business man needs somebody to praise him. He has done a great service in this country, and when he is steady and honest there is no greater force in all our life. A decade ago patriotism in America meant a reaction from an unsocial and selfish individualism to restraint and consideration for the general welfare, expressing itself in a cry for moderation and fairness and justice and sympathy in the use of power and wealth as the states of spirit and mind that alone can safeguard republican ideals. The emphasis, as I have said, was formerly on the rights of man; it is getting to be placed, as Mazzini preached, upon the duties of man. If in our youth and feverish strength there had grown up a spirit of avarice and a desire for quick wealth, and a theory of life in lesser minds that estimated money as everything and was willing to do anything for money, that very fact served to define the patriotic duty and mood of the National mind. This reawakened patriotism of the common good had the advantage of appeal to a sound public conscience, and of being supported by a valid public opinion. The part that vulgar cunning has played in creating great fortunes has been made known to this democracy and they are coming to know the genuine from the spurious, and some who were once looked at with admiration and approval as great ones, are not now seen in that light.

This very growth in discernment gave us power to see in a nobler and truer light, for the people of America, the names of those upright souls in business and in politics — and there are many noble men in business and politics — who have held true in a heady time and who have kept clean and kept human their public sympathies and their republican ideals and by so doing have kept sweet their country's fame. Democracy simply had met and outfaced one of the million moral crises that are likely to assail free government, and I believe that it is cleaner to-day in ruling passion, in motive, and in practice than it has been in fifty years.

It is now clear to all minds that the movement of our business operations in this Republic, unregulated and proceeding along individualistic lines, had come perilously near to developing a scheme of monopoly and a union of our political machinery with the forces of private gain that might easily have transformed our democracy into some ugly form of tyranny and injustice. We have halted this tendency somewhat tardily, but resolutely, and the nerves of the Nation were somewhat shaken by the very thought of what might have been, very much as a man gazes with gratitude and yet with fear upon a hidden precipice over which his pathway led. We had been saying over and over to ourselves with fierce determination that this Nation should remain democratic, and should not become plutocratic or autocratic or socialistic; and we should find the way to guarantee this. All about us were heard the voices of those who thought they saw the way and who were beckoning men to follow, but new dangers faced us, however, even as we left the ancient highway and attempted to cut new paths, for in endeavoring to make it possible for democracy, as we understood it, and a vast industrialism, as we had developed it, to live together justly under the same political roof, we had plainly come to a point where there was danger of our Government developing into a system of State socialism in conflict with our deepest traditions and convictions. The leadership of the future, therefore, would have a triple problem — to protect the people against privilege, to raise the levels of democratic living, and to preserve for the people the ancient guarantees and inestimable advantages of representative government and individual initiative.

You will observe that I have thus far spoken as a citizen preoccupied with the thoughts of that ancient world which ended on August 1, 1914, and I have not permitted myself to align and examine in full the perils and weaknesses of democratic society as they had manifested themselves under conditions of peace and apparent prosperity. These weaknesses had already begun, under the strain of ordinary industrial life, to reveal themselves under five general aspects, each aspect being in essence a sort of revulsion or excess of feeling from what were considered definite political virtues:—

1. A contempt of obedience as a virtue too closely allied to servility.

2. A disregard of discipline as smacking too much of docility.

3. An impatience with trained technical skill as seeming to affirm that one man is not as good as another.

4. A failure to understand the value of the common man as a moral and political asset and an inability to coördinate education to daily life as a means of forwarding national ends and ideals.

5. A crass individualism which exalted self and its rights above society and the solemn social obligation to coöperate for the common good.

The theory of democracy which alone among great human movements had known no setback for a century of time, was fast becoming self-critical and disposed to self-analysis, and especially in America these fundamental weaknesses were being assailed in practical forms. The liberal or progressive movement in our politics was striking at the theory of crass individualism, and after the unbalanced fashion of social reform was moving toward pure democracy of State socialism in the interest of communal welfare. Our old, original, intense American individualism, shamed by its ill-governed cities and lack of concern for popular welfare, had passed forever. Socialism, considered as a paternal form of government, exercising strict regulation over men's lives and destroying individual energy and initiative, was still feared and resisted; but the social goal of democracy was becoming even by the most conservative, to be considered the advancement and improvement of society by a protection of life and health, by a reformation of educational methods and by a large amount of governmental control of fundamentals for the common good. A multitude of laws, ranging from laws governing milk for babies, to public parks and free dispensaries and vast corporations, attested the vigor of this new attitude. And strange to say this new spirit was not wholly self-begotten. Plutocracy, with its common sense, its economies and hatred of waste, its organization and its energy, had taught us much. We, too, had caught a spirit from what we used to call effete Europe. Australia taught us how to vote; Belgium, Germany, and England that there was a democracy adapted to city and factory as well as to the farm and country-side.

The forces of education were pleading the cause of team work in modern life, scientifically directed, not by amateurs and demagogues, but by experts and scientists, whether in city government or public hygiene or scientific land culture, while seriousness and self-restraint were everywhere the themes of public teachers, pleading for order and organization as an ideal of public welfare, nearly as vital as liberty and self-direction. And then, without warning, fell out this great upheaval of the world, so vast, so fundamental, despite its sordid and stupid beginnings, that the dullest among us must dimly realize that a new epoch has registered itself in human affairs. War is a great pitiless flame. It sweeps its fiery torch along the ways of men, destroying but renovating, killing but quickening, and even amid its horrors of corruption and death leaving white ashes cleanly and fertile. War is also a ghastly mirror in which actualities and ideals and tendencies reflect themselves in awful vividness. Who caused this war, who will be aggrandized by this war — its triumphs and humiliations — are important and moving, but not vital questions. The fundamental question is what effect will its reactions have upon that movement of the human spirit called democracy, begun so simply, advanced so steadfastly, yesterday acclaimed as the highest development of human polity, but to-day already being sneered at and snarled at by a host of enemies. Will war, the harshest of human facts, destroy, weaken, modify, or strengthen essential democracy? It is my conviction that the Allies in this struggle are fighting for democracy — at least for the brand of democracy with which my spirit is familiar and which my soul has learned to love. Once more in the great human story, the choice is being made between contrasting civilizations, between ideals and institutions, between liberty and the lesser life. Every drop of my blood leaps to sympathy with those peoples who, heedless of inexorable efficiency, dream a mightier dream of an order directed by justice, invigorated by freedom, instinct with the higher happiness of individual liberty, self-directed to reason and coöperation. "For what avail the plough or sail, or land or life if freedom fail?" The very weaknesses of democratic government under the crucial test of war appeal to me. The tutelage of democracy breeds love of justice, the methods of persuasion and debate, and a conception of life which makes it sweet to live and in a way destroys the temperament for war, until horror and wrong and reversion to type create anew the savage impulse. Whatever way victory falls, democracy is destined to stand its trial, and to be submitted to a merciless crossexamination by the mind and spirit of man. It may and will yield up some of its aspirations; it will seize and adapt some of the weapons of its foes; it may relinquish some of its ancient theories and methods; it will shed some of its hampering weaknesses; but it will still remain democracy, and it is the king, the autocrat, and the mechanical State which will suffer in the end rather than the common man who, in sublime loyalty to race and flag, is now reddening the soil of Europe with his blood, or the great principle which has fascinated every generous thinking soul since freedom became the heritage of man.

The Germans are a mighty race, fecund in physical force and organizing genius. Like the French of 1789, they are now more possessed with a group of passionate creative impulses than any other nation. This grandiose idealism, for such it is, seems to me reactionary, but it is held with a sort of thrilling devotion and executed with undoubted genius. Nineteen hundred and fourteen is for the Prussians a sort of Prussian Elizabethan age, in which vast dreams and ideas glow in the hearts and minds of Teutonic Raleighs, Drakes, and Grenvilles, ready to die for them. The ideal of organization, the thought of a great whole uniting its members for effective work in building a powerful State, and the welding of a monstrous federal union of nations akin in interests and civilizations possess the Germanic mind. For the German the individual exists for the State, and his concept of the State is far more beautiful and spiritual than we Americans generally imagine. The State is to be the resultant of the best thought and efforts of all its units. They have a glorious concept of communal welfare, but to them parliamentarism is frankly a disease and suffrage a menace. To them, and

I am quoting a notable German scholar, "democracy is a thing, infirm of purpose, jealous, timid, changeable, unthorough, without foresight, blundering along in an age of lucidity guided by confused instincts." On the whole Germany is probably better governed in external forms than the United States or England. The material conditions of her people are better, her cities cleaner, her economies finer, her social life better administered, and her power to achieve amazing results under the fiercest of tests nearly marvelous. The world cannot and probably will not reject as vile all this German scholarship, concentration, and scientific power. The world may either slavishly imitate Germany, or wisely modify or set up a contrary system overtopping the German ideal in definite accomplishment, according to the inclination of the scales of victory. The fatality of the German Nation is that it does not behold the world as it is. It beholds its ideals and is logic-driven to their achievement. It has gone from the sand wastes of Brandenburg to world-power by force and the will to do, and by force and will it seeks its will and hacks its way through. It is enslaved by the majesty of plan and precision — the power of concert. Napoleon, "that ablest of historic men," as Lord Acton called him, tried all this once and failed. But here it all is again, with its weapons of flame and force. Germany, apparently, does not understand the fair doctrine of live and let live. Pride sustains its soul, and ambition directs its energy. In spite of all these concrete achievements Germany does not seem to me a progressive nation, but rather a Giant of Reaction — a sort of mixture, as some one has called it, of Ancient Sparta and Modern Science. And it is well to hold in mind that this mass-efficiency is brought to pass by subjecting even in the minutest particulars the individual to the supreme authority of the State. This subjection is scientific, well-meant, but very minute.,

The flaw of democracy is that it does understand and sympathize with the soul of man, but is so sympathetic with his yearning for free self-government and self-direction, so opposed to force as a moulding agent, so jealous of initiative, that it has not yet found the binding thread of social organization by which self-government and good government become one and the same thing. Let us confess that "*Les mœurs de la liberté*" cannot be the manners of absolutism. Debate, political agitation, bold, popular expression, are not the methods of smooth precision and relentless order. Napoleon revealed to the world the democratic passion and passed off the stage. Perhaps it is the destiny of the Prussian to teach us administration and order and to put us in the way of finding and achieving it without sacrificing our liberties, and then he, too, will pass.

To work out a free democratic, socialized life, wherein the individual is not lost in a metaphysical super-State, nor sunk in inaction and selfishness, by inducing desire for such life, by applying trained intelligence to its achievement, and by subjecting ourselves to the tests and disciplines that will bring it to pass — that is the task of American democracy and indeed of a fuller, deeper world-wide democracy. The center of gravity of the autocratic State is in the State itself, and in such ideals as self-anointed leaders suggest. The effect of the democracy has been to shift the center of gravity too much to the individual self and his immediate welfare.

There must be a golden mean somewhere and we must find it. When the great readjustment dawns, when the gaping wounds of war have healed, all the world will be seeking this golden mean. The social democrat of Germany, who is silent now in his splendid National devotion, will be seeking it; the Russian peasant, inarticulate, mystic, reflective; the Frenchman with his clear brain and forward-looking soul; the Englishman wrapped in his great tradition. Perhaps in our untouched and undreamed vigor, we shall become the champions of the great quest.

There would be fitness in such a result. Here continental democracy was born; here it has grown great upon an incomparable soil and with enormous waste. Let us prepare for our colossal moral and practical responsibilities in the world life, therefore, not alone by preparing common sense establishments of force on land and sea, until such time as human reason shall deem them not needed, but by the greater preparedness of self-restraint, self-analysis, and self-discipline. Let us not surrender our age-long dream of good, just self-government to any mechanical ideal of quickly obtaining material results erected into a crude dogma of efficiency. Democracy must know how to get material results economically and quickly. Democracy must and can be organized to that end, and this organization will undoubtedly involve certain surrenders, certain social and political self-abnegations in the interests of collectivism. But I hold the faith that all this can be done yet, retaining in the family of freedom that shining jewel of individual liberty which has glowed in our life since the beginning. The great democratic nations — America, England, France, Switzerland — have before them, therefore, the problem of retaining their standards of individual liberty, and yet contriving juster and finer administrative organs. Certainly the people that have built this Union can learn how to coördinate the activities of its people and obtain results as definite as those obtained under systems of mere authority.

Since my college days I have been hearing about and admiring the German genius for research, for adaptation of scientific truth and for organization. Now the whole world stands half astonished and half envious of their creed of efficiency. In so far as this creed is opposed to slipshodness and waste, it is altogether good, but the question arises, Is the ability to get things done well deadly to liberty, or is it consistent with personal liberty? In examining German progress, I do not find as many examples of supreme individual efficiency or independent spirit as I find in the democratic nations. The steam engine, the factory system, telegraph, telephone, wireless, electric light, the gasoline engine, aeroplane, machine gun, the submarine, uses of rubber, dreadnaught, the mighty names of Lister and Pasteur, come out of the democratic nations. The distinctive German genius is for administration and adaptation, rather than for independent creation. His civil service is the finest in the world. He knows what he wants. He decides what training is necessary to get that result. He universalizes that training. He enforces obedience to its discipline. A man must have skill; he must obey; he must work; he must coöperate. The freer nations desire the same results, but neglect to enforce their realization. Their theory of government forces them to plead for its attainment. Certain classes and individuals heed this persuasion, and in an atmosphere of precious freedom great personalities spring into being. In the conflict between achievement based on subjection and splendid obedience, and that based on political freedom, my belief is that the system of political and social freedom will triumphantly endure. In essence, it is the conflict between the efficiency of adaptation and organization and the efficiency of invention and creation. What autocracy needs is the thrill and push of individual liberty, and the continental peasant will get it as the result of this war, for the guns of autocracy are celebrating the downfall of autocracy, even in its most ancient fastness — Russia. These autocracies will realize their real greatness when they substitute humility for pride, freedom for accomplishment, as compelling national motives. What democracy needs is the discipline of patient labor, of trained skill, of thoroughness in work, and a more socialized conception of public duty. As President Eliot has pointed out, the German theory of social organization is very young, and her literature, philosophy, and art are fairly new. It is a bit premature to concede the supreme validity of her Kultur and of her political organization until she can point to such names as Dante and Angelo, Shakespeare and Milton, Newton and Darwin and Pasteur, and until such names appear in her political history as Washington and Jefferson and Burke. This is not meant to deny the surpassing greatness of her music and her philosophy, nor to minimize the glory of her Goethes or Schillers or Lessings or Steins, but to suggest that she has not yet reached the superlative. It is not yet quite sure that with all their genius for organization and efficiency, they may not be self-directed to ruin. Certainly the German has as much to learn from the freer nations as we have to learn from the Teutonic genius. Switzerland has organized her democracy and kept her personal liberty, and there is no finer spectacle on earth today than the spectacle of France, seed-sowing, torch-bearing France; France, that has touched the heights and sounded the depths of human experience and national tragedy; "*La belle France*," that has substituted duty for glory as a national motive, and has kept her soul free in the valley of humiliation; grim, patient, silent, far-seeing France, clinging to her republican ideals and reorganizing her life from hovel to palace in the very impact of conflict and death, so that it is enabled to present to the world the finest example of organized efficiency and military glory that the world has seen in some generations. In order to organize an autocracy, the rulers ordain that it shall get in order and provide the means to bring about that end. To organize a democracy, we must organize its soul, and give it power to create its own ideals. It is primarily a peace organization, and that is proof that it is the forward movement of the human soul and not the movement of scientific reaction. It is through a severe mental training in our schools and a return to the conception of public duty which guided the sword and uplifted the heart of the Founder of the Republic that we shall find strength to organize the democracy of the future, revolutionized by science and by urban life. The right to vote implies the duty to vote right; the right to legislate, the duty to legislate justly; the right to judge about foreign policy, the duty to fight if necessary; the right to come to college, the duty to carry one's self handsomely at college. Our youth must be taught to use their senses, to reason simply and correctly, from exact knowledge thus brought to them to attain to sincerity in thought and judgment through work and patience. In our home and civic life, we need some moral equivalent for the training which somehow issues out of war — the glory of self-sacrifice, obedience to just authority, contempt of ease, and a realization that through thoughtful, collective effort great results will be obtained. A great spiritual glory will come to these European nations through their sorrow and striving, which will express itself in great poems and great literature. They are preparing new shrines at which mankind will worship. Let us take care that prosperity is not our sole national endowment. War asks of men self-denials and sacrifice for ideals. Peace must somehow do the same. Autocracy orders men to forget self for an over-self called the State. Democracy must inspire men to forget self for a still higher thing called Humanity.

There stands upon the steps of the Sub-Treasury building, in Wall Street, the bronze figure of an old Virginia country gentleman looking out with his honest eyes upon that sea of hurrying, gain-getting men. This statue is a remarkable allegory, for in his grave, thoughtful person, Washington embodies that form of public spirit, that balance of character, that union of force and justice that redefines democracy. Out of his lips seems to issue the great creed which is the core of democratic society, and around which this finer organization shall be solidly built. Power rests on fitness to rule. Fitness to rule rests on trained minds and spirits. You can trust men if you will train them. The object of power is the public good. The ultimate judgment of mankind in the mass is a fairly good judgment.

CONSCRIPTION PROCLAMATION [1]

WOODROW WILSON

WHEREAS Congress has enacted and the President has, on the eighteenth day of May, one thousand nine hundred and seventeen, approved a law which contains the following provisions:—

Section 5. That all male persons between the ages of twenty-one and thirty, both inclusive, shall be subject to registration in accordance with regulations to be prescribed by the President, etc.

Now, therefore, I, WOODROW WILSON, President of the United States, do call upon the governor of each of the several States and Territories, the Board of Commissioners of the District of Columbia, and all officers and agents of the several States and Territories, of the District of Columbia, and of the counties and municipalities therein, to perform certain duties in the execution of the foregoing law, which duties will be communicated to them directly in regulations of even date herewith. . . .

The power against which we are arrayed has sought to impose its will upon the world by force. To this end it has increased armament until it has changed the face of war. In the sense in which we have been wont to think of armies there are no armies in this struggle. There are entire nations armed. Thus, the men who remain to till the soil and man the factories are no less a part of the army that is France than the men beneath the battle flags. It must be so with us.

[1] "Done at the city of Washington, this eighteenth day of May, in the year of our Lord one thousand nine hundred and seventeen and of the independence of the United States of America, the one hundred and forty-first."

It is not an army that we must shape and train for war; it is a nation. To this end our people must draw close in one compact front against a common foe. But this cannot be if each man pursues a private purpose. All must pursue one purpose. The nation needs all men; but it needs each man, not in the field that will most pleasure him, but in the endeavor that will best serve the common good. Thus, though a sharpshooter pleases to operate a trip-hammer for the forging of great guns, and an expert machinist desires to march with the flag, the Nation is being served only when the sharpshooter marches and the machinist remains at his levers. The whole Nation must be a team in which each man shall play the part for which he is best fitted. To this end, Congress has provided that the Nation shall be organized for war by selection and that each man shall be classified for service in the place to which it shall best serve the general good to call him.

The significance of this cannot be overstated. It is a new thing in our history and a landmark in our progress. It is a new manner of accepting and vitalizing our duty to give ourselves with thoughtful devotion to the common purpose of us all. It is in no sense a conscription of the unwilling; it is, rather, selection from a nation which has volunteered in mass. It is no more a choosing of those who shall march with the colors than it is a selection of those who shall serve an equally necessary and devoted purpose in the industries that lie behind the battle line.

The day here named is the time upon which all shall present themselves for assignment to their tasks. It is for that reason destined to be remembered as one of the most conspicuous moments in our history. It is nothing less than the day upon which the manhood of the country shall step forward in one solid rank in defense of the ideals to which this Nation is consecrated. It is important to those ideals no less than to the pride of this generation in manifesting its devotion to them, that there be no gaps in the ranks.

It is essential that the day be approached i. 'houghtful apprehension of its significance and that we accord to it the honor and the meaning that it deserves. Our industrial need prescribes that it be not made a technical holiday, but the stern sacrifice that is before us urges that it be carried in all our hearts as a great day of patriotic devotion and obligation when the duty shall lie upon every man, whether he is himself to be registered or not, to see to it that the name of every male person of the designated ages is written on these lists of honor.

AMERICANISM AND THE FOREIGN-BORN [1]

WOODROW WILSON

It warms my heart that you should give me such a reception, but it is not of myself that I wish to think to-night, but of those who have just become citizens of the United States. This is the only country in the world which experiences this constant and repeated rebirth. Other countries depend upon the multiplication of their own native people. This country is constantly drinking strength out of new sources by the voluntary association with it of great bodies of strong men and forward-looking women. And so by the gift of the free will of independent people it is constantly being renewed from generation to generation by the same process by which it was originally created. It is as if humanity had determined to see to it that this great nation, founded for the benefit of humanity, should not lack for the allegiance of the people of the world.

You have just taken an oath of allegiance to the United States. Of allegiance to whom? Of allegiance to no one, unless it be God. Certainly not of allegiance to those who temporarily represent this great Government. You have taken an oath of allegiance to a great ideal, to a great body of principles, to a great hope of the human race. You have said, "We are going to America," not only to earn a living, not only to seek the things which it was more difficult to obtain where you were born, but to help forward the great enterprises of the human spirit — to let man know that every-

[1] Delivered May 10, 1915, in Philadelphia, before an audience of naturalized Americans.

where in the world there are men who will cross strange oceans and go where a speech is spoken which is alien to them, knowing that, whatever the speech, there is but one longing and utterance of the human heart, and that is for liberty and justice.

And while you bring all countries with you, you come with a purpose of leaving all other countries behind you — bringing what is best of their spirit, but not looking over your shoulders and seeking to perpetuate what you intended to leave in them. I certainly would not be one even to suggest that a man ceases to love the home of his birth and the nation of his origin—these things are very sacred and ought not to be put out of our hearts—but it is one thing to love the place where you were born and it is another thing to dedicate yourself to the place to which you go. You cannot dedicate yourself to America unless you become in every respect and with every purpose of your will thorough Americans. You cannot become thorough Americans if you think of yourselves in groups. America does not consist of groups. A man who thinks of himself as belonging to a particular national group in America, has not yet become an American, and the man who goes among you to trade upon your nationality is no worthy son to live under the Stars and Stripes.

My urgent advice to you would be not only always to think first of America, but always, also, to think first of humanity. You do not love humanity if you seek to divide humanity into jealous camps. Humanity can be welded together only by love, by sympathy, by justice, not by jealousy and hatred. I am sorry for the man who seeks to make personal capital out of the passions of his fellow men. He has lost the touch and ideal of America, for America was created to unite mankind by those passions which lift and not by the passions which separate and debase.

We came to America, either ourselves or in the persons of our ancestors, to better the ideals of men, to make them see finer things than they had seen before, to get rid of things that divide, and to make sure of the things that unite. It was but an historical accident no doubt that this great country was called the "United States," and yet I am very thankful that it has the word "united" in its title; and the man who seeks to divide man from man, group from group, interest from interest, in the United States is striking at its very heart.

It is a very interesting circumstance to me, in thinking of those of you who have just sworn allegiance to this great Government, that you were drawn across the ocean by some beckoning finger of hope, by some belief, by some vision of a new kind of justice, by some expectation of a better kind of life.

No doubt you have been disappointed in some of us; some of us are very disappointing. No doubt you have found that justice in the United States goes only with a pure heart and a right purpose, as it does everywhere else in the world. No doubt what you found here did n't seem touched for you, after all, with the complete beauty of the ideal which you had conceived beforehand.

But remember this, if we had grown at all poor in the ideal, you brought some of it with you. A man does not go out to seek the thing that is not in him. A man does not hope for the thing that he does not believe in; and if some of us have forgotten what America believed in, you, at any rate, imported in your own hearts a renewal of the belief. That is the reason that I, for one, make you welcome.

If I have in any degree forgotten what America was intended for, I will thank God if you will remind me.

I was born in America. You dreamed dreams of what America was to be, and I hope you brought the dreams with you. No man that does not see visions will ever realize any high hope or undertake any high enterprise.

Just because you brought dreams with you, America is more likely to realize the dreams such as you brought. You are enriching us if you came expecting us to be better than we are.

See, my friends, what that means. It means that America must have a consciousness different from the consciousness of every other nation in the world. I am not saying this with even the slightest thought of criticism of other nations. You know how it is with a family. A family gets centered on itself if it is not careful and is less interested in the neighbors than it is in its own members.

So a nation that is not constantly renewed out of new sources is apt to have the narrowness and prejudice of a family. Whereas, America must have this consciousness, that on all sides it touches elbows and touches hearts with all the nations of mankind.

The example of America must be a special example. The example of America must be the example not merely of peace because it will not fight, but of peace because peace is the healing and elevating influence of the world and strife is not.

There is such a thing as a man being too proud to fight. There is such a thing as a nation being so right that it does not need to convince others by force that it is right.

So, if you come into this great nation as you have come, voluntarily seeking something that we have to give, all that we have to give is this: We cannot exempt you from work. No man is exempt from work anywhere in the world. I sometimes think he is fortunate if he has to work only with his hands and not with his head. It is very easy to do what other people give you to do, but it is very difficult to give other people things to do. We cannot exempt you from work; we cannot exempt you from the strife and the heart-breaking burden of the struggle of the day — that is common to mankind everywhere. We cannot exempt you from the loads you must carry; we can only make them light by the spirit in which they are carried. That is the spirit of hope, it is the spirit of liberty, it is the spirit of justice.

When I was asked, therefore, by the Mayor and the committee that accompanied him to come up from Washington to meet this great company of newly admitted citizens I could not decline the invitation. I ought not to be away from Washington, and yet I feel that it has renewed my spirit as an American.

In Washington men tell you so many things every day that are not so, and I like to come and stand in the presence of a great body of my fellow-citizens, whether they have been my fellow-citizens a long time or a short time, and drink, as it were, out of the common fountains with them and go back feeling that you have so generously given me the sense of your support and of the living vitality in your hearts, of its great ideals which made America the hope of the world.

IV

AMERICAN FOREIGN POLICY

COUNSEL ON ALLIANCES[1]

GEORGE WASHINGTON

Observe good faith and justice toward all nations; cultivate peace and harmony with all. Religion and morality
enjoin this conduct; and can it be, that good policy does not
equally enjoin it? It will be worthy of a free, enlightened,
and, at no distant period, a great nation, to give to mankind
the magnanimous and too novel example of a people always
guided by an exalted justice and benevolence. Who can
doubt that, in the course of time and things, the fruits of
such a plan would richly repay any temporary advantages
which might be lost by a steady adherence to it? Can it be,
that Providence has not connected the permanent felicity
of a nation with its virtue? The experiment, at least, is recommended by every sentiment which ennobles human nature. Alas! is it rendered impossible by its vices?

In the execution of such a plan, nothing is more essential
than that permanent, inveterate antipathies against particular nations, and passionate attachments for others, should
be excluded; and that, in place of them, just and amicable
feelings towards all should be cultivated. The nation which
indulges towards another an habitual hatred, or an habitual
fondness, is in some degree a slave. It is a slave to its animosity or to its affection, either of which is sufficient to lead
it astray from its duty and its interest. Antipathy in one

---

[1] From the "Farewell Address," September, 1796. The address was probably written by Hamilton and Madison. The familiar phrase "entangling
alliances," popularly attributed to Washington, is to be found in Jefferson's
"First Inaugural Address" (see p. 59 of the present volume).

nation against another disposes each more readily to offer insult and injury, to lay hold of slight causes of umbrage, and to be haughty and intractable when accidental or trifling occasions of dispute occur. Hence frequent collisions, obstinate, envenomed, and bloody contests. The nation, prompted by ill-will and resentment, sometimes impels to war the government, contrary to the best calculations of policy. The government sometimes participates in the national propensity, and adopts through passion what reason would reject; at other times, it makes the animosity of the nation subservient to projects of hostility instigated by pride, ambition, and other sinister and pernicious motives. The peace often, sometimes perhaps the liberty, of nations has been the victim.

So likewise, a passionate attachment of one nation for another produces a variety of evils. Sympathy for the favorite nation facilitating the illusion of an imaginary common interest, in cases where no real common interest exists, and infusing into one the enmities of the other, betrays the former into a participation in the quarrels and wars of the latter, without adequate inducement or justification. It leads also to concessions to the favorite nation of privileges denied to others, which is apt doubly to injure the nation making the concessions: by unnecessarily parting with what ought to have been retained; and by exciting jealousy, ill-will, and a disposition to retaliate, in the parties from whom equal privileges are withheld. And it gives to ambitious, corrupted or deluded citizens (who devote themselves to the favorite nation), facility to betray or sacrifice the interests of their own country, without odium, sometimes even with popularity; gilding, with the appearances of a virtuous sense of obligation, a commendable deference for public opinion, or a laudable zeal for public good, the base of foolish compliances of ambition, corruption, or infatuation.

As avenues to foreign influence in innumerable ways, such attachments are particularly alarming to the truly enlightened and independent patriot. How many opportunities do they afford to tamper with domestic factions, to practise the arts of seduction, to mislead public opinion, to influence or awe the public councils. Such an attachment of a small or weak, towards a great and powerful nation, dooms the former to be the satellite of the latter.

Against the insidious wiles of foreign influence (I conjure you to believe me, fellow-citizens), the jealousy of a free people ought to be *constantly* awake; since history and experience prove that foreign influence is one of the most baneful foes of republican government. But that jealousy, to be useful, must be impartial; else it becomes the instrument of the very influence to be avoided, instead of a defence against it. Excessive partiality for one foreign nation, and excessive dislike of another, cause those whom they actuate to see danger only on one side, and serve to veil and even second the arts of influence on the other. Real patriots, who may resist the intrigues of the favorite, are liable to become suspected and odious; while its tools and dupes usurp the applause and confidence of the people, to surrender their interests.

The great rule of conduct for us, in regard to foreign nations, is, in extending our commercial relations, to have with them as little *political* connection as possible. So far as we have already formed engagements, let them be fulfilled with perfect good faith. Here let us stop.

Europe has a set of primary interests which to us have none, or a very remote relation. Hence she must be engaged in frequent controversies, the causes of which are essentially foreign to our concerns. Hence, therefore, it must be unwise in us to implicate ourselves, by artificial ties, in the ordinary vicissitudes of her politics, or the ordinary combinations and collisions of her friendships or enmities.

Our detached and distant situation invites and enables us to pursue a different course. If we remain one people, under an efficient government, the period is not far off, when we may defy material injury from external annoyance; when we may take such an attitude as will cause the neutrality we may at any time resolve upon, to be scrupulously respected; when belligerent nations, under the impossibility of making acquisitions upon us, will not lightly hazard the giving us provocation; when we may choose peace or war, as our interest, guided by justice, shall counsel.

Why forego the advantages of so peculiar a situation? Why quit our own to stand upon foreign ground? Why, by interweaving our destiny with that of any part of Europe, entangle our peace and prosperity in the toils of European ambition, rivalship, interest, humor, or caprice?

It is our true policy to steer clear of permanent alliances with any portion of the foreign world; so far, I mean, as we are now at liberty to do it; for let me not be understood as capable of patronizing infidelity to existing engagements. I hold the maxim no less applicable to public than to private affairs, that honesty is always the best policy. I repeat it, therefore, let those engagements be observed in their genuine sense. But, in my opinion, it is unnecessary and would be unwise to extend them.

Taking care always to keep ourselves, by suitable establishments, on a respectable defensive posture, we may safely trust to temporary alliances for extraordinary emergencies.

Harmony, liberal intercourse with all nations, are recommended by policy, humanity, and interest. But even our commercial policy should hold an equal and impartial hand: neither seeking nor granting exclusive favors or preferences; consulting the natural course of things; diffusing and diver-

sifying by gentle means the streams of commerce, but forc-
ing nothing; establishing, with powers so disposed, in order
to give trade a stable course, to define the rights of our merchants, and to enable the government to support them, conventional rules of intercourse, the best that present circumstances and mutual opinion will permit, but temporary, and
liable to be from time to time abandoned or varied, as experience and circumstances shall dictate; constantly keeping in view, that it is folly in one nation to look for disinterested favors from another; that it must pay with a portion
of its independence for whatever it may accept under that
character; that, by such acceptance, it may place itself in the
condition of having given equivalents for nominal favors,
and yet of being reproached with ingratitude for not giving
more. There can be no greater error than to expect or calcu-
late upon real favors from nation to nation. It is an illusion, which experience must cure, which a just pride ought
to discard.

THE MONROE DOCTRINE [1]

JAMES MONROE

AT the proposal of the Russian Imperial Government, made through the minister of the Emperor residing here, a full power and instructions have been transmitted to the minister of the United States at St. Petersburg to arrange by amicable negotiation the respective rights and interests of the two nations on the northwest coast of this continent. A similar proposal had been made by His Imperial Majesty to the Government of Great Britain, which has likewise been acceded to. The Government of the United States has been desirous by this friendly proceeding of manifesting the great value which they have invariably attached to the friendship of the Emperor and their solicitude to cultivate the best understanding with his Government. In the discussions to which this interest has given rise and in the arrangements by which they may terminate the occasion has been judged proper for asserting, as a principle in which the rights and interests of the United States are involved, that the American continents, by the free and independent condition which they have assumed and maintain, are henceforth not to be considered as subjects for future colonization by any European powers. . . .

It was stated at the commencement of the last session that a great effort was then making in Spain and Portugal to improve the condition of the people of those countries, and that it appeared to be conducted with extraordinary

[1] From the Message of December 2, 1823, outlining the Monroe Doctrine.

moderation. It need scarcely be remarked that the result
has been so far very different from what was then anticipated. Of events in that quarter of the globe, with which
we have so much intercourse and from which we derive our
origin, we have always been anxious and interested spectators. The citizens of the United States cherish sentiments
the most friendly in favor of the liberty and happiness of
their fellow-men on that side of the Atlantic. In the wars of
the European powers in matters relating to themselves we
have never taken any part, nor does it comport with our
policy so to do. It is only when our rights are invaded or
seriously menaced that we resent injuries or make preparation for our defense. With the movements in this hemisphere we are of necessity more immediately connected, and
by causes which must be obvious to all enlightened and impartial observers. The political system of the allied powers
is essentially different in this respect from that of America.
This difference proceeds from that which exists in their respective Governments; and to the defense of our own, which
has been achieved by the loss of so much blood and treasure,
and matured by the wisdom of their most enlightened citizens, and under which we have enjoyed unexampled felicity,
this whole nation is devoted. We owe it, therefore, to candor and the amicable relations existing between the United
States and those powers to declare that we should consider
any attempt on their part to extend their system to any portion of this hemisphere as dangerous to our peace and safety.
With the existing colonies or dependencies of any European
power we have not interfered and shall not interfere. But
with the Governments who have declared their independence and maintained it, and whose independence we have,
on great consideration and on just principles, acknowledged,
we could not view any interposition for the purpose of
oppressing them, or controlling in any other manner their

destiny, by any European power, in any other light than as
the manifestation of an unfriendly disposition toward the
United States. In the war between those new Governments
and Spain we declared our neutrality at the time of their
recognition, and to this we have adhered, and shall continue
to adhere, provided no change shall occur which, in the
judgment of the competent authorities of this Government,
shall make a corresponding change on the part of the United
States indispensable to their security.

The late events in Spain and Portugal show that Europe
is still unsettled. Of this important fact no stronger proof
can be adduced than that the allied powers should have
thought it proper, on any principle satisfactory to themselves, to have interposed by force in the internal concerns
of Spain. To what extent such interposition may be carried,
on the same principle, is a question in which all independent
powers whose governments differ from theirs are interested,
even those most remote, and surely none more so than the
United States. Our policy in regard to Europe, which was
adopted at an early stage of the wars which have so long
agitated that quarter of the globe, nevertheless remains the
same, which is, not to interfere in the internal concerns of
any of its powers; to consider the government *de facto* as the
legitimate government for us; to cultivate friendly relations
with it, and to preserve those relations by a frank, firm, and
manly policy, meeting in all instances the just claims of every
power, submitting to injuries from none. But in regard to
those continents circumstances are eminently and conspicu-
ously different. It is impossible that the allied powers should
extend their political system to any portion of either continent without endangering our peace and happiness; nor can
any one believe that our southern brethren, if left to themselves, would adopt it of their own accord. It is equally impossible, therefore, that we should behold such interposition

in any form with indifference. If we look to the comparative strength and resources of Spain and those new Governments, and their distance from each other, it must be obvious that she can never subdue them. It is still the true policy of the United States to leave the parties to themselves, in the hope that other powers will pursue the same course.

THE EMANCIPATION OF SOUTH AMERICA [1]

HENRY CLAY

THREE hundred years ago, upon the ruins of the thrones of Montezuma and the Incas of Peru, Spain erected the most stupendous system of colonial despotism that the world has ever seen — the most vigorous, the most exclusive. The great principle and object of this system has been to render one of the largest portions of the world exclusively subservient, in all its faculties, to the interests of an inconsiderable spot in Europe. To effectuate this aim of her policy, she locked up Spanish America from all the rest of the world, and prohibited, under the severest penalties, any foreigner from entering any part of it. To keep the natives themselves ignorant of each other, and of the strength and resources of the several parts of her American possessions, she next prohibited the inhabitants of one viceroyalty or government from visiting those of another; so that the inhabitants of Mexico, for example, were not allowed to enter the viceroyalty of New Granada. The agriculture of those vast regions was so regulated and restrained, as to prevent all collision with the agriculture of the peninsula. Where nature, by the character and composition of the soil, had commanded, the abominable system of Spain has forbidden, the growth of certain articles. Thus the olive and the vine, to which Spanish America is so well adapted, are prohibited, wherever

---

[1] From a speech delivered before the House of Representatives, March 24, 1818. His ideas, though rejected by Congress, were endorsed in 1820, and in 1822 certain of the Latin American countries were formally recognized.

their culture can interfere with the olive and the vine of the peninsula. The commerce of the country, in the direction and objects of the exports and imports, is also subjected to the narrow and selfish views of Spain, and fettered by the odious spirit of monopoly, existing in Cadiz. She has sought by scattering discord among the several castes of her American population, and by a debasing course of education, to perpetuate her oppression. Whatever concerns public law, or the science of government, all writings upon political economy, or that tend to give vigor, and freedom, and expansion, to the intellect, are prohibited. Gentlemen would be astonished by the long list of distinguished authors, whom she proscribes, to be found in Depons' and other works. A main feature in her policy is that which constantly elevates the European and depresses the American character. Out of upwards of seven hundred and fifty viceroys and captains-general, whom she has appointed since the conquest of America, about eighteen only have been from the body of the American population. On all occasions she seeks to raise and promote her European subjects, and to degrade and humiliate the Creoles. Wherever in America her sway extends, everything seems to pine and wither beneath its baneful influence. The richest regions of the earth, man, his happiness and his education, all the fine faculties of his soul, are regulated and modified, and moulded, to suit the execrable purposes of an inexorable despotism.

Such is a brief and imperfect picture of the state of things in Spanish America, in 1808, when the famous transactions of Bayonne occurred. The King of Spain and the Indies (for Spanish America has always constituted an integral part of the Spanish empire) abdicated his throne and became a voluntary captive. Even at this day one does not know whether he should most condemn the baseness and perfidy of the one party, or despise the meanness and imbecility of the other.

If the obligation of obedience and allegiance existed on the part of the colonies to the King of Spain, it was founded on the duty of protection which he owed them. By disqualifying himself for the performance of this duty, they became released from that obligation. The monarchy was dissolved; and each integral part had a right to seek its own happiness, by the institution of any new government adapted to its wants. Joseph Bonaparte, the successor *de facto* of Ferdinand, recognized this right on the part of the colonies, and recommended them to establish their independence. Thus, upon the ground of strict right, upon the footing of a mere legal question, governed by forensic rules, the colonies, being absolved by the acts of the parent country from the duty of subjection to it, had an indisputable right to set up for themselves. But I take a broader and a bolder position. I maintain, that an oppressed people are authorized, whenever they can, to rise and break their fetters. This was the great principle of the English revolution. It was the great principle of our own. Vattel, if authority were wanting, expressly supports this right. We must pass sentence of condemnation upon the founders of our liberty, say that they were rebels, traitors, and that we are at this moment legislating without competent powers, before we can condemn the cause of Spanish America. Our revolution was mainly directed against the mere theory of tyranny. We had suffered comparatively but little; we had, in some respects, been kindly treated; but our intrepid and intelligent fathers saw, in the usurpation of the power to levy an inconsiderable tax, the long train of oppressive acts that were to follow. They rose; they breasted the storm; they achieved our freedom. Spanish America for centuries has been doomed to the practical effects of an odious tyranny. If we were justified, she is more than justified.

I am no propagandist. I would not seek to force upon

other nations our principles and our liberty, if they do not want them. I would not disturb the repose even of a detestable despotism. But if an abused and oppressed people will their freedom; if they seek to establish it; if, in truth, they have established it; we have a right, as a sovereign power, to notice the fact, and to act as circumstances and our interest require. I will say, in the language of the venerated father of my country, "born in a land of liberty, my anxious recollections, my sympathetic feelings, and my best wishes, are irresistibly excited, whensoever, in any country, I see an oppressed nation unfurl the banners of freedom." Whenever I think of Spanish America, the image irresistibly forces itself upon my mind, of an elder brother, whose education has been neglected, whose person has been abused and maltreated, and who has been disinherited by the unkindness of an unnatural parent. And, when I contemplate the glorious struggle which that country is now making, I think I behold that brother rising, by the power and energy of his fine native genius, to the manly rank which nature and nature's God intended for him. . . .

In the establishment of the independence of Spanish America, the United States have the deepest interest. I have no hesitation in asserting my firm belief that there is no question in the foreign policy of this country which has ever arisen, or which I can conceive as ever occurring, in the decision of which we have had or can have so much at stake. This interest concerns our politics, our commerce, our navigation. There cannot be a doubt that, Spanish America once independent, whatever may be the form of the governments established in its several parts, these governments will be animated by an American feeling, and guided by an American policy. They will obey the laws of the system of the new world, of which they will compose a part, in contradistinction to that of Europe. Without the influence of that vortex in Europe, the balance of power between its several parts, the preservation of which has so often drenched Europe in blood, America is sufficiently remote to contemplate the new wars which are to afflict that quarter of the globe, as a calm if not a cold and indifferent spectator. In relation to those wars, the several parts of America will generally stand neutral. And as, during the period when they rage, it will be important that a liberal system of neutrality should be adopted and observed, all America will be interested in maintaining and enforcing such a system. The independence of Spanish America, then, is an interest of primary consideration. Next to that, and highly important in itself, is the consideration of the nature of their governments. That is a question, however, for themselves. They will, no doubt, adopt those kinds of governments which are best suited to their condition, best calculated for their happiness. Anxious as I am that they should be free governments, we have no right to prescribe for them. They are, and ought to be, the sole judges for themselves. I am strongly inclined to believe that they will in most, if not all parts of their country, establish free governments. We are their great example. Of us they constantly speak as of brothers, having a similar origin. They adopt our principles, copy our institutions, and, in many instances, employ the very language and sentiments of our revolutionary papers.

But it is sometimes said that they are too ignorant and too superstitious to admit of the existence of free governments. This charge of ignorance is often urged by persons themselves actually ignorant of the real condition of that people. I deny the alleged fact of ignorance; I deny the inference from that fact, if it were true, that they want capacity for free government; and I refuse assent to the further conclusion, if the fact were true, and the inference just, that we are to be indifferent to their fate. All the writers of the most established authority, Depons, Humboldt, and others, concur in assigning to the people of Spanish America great quickness, genius, and particular aptitude for the acquisition of the exact sciences, and others which they have been allowed to cultivate. In astronomy, geology, mineralogy, chemistry, botany, and so forth, they are allowed to make distinguished proficiency. They justly boast of their Abzate, Velasques, and Gama and other illustrious contributors to science. They have nine universities, and in the city of Mexico, it is affirmed by Humboldt, that there are more solid scientific establishments than in any city even of North America. I would refer to the message of the supreme director of La Plata, which I shall hereafter have occasion to use for another purpose, as a model of fine composition of a state paper, challenging a comparison with any, the most celebrated, that ever issued from the pens of Jefferson or Madison. Gentlemen will egregiously err, if they form their opinions of the present moral condition of Spanish America, from what it was under the debasing system of Spain. The eight years' revolution in which it has been engaged, has already produced a powerful effect. Education has been attended to, and genius developed.

PAN–AMERICANISM [1]

ROBERT LANSING

MR. PRESIDENT, AND GENTLEMEN OF THE CONGRESS: —

It is an especial gratification to me to address you to-day, not only as the officer of the United States who invited you to attend this great Scientific Congress of the American Republics, but also as the presiding member of the Governing Board of the Pan-American Union. In this dual capacity I have the honor and the pleasure to welcome you, gentlemen, to the capital of this country, in the full confidence that your deliberations will be of mutual benefit in your various spheres of thought and research — and not only in your individual spheres but in the all-embracing sphere of Pan-American unity and fraternity which is so near to the hearts of us all.

It is the Pan-American spirit and the policy of Pan-Americanism to which I would for a few moments direct your attention at this early meeting of the Congress, since it is my earnest hope that "Pan-America" will be the keynote which will influence your relations with one another and inspire your thoughts and words.

Nearly a century has passed since President Monroe proclaimed to the world his famous doctrine as the National policy of the United States. It was founded on the principle that the safety of this Republic would be imperiled by the extension of sovereign right by a European power over territory in this hemisphere. Conceived in a suspicion of monarchical institutions and in a full sympathy with the re-

[1] Address of welcome by the Secretary of State, December 27, 1915, at the Second Pan-American Scientific Congress.

publican idea, it was uttered at a time when our neighbors to
the south had won their independence and were gradually
adapting themselves to the exercise of their newly acquired
rights. To those struggling nations the doctrine became a
shield against the great European powers, which in the spirit
of the age coveted political control over the rich regions
which the new-born States had made their own.

The United States was then a small nation, but a nation
which had been tried in the fire; a nation whose indomitable
will had remained unshaken by the dangers through which
it had passed. The announcement of the Monroe Doctrine
was a manifestation of this will. It was a courageous thing
for President Monroe to do. It meant much in those early
days, not only to this country, but to those nations which
were commencing a new life under the standard of liberty.
How much it meant we can never know, since for four decades it remained unchallenged.

During that period the younger Republics of America,
giving expression to the virile spirit born of independence
and liberal institutions, developed rapidly and set their feet
firmly on the path of national progress which has led them
to that plane of intellectual and material prosperity which
they to-day enjoy.

Within recent years the Government of the United States
has found no occasion, with the exception of the Venezuela
boundary incident, to remind Europe that the Monroe Doctrine continues unaltered a National policy of this Republic.
The Republics of America are no longer children in the great
family of nations. They have attained maturity. With enterprise and patriotic fervor they are working out their several destinies.

During this later time when the American Nations have
come into a realization of their nationality and are fully conscious of the responsibilities and privileges which are theirs

as sovereign and independent States, there has grown up a feeling that the Republics of this hemisphere constitute a group separate and apart from the other nations of the world, a group which is united by common ideals and common aspirations. I believe that this feeling is general throughout North and South America, and that year by year it has increased until it has become a potent influence over our political and commercial intercourse. It is the same feeling which, founded on sympathy and mutual interest, exists among the members of a family. It is the tie which draws together the twenty-one Republics and makes of them the American Family of Nations.

This feeling, vague at first, has become to-day a definite and certain force. We term it the "Pan-American" spirit, from which springs the international policy of Pan-Americanism. It is that policy which is responsible for this great gathering of distinguished men, who represent the best and most advanced thought of the Americas. It is a policy which this Government has unhesitatingly adopted and which it will do all in its power to foster and promote.

When we attempt to analyze Pan-Americanism we find that the essential qualities are those of the family — sympathy, helpfulness and a sincere desire to see another grow in prosperity, absence of covetousness of another's possessions, absence of jealousy of another's prominence, and, above all, absence of that spirit of intrigue which menaces the domestic peace of a neighbor. Such are the qualities of the family tie among individuals, and such should be, and I believe are, the qualities which compose the tie which unites the American Family of Nations.

I speak only for the Government of the United States, but in doing so I am sure that I express sentiments which will find an echo in every Republic represented here, when I say that the might of this country will never be exercised in a spirit of greed to wrest from a neighboring state its territory or possessions. The ambitions of this Republic do not lie in the path of conquest but in the paths of peace and justice. Whenever and wherever we can, we will stretch forth a hand to those who need help. If the sovereignty of a sister Republic is menaced from overseas, the power of the United States and, I hope and believe, the united power of the American Republics will constitute a bulwark which will protect the independence and integrity of their neighbor from unjust invasion or aggression. The American Family of Nations might well take for its motto that of Dumas's famous musketeers, "One for all; all for one."

If I have correctly interpreted Pan-Americanism from the standpoint of the relations of our Governments with those beyond the seas, it is in entire harmony with the Monroe Doctrine. The Monroe Doctrine is a national policy of the United States; Pan-Americanism is an international policy of the Americas. The motives are to an extent different; the ends sought are the same. Both can exist without impairing the force of either. And both do exist and, I trust, will ever exist in all their vigor.

But Pan-Americanism extends beyond the sphere of politics and finds its application in the varied fields of human enterprise. Bearing in mind that the essential idea manifests itself in coöperation, it becomes necessary for effective coöperation that we should know each other better than we do now. We must not only be neighbors, but friends; not only friends, but intimates. We must understand one another. We must comprehend our several needs. We must study the phases of material and intellectual development which enter into the varied problems of national progress. We should, therefore, when opportunity offers, come together and familiarize ourselves with each other's processes of thought in dealing with legal, economic, and educational questions.

Commerce and industry, science and art, public and private law, government and education, all those great fields which invite the intellectual thought of man, fall within the province of the deliberations of this congress. In the exchange of ideas and comparison of experiences we will come to know one another and to carry to the nations which we represent a better and truer knowledge of our neighbors than we have had in the past. I believe that from that wider knowledge a mutual esteem and trust will spring which will unite these Republics more closely politically, commercially, and intellectually, and will give to the Pan-American spirit an impulse and power which it has never known before.

The present epoch is one which must bring home to every thinking American the wonderful benefits to be gained by trusting our neighbors and by being trusted by them, by coöperation and helpfulness, by a dignified regard for the rights of all, and by living our national lives in harmony and good-will.

Across the thousands of miles of the Atlantic we see Europe convulsed with the most terrible conflict which this world has ever witnessed; we see the manhood of these great nations shattered, their homes ruined, their productive energies devoted to the one purpose of destroying their fellow-men. When we contemplate the untold misery which these once happy people are enduring and the heritage which they are transmitting to succeeding generations, we cannot but contrast a continent at war and a continent at peace. The spectacle teaches a lesson we cannot ignore.

If we seek the dominant ideas in world-politics since we became independent nations, we will find that we won our liberties when individualism absorbed men's thoughts and inspired their deeds. This idea was gradually supplanted by that of nationalism, which found expression in the ambitions of conquest and the greed for territory so manifest in the nineteenth century. Following the impulse of nationalism the idea of internationalism began to develop. It appeared to be an increasing influence throughout the civilized world, when the present war of empires, that great manifestation of nationalism, stayed its progress in Europe and brought discouragement to those who had hoped that the new idea would usher in an era of universal peace and justice.

While we are not actual participants in the momentous struggle which is shattering the ideals toward which civilization was moving and is breaking down those principles on which internationalism is founded, we stand as anxious spectators of this most terrible example of nationalism. Let us hope that it is the final outburst of the cardinal evils of that idea which has for nearly a century spread its baleful influence over the world.

Pan-Americanism is an expression of the idea of internationalism. America has become the guardian of that idea, which will in the end rule the world. Pan-Americanism is the most advanced as well as the most practical form of that idea. It has been made possible because of our geographical isolation, of our similar political institutions, and of our common conception of human rights. Since the European War began, other factors have strengthened this natural bond and given impulse to the movement. Never before have our people so fully realized the significance of the words "peace" and "fraternity." Never have the need and benefit of international coöperation in every form of human activity been so evident as they are to-day.

The path of opportunity lies plain before us Americans. The government and people of every Republic should strive to inspire in others confidence and coöperation by exhibiting integrity of purpose and equity in action. Let us as members of this congress, therefore, meet together on the plane of common interests, and together seek the common good.

Whatever is of common interest, whatever makes for the common good, whatever demands united effort is a fit subject for applied Pan-Americanism. Fraternal helpfulness is the keystone to the arch. Its pillars are faith and justice.

In this great movement this congress will, I believe, play an exalted part. You, gentlemen, represent powerful intellectual forces in your respective countries. Together you represent the enlightened thought of the continent. The policy of Pan-Americanism is practical. The Pan-American spirit is ideal. It finds its source and being in the minds of thinking men. It is the offspring of the best, the noblest conception of international obligation.

With all earnestness, therefore, I commend to you, gentlemen, the thought of the American Republics, twenty-one sovereign and independent nations, bound together by faith and justice, and firmly cemented by a sympathy which knows no superior and no inferior, but which recognizes only equality and fraternity.

A LEAGUE TO ENFORCE PEACE [1]

A. LAWRENCE LOWELL

In spite of its ominous sound, the suggestion of a league of nations to enforce peace has no connection with any effort to stop the present war. It is aimed solely at preventing future conflicts after the terrific struggle now raging has come to an end; and yet this is not a bad time for people in private life to bring forward proposals of such a nature. Owing to the vast number of soldiers under arms, to the proportion of men and women in the warring countries who suffer acutely, to the extent of the devastation and misery, it is probable that, whatever the result may be, the people of all nations will be more anxious to prevent the outbreak of another war than ever before in the history of the world. The time is not yet ripe for governments to take action, but it is ripe for public discussion of practicable means to reduce the danger of future breaches of international peace.

The nations of the world to-day are in much the position of frontier settlements in America half a century ago, before orderly government was set up. The men there were in the main well disposed, but in the absence of an authority that could enforce order each man, feeling no other security from attack, carried arms which he was prepared to use if danger threatened. The first step, when affrays became unbearable, was the formation of a vigilance committee, supported by the enrollment of all good citizens, to prevent men from shooting one another and to punish offenders. People did

[1] Reprinted from the *Atlantic Monthly*, September, 1915, through the generous permission of the author and of the Atlantic Monthly Publishing Company.

not wait for a gradual improvement by the preaching of higher ethics and a better civilization. They felt that violence must be met by force, and, when the show of force was strong enough, violence ceased. In time the vigilance committee was replaced by the policeman and by the sheriff with the *posse comitatus*. The policeman and the sheriff maintain order because they have the bulk of the community behind them, and no country has yet reached, or is likely for an indefinite period to reach, such a state of civilization that it can wholly dispense with the police.

Treaties for the arbitration of international disputes are good. They have proved an effective method of settling questions that would otherwise have bred ill-feeling without directly causing war; but when passion runs high, and deep-rooted interests or sentiments are at stake, there is need of the sheriff with his *posse* to enforce the obligation. There are, no doubt, differences in the conception of justice and right, divergencies of civilization, so profound that people will fight over them, and face even the prospect of disaster in war rather than submit. Yet even in such cases it is worth while to postpone the conflict, to have a public discussion of the question at issue before an impartial tribunal, and thus give to the people of the countries involved a chance to consider, before hostilities begin, whether the risk and suffering of war is really worth while. No sensible man expects to abolish wars altogether, but we ought to seek to reduce the probability of war as much as possible. It is on these grounds that the suggestion has been put forth of a league of nations to enforce peace.

Without attempting to cover details of operation, which are, indeed, of vital importance and will require careful study by experts in international law and diplomacy, the proposal contains four points stated as general objects. The first is that before resorting to arms the members of the league shall submit disputes with one another, if justiciable, to an international tribunal; second, that in like manner they shall submit non-justiciable questions (that is, such as cannot be decided on the basis of strict international law) to an international council of conciliation, which shall recommend a fair and amicable solution; third, that if any member of the league wages war against another before submitting the question in dispute to the tribunal or council, all the other members shall jointly use forthwith both their economic and military forces against the state that so breaks the peace; and, fourth, that the signatory powers shall endeavor to codify and improve the rules of international law.

The kernel of the proposal, the feature in which it differs from other plans, lies in the third point, obliging all the members of the league to declare war on any member violating the pact of peace. This is the provision that provokes both adherence and opposition; and at first it certainly gives one a shock that a people should be asked to pledge itself to go to war over a quarrel which is not of its making, in which it has no interest, and in which it may believe that substantial justice lies on the other side. If, indeed, the nations of the earth could maintain complete isolation, could pursue each its own destiny without regard to the rest, if they were not affected by a war between two others or liable to be drawn into it; if, in short, there were no overwhelming common interest in securing universal peace, the provision would be intolerable. It would be as bad as the liability of an individual to take part in the *posse comitatus* of a community with which he had nothing in common. But in every civilized country the public force is employed to prevent any man, however just his claim, from vindicating his own right with his own hand instead of going to law; and every citizen is bound, when needed, to assist in preventing him, because that is the only way to restrain private war, and the maintenance of order is of paramount importance for every one. Surely the family of nations has a like interest in restraining war between states.

It will be observed that the members of the league are not to bind themselves to enforce the decision of the tribunal or the award of the council of conciliation. That may come in the remote future, but it is no part of this proposal. It would be imposing obligations far greater than the nations can reasonably be expected to assume at the present day; for the conceptions of international morality and fair play are still so vague and divergent that a nation can hardly bind itself to wage war on another, with which it has no quarrel, to enforce a decision or a recommendation of whose justice or wisdom it may not be itself heartily convinced. The proposal goes no farther than obliging all the members to prevent by threat of armed intervention a breach of the public peace before the matter in dispute has been submitted to arbitration, and this is neither unreasonable nor impracticable. There are many questions, especially of a non-justiciable nature, on which we should not be willing to bind ourselves to accept the decision of an arbitration, and where we should regard compulsion by armed intervention of the rest of the world as outrageous. Take, for example, the question of Asiatic immigration, or a claim that the Panama Canal ought to be an unfortified neutral highway, or the desire by a European power to take possession of Colombia. But we ought not, in the interest of universal peace, to object to making a public statement of our position in an international court or council before resorting to arms; and in fact the treaty between the United States and Great Britain, ratified on November 14, 1914, provides that all disputes between the high contracting parties, of every nature whatsoever, shall, failing other methods of adjustment, be referred for investigation and report to a Permanent International Commission with a stipulation that neither country shall declare war or begin hostilities during such investigation and before the report is submitted.

What is true of this country is true of others. To agree to abide by the result of an arbitration, on every non-justiciable question of every nature whatsoever, on pain of compulsion in any form by the whole world, would involve a greater cession of sovereignty than nations would now be willing to concede. This appears, indeed, perfectly clearly from the discussions at the Hague Conference of 1907. But to exclude differences that do not turn on questions of international law from the cases where a state must present the matter to a tribunal or council of conciliation before beginning hostilities, would leave very little check upon the outbreak of war. Almost every conflict between European nations for more than half a century has been based upon some dissension which could not be decided by strict rules of law, and in which a violation of international law or of treaty rights has usually not even been used as an excuse. This was true of the war of France and Sardinia against Austria in 1859, and in substance of the war between Prussia and Austria in 1866. It was true of the Franco-Prussian War in 1870, of the Russo-Turkish War in 1876, of the Balkan War against Turkey in 1912, and of the present war.

No one will claim that a league to enforce peace, such as is proposed, would wholly prevent war, but it would greatly reduce the probability of hostilities. It would take away the advantage of surprise, of catching the enemy unprepared for a sudden attack. It would give a chance for public opinion on the nature of the controversy to be formed throughout the world and in the militant country. The latter is of great importance, for the moment war is declared argument about its merits is at once stifled. Passion runs too high for calm debate, and patriotism forces people to support their government. But a trial before an international tribunal would give time for discussion while emotion is not yet highly inflamed. Men opposed to war would be able to urge its injustice, to ask whether, after all, the object is worth the sacrifice, and they would get a hearing from their fellow citizens which they cannot get after war begins. The mere delay, the interval for consideration, would be an immense gain for the prospect of a peaceful settlement.

In this connection it may be of interest to recall the way in which the medieval custom of private war was abolished in England. It was not done at one step, but gradually, by preventing men from avenging their own wrongs before going to court. The trial by battle long remained a recognized part of judicial procedure, but only after the case had been presented to the court, and only in accordance with judicial forms. This had the effect of making the practice far less common, and of limiting it to the principals in the quarrel instead of involving a general breach of the peace in which their retainers and friends took part. Civilization was still too crude to give up private war, but the arm of the law and the force in the hands of the Crown were strong enough to delay a personal conflict until the case had been presented to court. Without such a force the result could not have been attained.

Every one will admit this in the case of private citizens, but many people shrink from the use of international force to restrain war; some of them on the principle of strict non-resistance, that any taking of life in war cannot be justified, no matter what its purpose or effect. Such people have the most lofty moral ideals, but these are not the whole of true statesmanship, which must aim at the total welfare and strive to lessen the scourges of mankind even by forcible means. Many years ago when an Atlantic steamship was wrecked, it was said that some of the crew made a rush for the boats, beating the passengers off, and that the captain, when he was urged to restore order by shooting a mutineer, replied that he was too near eternity to take life. The result was a far greater loss of life than would have been suffered had he restored order by force. Probably no man with the instincts of a statesman would defend his conduct to-day. He was not a coward, but his sentiments unfitted him for a responsible post in an emergency.

Most people who have been thinking seriously about the maintenance of peace are tending to the opinion that a sanction of some kind is needed to enforce the observance of treaties and of agreements for arbitration. Among the measures proposed has been that of an international police force, under the control of a central council which could use it to preserve order throughout the world. At present such a plan seems visionary. The force would have to be at least large enough to cope with the army that any single nation could put into the field — under existing conditions let us say five millions of men fully equipped and supplied with artillery and ammunition for a campaign of several months. These troops need not be under arms, or quartered near The Hague, but they must be thoroughly trained and ready to be called out at short notice. Practically that would entail yearly votes of the legislative bodies of each of the nations supplying a quota, and if any one of them failed to make the necessary appropriation there would be great difficulty in preventing others from following its example. The whole organization would, therefore, be in constant danger of going to pieces.

But quite apart from the practical difficulties in the permanent execution of such a plan, let us see how it would affect the United States. The amount of the contingents of the various countries would be apportioned with some regard to population, wealth and economic resources; and if the total were five million men, our quota on a moderate estimate might be five hundred thousand men. Is it conceivable that the United States would agree to keep anything like that number drilled, equipped and ready to take the field on the order of an international council composed mainly of foreign nations? Of course it will be answered that these figures are exaggerated because any such plan will be accompanied by a reduction in armaments. But that is an easier thing to talk about than to effect, and especially to maintain. One must not forget that the existing system of universal compulsory military service on the continent of Europe arose from Napoleon's attempt to limit the size of the Prussian army. He would be a bold or sanguine man who should assert that any treaty to limit armaments could not in like manner be evaded; and, however much they were limited, the quantity of troops to be held at the disposal of a foreign council would of necessity be large, while no nation would be willing to pledge for the purpose the whole of its military force. Such a plan may be practicable in some remote future when the whole world is a vast federation under a central government, but that would seem to be a matter for coming generations, not for the men of our day.

Moreover, the nations whose troops were engaged in fighting any country would inevitably find themselves at war with that country.

One cannot imagine saying to some foreign state, "Our troops are killing yours, they are invading your land, we are supplying them with recruits and munitions of war, but otherwise we are at peace with you. You must treat us as a neutral, and accord to our citizens, to their commerce and property, all the rights of neutrality." In short, the plan of an international police force involves all the consequences of the proposal of a league to enforce peace, with other complex provisions extremely hard to execute.

A suggestion more commonly made is that the members of the league of nations, instead of pledging themselves to use their military forces forthwith against any of their number that commits a breach of the peace, should agree to hold at once a conference, and take such measures — diplomatic, economic, or military — as may be necessary to prevent war. The objection to this is that it weakens very seriously the sanction. Conferences are apt to shrink from decisive action. Some of the members are timid, others want delay, and much time is consumed in calling the body together and in discussions after it meets. Meanwhile the war may have broken out, and be beyond control. It is much easier to prevent a fire than to put it out. The country that is planning war is likely to think it has friends in the conference, or neighbors that it can intimidate, who will prevent any positive decision until the fire is burning. Even if the majority decide on immediate action, the minority is not bound thereby. One great power refuses to take part; a second will not do so without her, the rest hesitate and nothing is done to prevent the war.

A conference is an excellent thing. The proposal of a league to enforce peace by no means excludes it; but the important matter, the effective principle, is that every member of the league should know that whether a conference meets or not, or whatever action it may take or fail to take, all the members of the league have pledged themselves to declare war forthwith on any member that commits a breach of the peace before submitting its case to the international tribunal or council of conciliation. Such a pledge, and such a pledge alone, can have the strong deterrent influence, and thus furnish the sanction that is needed. Of course the pledge may not be kept. Like other treaties it may be broken by the parties to it. Nations are composed of human beings with human weaknesses, and one of these is a disinclination to perform an agreement when it involves a sacrifice. Nevertheless, nations, like men, often do have enough sense of honor, of duty, or of ultimate self-interest to carry out their contracts at no little immediate sacrifice. They are certainly more likely to do a thing if they have pledged themselves to it than if they have not; and any nation would be running a terrible risk that went to war in the hope that the other members of the league would break their pledges.

The same objection applies to another alternative proposed in place of an immediate resort to military force; that is the use of economic pressure, by a universal agreement, for example, to have no commercial intercourse with the nation breaking the peace. A threat of universal boycott is, no doubt, formidable, but by no means so formidable as a threat of universal war. A large country with great natural resources which has determined to make war might be willing to face commercial nonintercourse with the other members of the league during hostilities, when it would not for a moment contemplate the risk of fighting them. A threat, for example, by England, France, and Germany to stop all trade with the United States might or might not have prevented our going to war with Spain, but a declaration that they would take part with all their armies and navies against us would certainly have done so.

It has often been pointed out that the threat of general nonintercourse would bear much more hardly on some countries than on others. That may not in itself be a fatal objection, but a very serious consideration arises from the fact that there would be a premium on preparation for war. A nation which had accumulated vast quantities of munitions, food and supplies of all kinds, might afford to disregard it; while another less fully prepared could not.

Moreover, economic pressure, although urged as a milder measure, is in fact more difficult to apply and maintain. A declaration of war is a single act, and when made sustains itself by the passion it inflames; while commercial nonintercourse is a continuous matter, subject to constant opposition exerted in an atmosphere relatively cool. Our manufacturers would complain bitterly at being deprived of dyestuffs and other chemical products on account of a quarrel in which we had no interest; the South would suffer severely by the loss of a market for cotton; the shipping firms and the exporters and importers of all kinds would be gravely injured; and all these interests would bring to bear upon Congress a pressure well-nigh irresistible. The same would be true of every other neutral country, a fact which would be perfectly well known to the intending belligerent and reduce its fear of a boycott.

But, it is said, why not try economic pressure first, and, if that fails, resort to military force, instead of inflicting at once on unoffending members of the league the terrible calamity of war? What do we mean by "if that fails"? Do we mean, if in spite of the economic pressure the war breaks out? But then the harm is done, the fire is ablaze and can be put out only by blood. The object of the league is not to chastise a country guilty of breaking the peace, but to prevent the outbreak of war, and to prevent it by the immediate prospect of such appalling consequences to the offender that he will not venture to run the risk. If a number of great powers were to pledge themselves, with serious intent, to wage war jointly and severally on any one of their members that attacked another before submitting the case to arbitration, it is in the highest degree improbable that the *casus fœderis* would ever occur, while any less drastic provision would be far less effective.

An objection has been raised to the proposal for a league to enforce peace on the ground that it has in the past often proved difficult, if not impossible, to determine which of two belligerents began a war. The criticism is serious, and presents a practical difficulty, grave but probably not insurmountable. The proposal merely lays down a general principle, and if adopted the details would have to be worked out very fully and carefully in a treaty which would specify the acts that would constitute the waging of war by one member upon another. These would naturally be, not the mere creating of apprehension, but specific acts, such as a declaration of war, invasion of territory, the use of force at sea not disowned within forty-eight hours, or an advance into a region in dispute. This last is an especially difficult point, but the portions of the earth's surface in which different nations have conflicting claims is growing less decade by decade. It must be remembered that the cases which would arise under a league of peace are not like those which have arisen in the past, where one nation was determined to go to war and merely sought to throw the moral responsibility on the other while getting the advantage of actually beginning hostilities. It is a case where each will strive to avoid the specific acts of war that may involve the penalty. The reader may have seen, in a country where personal violence is severely punished, two men shaking their fists in each other's faces, each trying to provoke the other to strike the first blow, and no fight after all.

There are many agreements in private business which are not easy to embody in formal contracts; agreements where, as in this case, the execution of the terms calls for immediate action, and where redress after an elaborate trial of the facts affords no real reparation. But, if the object sought is good, men do not condemn it on account of the difficulty in devising provisions that will accomplish the result desired; certainly not until they have tried to devise them. It may, indeed, prove impossible to draft a code of specific acts that will cover the ground; it may be impracticable to draft it so as to avoid issues of fact that can be determined only after a long sifting of evidence which would come too late; but surely that is no reason for failure to make the attempt. We are not making a treaty among nations. We are merely putting forward a suggestion for reducing war which seems to merit consideration.

A second difficulty that will sometimes arise is the rule of conduct to be followed pending the presentation of the question to the international tribunal. The continuance or cessation of the acts complained of may appear to be, and may even be in fact, more important than the final decision. This has been brought to our attention forcibly by the sinking of the Lusitania. We should have no objection to submitting to arbitration the question of the right of submarines to torpedo merchant ships without warning, provided Germany abandoned the practice pending the arbitration; and Germany would probably have no objection to submitting the question to a tribunal on the understanding that the practice was to continue until the decision was rendered, because by that time the war would be over. This difficulty is inherent in every plan for the arbitration of international disputes, although more serious in a league whose members bind themselves to prevent by force the outbreak of war. It would be necessary to give the tribunal summary authority to decree a *modus vivendi*, to empower it, like a court of equity, to issue a temporary injunction.

In short, the proposal for a league to enforce peace cannot meet all possible contingencies. It cannot prevent all future wars, nor does any sensible person believe that any plan can do so in the present state of civilization. But it can prevent some wars that would otherwise take place, and, if it does that, it will have done much good.

People have asked how such a league would differ from the Triple Alliance or Triple Entente, whether it would not be nominally a combination for peace which might have quite a different effect. But in fact its object is quite contrary to those alliances. They are designed to protect their members against outside powers. This is intended to insure peace among the members themselves. If it grew strong enough, by including all the great powers, it might well insist on universal peace by compelling the outsiders to come in. But that is not its primary object, which is simply to prevent its members from going to war with one another. No doubt if several great nations, and some of the smaller ones, joined it, and if it succeeded in preserving constant friendly relations among its members, there would grow up among them a sense of solidarity, which would make any outside power chary of attacking one of them; and, what is more valuable, would make outsiders want to join it. But there is little use in speculating about probabilities. It is enough if such a league were a source of enduring peace among its own members.

How about our own position in the United States? The proposal is a radical and subversive departure from the traditional policy of our country. Would it be wise for us to be parties to such an agreement? At the threshold of such a discussion one thing is clear. If we are not willing to urge our own government to join a movement for peace, we have no business to discuss any plan for the purpose. It is worse than futile, it is an impertinence, for Americans to advise the people of Europe how they ought to conduct their affairs if we have nothing in common with them; to suggest to them conventions with burdens which are well enough for them, but which we are not willing to share. If our peace organizations are not prepared to have us take part in the plans they devise, they had better disband, or confine their discussions to Pan-American questions.

To return to the question; would it be wise for the United

States to make so great a departure from its traditional policy? The wisdom of consistency lies in adherence to a principle so long as the conditions upon which it is based remain unchanged. But the conditions that affect the relation of America to Europe have changed greatly in the last hundred and twenty years. At that time it took about a month to cross the ocean to our shores. Ships were small and could carry few troops. Their guns had a short range. No country had what would now be called more than a very small army; and it was virtually impossible for any foreign nation to make more than a raid upon our territory before we could organize and equip a sufficient force to resist, however unprepared we might be at the outset. But now, by the improvements in machinery, the Atlantic has shrunk to a lake, and before long will shrink to a river. Except for the protection of the navy, and perhaps in spite of it, a foreign nation could land on our coast an army of such a size, and armed with such weapons, that unless we maintain troops several times larger than our present forces, we should be quite unable to oppose them before we had suffered incalculable damage.

It is all very well to assert that we have no desire to quarrel with any one, or any one with us; but good intentions in the abstract, even if accompanied by long-suffering and a disposition to overlook affronts, will not always keep us out of strife. When a number of great nations are locked in a death grapple they are a trifle careless of the rights of the bystander. Within fifteen years of Washington's Farewell Address we were drawn into the wars of Napoleon, and a sorry figure we made for the most part of the fighting on land. A hundred years later our relations with the rest of the world are far closer, our ability to maintain a complete isolation far less. Except by colossal self-deception we cannot believe that the convulsions of Europe do not affect us profoundly, that wars there need not disturb us, that we are not in danger of being drawn into them; or even that we may not some day find ourselves in the direct path of the storm. If our interest in the maintenance of peace is not quite so strong as that of some other nations, it is certainly strong enough to warrant our taking steps to preserve it, even to the point of joining a league to enforce it. The cost of the insurance is well worth the security to us.

If mere material self-interest would indicate such a course, there are other reasons to confirm it. Civilization is to some extent a common heritage which it is worth while for all nations to defend, and war is a scourge which all peoples should use every rational means to reduce. If the family of nations can by standing together make wars less frequent, it is clearly their duty to do so, and in such a body we do not want the place of our own country to be vacant.

To join such a league would mean, no doubt, a larger force of men trained for arms in this country, more munitions of war on hand, and better means of producing them rapidly; for although it may be assumed that the members of the league would never be actually called upon to carry out their promise to fight, they ought to have a potential force for the purpose. But in any case this country ought not to be so little prepared for an emergency as it is to-day, and it would require to be less fully armed if it joined a league pledged to protect its members against attack, than if it stood alone and unprotected. In fact the tendency of such a league, by procuring at least delay before the outbreak of hostilities, would be to lessen the need of preparation for immediate war, and thus have a more potent effect in reducing armaments than any formal treaties, whether made voluntarily or under compulsion.

The proposal for a league to enforce peace does not conflict with plans to go farther, to enforce justice among nations by compelling compliance with the decisions of a tribunal by diplomatic, economic or military pressure. Nor, on the other hand, does it imply any such action, or interfere with the independence or sovereignty of states except in this one respect, that it would prohibit any member, before submitting its claims to arbitration, from making war upon another on pain of finding itself at war with all the rest. The proposal is only a suggestion, defective probably, crude certainly, but if, in spite of that, it is the most promising plan for maintaining peace now brought forward, it merits sympathetic consideration both here and abroad.

THE MONROE DOCTRINE AND THE PROGRAM OF THE LEAGUE TO ENFORCE PEACE [1]

BY GEORGE GRAFTON WILSON

THERE have been some arguments against the platform of the League to Enforce Peace. One of the most frequently advanced of these arguments is that the carrying out of the platform of the league would violate the so-called Monroe Doctrine. These words, the Monroe Doctrine, have been used to designate or to conceal such a variety of ideas and practices that it is necessary to start with some premise as to what the Monroe Doctrine may be.

If the Monroe Doctrine is, as Professor Bingham says, an "obsolete shibboleth," it is clear that the relation of the platform of the league to the content of the doctrine would be one of historical and speculative interest only. If on the other hand it is, as M. Pétin says, the substitution by the United States of an "American law for the general law of nations," the relation of the Monroe Doctrine to the platform of the league would be a fundamental question. If the Monroe Doctrine is an assertion of the "supremacy of the United States in the Western Hemisphere" or "supremacy in political leadership," there would also be reason for careful deliberation.

[1] This paper, by the Professor of International Law at Harvard University, was read at the First National Assemblage of the League to Enforce Peace at Washington on May 26, 1916, under the general topic "Practicability of the League Program." Professor Wilson has revised the paper for inclusion in this book.

In any case, a careful investigation would show that the Monroe Doctrine is not a part of international law. The statement of the doctrine has varied. Early discussions in the Cabinet before the doctrine was set forth in Monroe's Message seem to have been as lively as some later ones upon the same subject. Jefferson, when consulted upon the advisability of a policy which would not "suffer Europe to intermeddle with cis-Atlantic affairs," comparing the Declaration of Independence with this doctrine, said: "That [the Declaration] made us a nation, this sets our compass and points the course which we are to steer through the ocean of time opening on us." In the early days of the Monroe Doctrine the aim was to avoid further European interference in American affairs. Later, particularly from the days of President Polk, the doctrine assumed a more positive form. Bismarck is reported to have called the doctrine a piece of "international impertinence." In 1901 President Roosevelt in his Annual Message declared: "The Monroe Doctrine should be the cardinal feature of the foreign policy of all the nations of the two Americas, as it is of the United States," and in 1904 he said that "the Monroe Doctrine may force the United States, however reluctantly, in flagrant cases of such wrongdoing or impotence to the exercise of an international police power." President Taft intimated in his Message in 1909 that "the apprehension which gave rise to the Monroe Doctrine may be said to have already disappeared and neither the doctrine as it exists nor any other doctrine of American policy should be permitted to operate for the perpetuation of irresponsible government, the escape of just obligations or the insidious allegation of dominating ambitions on the part of the United States."

The construction of the Panama Canal gave rise to new problems. The rumor that foreigners were making purchases of land about Magdalena Bay in Mexico led to pronouncements in the United States Senate, in 1912, that the United States could not view foreign possession of this or any such harbor "without grave concern," and it was admitted that this is a "statement of policy, allied to the Monroe Doctrine, of course, but not necessarily dependent upon it or growing out of it."

As in the early days the United States considered it within its rights to assert a policy defensive in its nature, but for the preservation of its well-being, so in later days the same general policy has taken differing forms. President Wilson early in his Administration endeavored to assure the Americas of his desire for the cordial coöperation of the people of the different nations, and a little later he asserted, "we are friends of constitutional government in America; we are more than its friends, we are its champions"; and, in the same message, he declared that the United States "must regard it as one of the duties of friendship to see that from no quarter are material interests made superior to human liberty and national opportunity." [1] President Roosevelt had in 1901 asserted that the doctrine referred not merely to European, but to "any non-American power." This was recognized abroad, as Sir Edward Grey said in 1911 of the United States: "They had a policy associated with the name of Monroe, the cardinal point of which was that no European or non-American nation should acquire fresh territory on the continent of America."

In December, 1913, Mr. Page, the American Ambassador to Great Britain, announced a late form of policy, saying: "We have now developed subtler ways than taking their lands. There is the taking of their bonds, for instance. Therefore, the important proposition is that no sort of financial control can, without the consent of the United

[1] Since this paper was written President Wilson has proposed a "Monroe Doctrine for the whole world." [Author's note.]

States, be obtained over these weaker nations which would in effect control their government."

These and many other views as to the significance of the Monroe Doctrine show the varying forms in which the United States has stated its opposition to the permanent occupation of territory or acquisition of political control in the American hemisphere by non-American powers. It has seemed necessary to present these differing ideas of the Monroe Doctrine to show that it is not law and to show that, as a manifestation of policy, it is not set forth in any single formula.

As single nations and as groups of nations have policies which vary in different parts of the world, and as the conflict of policies rather than the violation of established law is the frequent cause of international differences, it is evident that, if the League to Enforce Peace cannot provide any aid in case of conflict of policies, its function will be comparatively restricted. The conflict of policy would rarely take a form which would make justiciable methods practicable as a means to settlement.

This being the case, reference of such matters would be to the council of conciliation provided for in the second article of the platform of the League to Enforce Peace. The first article provides for justiciable questions and the second states: —

All other questions arising between the signatories and not settled by negotiation shall be submitted to a council of conciliation for hearing, consideration and recommendation.

Here it should be repeated that the League to Enforce Peace does not bind itself to carry out the recommendation which the council of conciliation may make but merely binds itself to see that no power goes to war over such a matter until the question has been submitted.

The conflicts of policy would, in most cases, be settled

by ordinary diplomatic negotiations between the parties concerned. Even the Hague Conventions of 1899 and of 1907 for the Pacific Settlement of International Disputes, ratified by twenty-seven or more of the leading states of the world, provide that, "in case of serious disagreement or dispute, before an appeal to arms, the signatory powers agree to have recourse, as far as circumstances allow, to the good offices or mediation of one or more friendly powers" (Art. 2). The Convention of 1907 deems it "expedient and desirable that one or more powers, strangers to the dispute, should, on their own initiative," tender such good offices. The United States, however, in signing this Convention made reservation that "nothing contained in this Convention shall be so construed as to require the United States of America to depart from its traditional policy of not intruding upon, interfering with, or entangling itself in political questions or policy or internal administration of any foreign state; nor shall anything contained in the said Convention be construed to imply a relinquishment by the United States of America of its traditional attitude toward purely American questions."

The United States has, however, also within recent years, particularly since 1913, become a party to numerous treaties in which "the high contracting parties agree that all disputes between them, of every nature whatsoever, to the settlement of which previous arbitration treaties or agreements do not apply in their terms or are not applied in fact, shall, when diplomatic methods of adjustment have failed, be referred for investigation and report to an international commission"; and "they agree not to declare war or begin hostilities during such investigation and before the report is submitted." The report shall be presented in the maximum period of one year, but "the high contracting parties, by mutual accord, may shorten or extend this period." Some of these treaties are to remain effective for five years from

the date of ratification and then till twelve months from
notice of intention to terminate the treaty. These treaties
have still some time to run. Plainly, therefore, the United
States is bound already, possibly in some cases under the
Hague Convention and certainly under these other treaties,
of which there are a large number, to submit disputes even
involving the Monroe Doctrine to a body which would meet
the requirements of the platform of the League to Enforce
Peace. These treaties are with France, Great Britain, and
Russia, as well as with other European States and with
South and Central American States. The President, in pro-
claiming these treaties, declares that he has "caused the
said treaty to be made public, to the end that the same and
every article and clause thereof may be observed and fulfilled with good faith by the United States and by the citizens thereof."

A dispute in regard to the Monroe Doctrine or involving
its principles, whatever they may be, would surely be included in the agreement made by the United States to refer
disputes "of every nature whatsoever" to an international
commission for investigation and report. This principle has
had endorsement by leaders in preceding Administrations
as well as in the action upon these treaties by the present
Administration, and is therefore not to be regarded as em-
bodying partisan policies. The United States is already
bound to act as regards the Monroe Doctrine in disputes
which may arise with most states in a fashion in exact accord
with the second article of the platform of the League to Enforce Peace. The aim of the league is secured when the question which negotiation has been unable to settle is submitted "for hearing, consideration and recommendation,"
and it makes little difference whether the body to which it
is submitted is called an "international commission" or a
"council of conciliation."

-If, then, the United States and thirty or more nations are already bound to the principle of the second article of the league's platform so far as the Monroe Doctrine and other matters are subjects of dispute, there would seem to be no reason for raising the question of the practicability of that part of the program at the present time. Its practicability has already been formally declared, and, as embodied in treaty provisions, is a part of the law of the land.

Any further discussion as to the practicability of the application of the league's program to differences arising in regard to the Monroe Doctrine would involve the question as to whether treaties already made will be observed when put to the test. Put concretely, the question may be, will the United States, which has made treaties with certain states agreeing to submit to an international commission disputes "of every nature whatsoever," find it practicable to submit a dispute arising in regard to the Monroe Doctrine to such a commission, or will the United States disregard the treaty, and did the United States so intend in making the treaty. It is to be hoped, and it must be believed, that these treaties were made in good faith and that the parties to the treaties intend to observe their provisions. It has even been announced that the United States proposes to observe in principle toward other nations not parties to such treaties the conduct prescribed in these treaties. These treaties are called treaties for the "Advancement of Peace" and declare as their object "to contribute to the development of the spirit of universal peace." or "to serve the cause of general peace." Accordingly, the enforcement of these treaties is regarded by these states as at least desirable for the sake of peace.

Under the general practice and law of nations the violation of a treaty may be a just cause of war. If this be so, then it is particularly essential that treaties for "the de-

velopment of the spirit of universal peace" be kept. It
would seem to be a simple proposition that the greater the
risk of violation of a treaty the less ready a state will be to
violate the treaty. This principle generally prevails, though
at times states disregard all risks. If there is behind a treaty
the compelling force of the fact of a signed agreement and
the physical resources of the other signatory only, the fact
of the agreement seems often, even in modern times, to have
had little weight, and the sole deterrent seems to have been
the physical power which might be felt if the agreement was
not observed. This has given rise to the maxim often quoted
that "a treaty is as strong as the force behind it." There is
undoubtedly some truth in the maxim. The program of
the League to Enforce Peace proposes to adopt what is beneficial in the maxim and to put behind treaties a degree of
force which weak states might by themselves be unable to
command. If, under the provision by which the United
States and other states have agreed to refer to an international commission all differences, there is a reservation as
regards matters affecting the Monroe Doctrine, this reservation is not expressed or implied.

There has been for many years evidence that treaties
needed behind them some sanction. The one sanction which
all nations recognize is that of force, whether it be economic,
physical or other force. By the state which scrupulously
observes its treaty engagements this force is never felt or
feared. By the state that is not considerate of its treaty
obligations this force is feared and may be felt. The state
that proposed to observe its international obligations would
seem to have almost a right to demand that it be secured
against violation of its rights by a party which has agreed
by treaty to observe them, particularly when the party
which observes its international obligations has, in reliance
upon the promise of the other party, refrained from building

up a force to inspire fear in that party. All that a state can reasonably demand is that its side of a controversy be heard and considered impartially. The League to Enforce Peace proposes to secure such hearing and consideration for both parties but beyond that does not propose to go, even if the subject of the controversy be the Monroe Doctrine.

Further, it may be said if, when in dispute, the Monroe Doctrine as applied by the United States is not a policy upon which the United States is willing to await hearing, consideration and recommendation, then the United States has not acted in good faith in signing these recent treaties; and it may also be said, if the American policy as embodied in the Monroe Doctrine will not stand the test of investigation and consideration, that it is time for the United States to be determining why it should longer give to the doctrine its support.

As the plan of the league for submission of controversies such as might arise over the Monroe Doctrine has, on the initiative of the United States, already been embodied in treaties with a greater part of the states of the world, such a plan cannot be regarded as impracticable without condemnation of the judgment of those who are in control of the affairs of the world, and this judgment the League to Enforce Peace, having the well-being of the world in view, does not criticize and condemn, but supports and commends.

THE CONDITIONS OF PEACE [1]

WOODROW WILSON

GENTLEMEN OF THE SENATE: On the 18th of December last I addressed an identic note to the Governments of the nations now at war, requesting them to state, more definitely than they had yet been stated by either group of belligerents, the terms upon which they would deem it possible to make peace. I spoke on behalf of humanity and of the rights of all neutral nations like our own, many of whose most vital interests the war puts in constant jeopardy.

The Central Powers united in a reply which stated merely that they were ready to meet their antagonists in conference to discuss terms of peace.

The Entente Powers have replied much more definitely, and have stated, in general terms, indeed, but with sufficient definiteness to imply details, the arrangements, guarantees, and acts of reparation which they deem to be the indispensable conditions of a satisfactory settlement.

We are that much nearer a definite discussion of the peace which shall end the present war. We are that much nearer the discussion of the international concert which must thereafter hold the world at peace. In every discussion of the peace that must end this war it is taken for granted that that peace must be followed by some definite concert of power, which will make it virtually impossible that any such catastrophe should ever overwhelm us again. Every lover of mankind, every sane and thoughtful man, must take that for granted.

[1] Address to the Senate, January 22, 1917.

I have sought this opportunity to address you because I thought that I owed it to you, as the council associated with me in the final determination of our international obligations, to disclose to you without reserve the thought and purpose that have been taking form in my mind in regard to the duty of our Government in those days to come when it will be necessary to lay afresh and upon a new plan the foundations of peace among the nations.

It is inconceivable that the people of the United States should play no part in that great enterprise. To take part in such a service will be the opportunity for which they have sought to prepare themselves by the very principles and purposes of their polity and the approved practices of their Government, ever since the days when they set up a new nation in the high and honorable hope that it might in all that it was and did show mankind the way to liberty. They cannot, in honor, withhold the service to which they are now about to be challenged. They do not wish to withhold it. But they owe it to themselves and to the other nations of the world to state the conditions under which they will feel free to render it.

That service is nothing less than this — to add their authority and their power to the authority and force of other nations to guarantee peace and justice throughout the world. Such a settlement cannot now be long postponed. It is right that before it comes this Government should frankly formulate the conditions upon which it would feel justified in asking our people to approve its formal and solemn adherence to a league for peace. I am here to attempt to state those conditions.

The present war must first be ended, but we owe it to candor and to a just regard for the opinion of mankind to say that, so far as our participation in guarantees of future peace is concerned, it makes a great deal of difference in what way and upon what terms it is ended. The treaties and agreements which bring it to an end must embody terms which will create a peace that is worth guaranteeing and preserving, a peace that will win the approval of mankind, not merely a peace that will serve the several interests and immediate aims of the nations engaged.

We shall have no voice in determining what those terms shall be, but we shall, I feel sure, have a voice in determining whether they shall be made lasting or not by the guarantees of a universal covenant, and our judgment upon what is fundamental and essential as a condition precedent to permanency should be spoken now, not afterward, when it may be too late.

No covenant of coöperative peace that does not include the peoples of the new world can suffice to keep the future safe against war, and yet there is only one sort of peace that the peoples of America could join in guaranteeing.

The elements of that peace must be elements that engage the confidence and satisfy the principles of the American Governments, elements consistent with their political faith and the practical conviction which the peoples of America have once for all embraced and undertaken to defend.

I do not mean to say that any American Government would throw any obstacle in the way of any terms of peace the Governments now at war might agree upon, or seek to upset them when made, whatever they might be. I only take it for granted that mere terms of peace between the belligerents will not satisfy even the belligerents themselves. Mere agreements may not make peace secure. It will be absolutely necessary that a force be created as a guarantor of the permanency of the settlement so much greater than the force of any nation now engaged or any alliance hitherto formed or projected, that no nation, no probable combination of nations, could face or withstand it. If the peace presently to be made is to endure, it must be a peace made secure by the organized major force of mankind.

The terms of the immediate peace agreed upon will determine whether it is a peace for which such a guarantee can be secured. The question upon which the whole future peace and policy of the world depends is this: —

Is the present war a struggle for a just and secure peace or only for a new balance of power? If it be only a struggle for a new balance of power, who will guarantee, who can guarantee, the stable equilibrium of the new arrangement? Only a tranquil Europe can be a stable Europe. There must be not only a balance of power, but a community of power; not organized rivalries, but an organized common peace.

Fortunately, we have received very explicit assurances on this point. The statesmen of both of the groups of nations, now arrayed against one another, have said, in terms that could not be misinterpreted, that it was no part of the purpose they had in mind to crush their antagonists. But the implication of these assurances may not be equally clear to all, may not be the same on both sides of the water. I think it will be serviceable if I attempt to set forth what we understand them to be.

They imply, first of all, that it must be a peace without victory. It is not pleasant to say this. I beg that I may be permitted to put my own interpretation upon it and that it may be understood that no other interpretation was in my thought. I am seeking only to face realities and to face them without soft concealments. Victory would mean peace forced upon the loser, a victor's terms imposed upon the vanquished. It would be accepted in humiliation, under duress, at an intolerable sacrifice, and would leave a sting, a resentment, a bitter memory, upon which terms of peace would rest, not permanently, but only as upon quicksand.

Only a peace between equals can last; only a peace the

very principle of which is equality and a common participation in a common benefit. The right state of mind, the right feeling, between nations, is as necessary for a lasting peace as is the just settlement of vexed questions of territory or of racial and national allegiance.

The equality of nations upon which peace must be founded, if it is to last, must be an equality of rights; the guarantees exchanged must neither recognize nor imply a difference between big nations and small, between those that are powerful and those that are weak. Right must be based upon the common strength, not upon the individual strength, of the nations upon whose concert peace will depend.

Equality of territory, of resources, there, of course, cannot be; nor any other sort of equality not gained in the ordinary peaceful and legitimate development of the peoples themselves. But no one asks or expects anything more than an equality of rights. Mankind is looking now for freedom of life, not for equipoises of power.

And there is a deeper thing involved than even equality of rights among organized nations. No peace can last, or ought to last, which does not recognize and accept the principle that Governments derive all their just powers from the consent of the governed, and that no right anywhere exists to hand peoples about from sovereignty to sovereignty as if they were property.

I take it for granted, for instance, if I may venture upon a single example, that statesmen everywhere are agreed that there should be a united, independent, and autonomous Poland, and that henceforth inviolable security of life, of worship, and of industrial and social development should be guaranteed to all peoples who have lived hitherto under the power of Governments devoted to a faith and purpose hostile to their own.

I speak of this not because of any desire to exalt an ab-

stract political principle which has always been held very
dear by those who have sought to build up liberty in America, but for the same reason that I have spoken of the other
conditions of peace, which seem to me clearly indispensable
— because I wish frankly to uncover realities. Any peace
which does not recognize and accept this principle will inevitably be upset. It will not rest upon the affections or the
convictions of mankind. The ferment of spirit of whole popu-
lations will fight subtly and constantly against it, and all the
world will sympathize. The world can be at peace only if its
life is stable, and there can be no stability where the will is in
rebellion, where there is not tranquillity of spirit and a sense
of justice, of freedom, and of right.

So far as practicable, moreover, every great people now
struggling toward a full development of its resources and of
its powers should be assured a direct outlet to the great highways of the sea. Where this cannot be done by the cession
of territory it can no doubt be done by the neutralization of
direct rights of way under the general guarantee which will
assure the peace itself. With a right comity of arrangement
no nation need be shut away from free access to the open
paths of the world's commerce.

And the paths of the sea must alike in law and in fact be
free. The freedom of the seas is the *sine qua non* of peace,
equality, and coöperation. No doubt a somewhat radical
reconsideration of many of the rules of international practice hitherto sought to be established may be necessary in
order to make the seas indeed free and common in practically all circumstances for the use of mankind, but the motive for such changes is convincing and compelling. There
can be no trust or intimacy between the peoples of the world
without them.

The free, constant, unthreatened intercourse of nations
is an essential part of the process of peace and of develop-

ment. It need not be difficult to define or to secure the freedom of the seas if the Governments of the world sincerely desire to come to an agreement concerning it.

It is a problem closely connected with the limitation of naval armaments and the coöperation of the navies of the world in keeping the seas at once free and safe.

And the question of limiting naval armaments opens the wider and perhaps more difficult question of the limitation of armies and of all programs of military preparation. Difficult and delicate as those questions are, they must be faced with the utmost candor and decided in a spirit of real accommodation if peace is to come with healing in its wings and come to stay.

Peace cannot be had without concession and sacrifice. There can be no sense of safety and equality among the nations if great preponderating armies are henceforth to continue here and there to be built up and maintained. The statesmen of the world must plan for peace and nations must adjust and accommodate their policy to it as they have planned for war and made ready for pitiless contest and rivalry. The question of armaments, whether on land or sea, is the most immediately and intensely practical question connected with the future fortunes of nations and of mankind.

I have spoken upon these great matters without reserve and with the utmost explicitness because it has seemed to me to be necessary if the world's yearning desire for peace was anywhere to find free voice and utterance. Perhaps I am the only person in high authority among all the peoples of the world who is at liberty to speak and hold nothing back. I am speaking as an individual, and yet I am speaking also, of course, as the responsible head of a great Government, and I feel confident that I have said what the people of the United States would wish me to say.

May I not add that I hope and believe that I am, in effect, speaking for liberals and friends of humanity in every nation and of every program of liberty? I would fain believe that I am speaking for the silent mass of mankind everywhere who have as yet had no place or opportunity to speak their real hearts out concerning the death and ruin they see to have come already upon the persons and the homes they hold most dear.

And in holding out the expectation that the people and the Government of the United States will join the other civilized nations of the world in guaranteeing the permanence of peace upon such terms as I have named, I speak with the greater boldness and confidence because it is clear to every man who can think that there is in this promise no breach in either our traditions or our policy as a nation, but a fulfillment rather of all that we have professed or striven for.

I am proposing, as it were, that the nations should with one accord adopt the doctrine of President Monroe as the doctrine of the world: That no nation should seek to extend its policy over any other nation or people, but that every people should be left free to determine its own policy, its own way of development, unhindered, unthreatened, unafraid, the little along with the great and powerful.

I am proposing that all nations henceforth avoid entangling alliances which would draw them into competition of power, catch them in a net of intrigue and selfish rivalry, and disturb their own affairs with influences intruded from without. There is no entangling alliance in a concert of power. When all unite to act in the same sense and with the same purpose, all act in the common interest and are free to live their own lives under a common protection.

I am proposing government by the consent of the governed; that freedom of the seas which in international conference after conference representatives of the United States have urged with the eloquence of those who are the convinced disciples of liberty; and that moderat.... of armaments which makes of armies and navies a power for order merely, not an instrument of aggression or of selfish violence.

These are American principles, American policies. We can stand for no others. And they are also the principles and policies of forward-looking men and women everywhere, of every modern nation, of every enlightened community. They are the principles of mankind and must prevail.

WAR FOR DEMOCRACY AND PEACE.[1]

WOODROW WILSON

GENTLEMEN OF THE CONGRESS: I have called the Congress into extraordinary session because there are serious, very serious, choices of policy to be made, and made immediately, which it was neither right nor constitutionally permissible that I should assume the responsibility of making.

On the 3d of February last I officially laid before you the extraordinary announcement of the Imperial German Government that on and after the first day of February it was its purpose to put aside all restraints of law or of humanity and use its submarines to sink every vessel that sought to approach either the ports of Great Britain and Ireland or the western coasts of Europe or any of the ports controlled by the enemies of Germany within the Mediterranean. That had seemed to be the object of the German submarine warfare earlier in the war, but since April of last year the Imperial Government had somewhat restrained the commanders of its undersea craft, in conformity with its promise, then given to us, that passenger boats should not be sunk and that due warning would be given to all other vessels which its submarines might seek to destroy, when no resistance was offered or escape attempted, and care taken that their crews were given at least a fair chance to save their lives in their open boats. The precautions taken were meagre and haphazard enough, as was proved in distressing instance

[1] The War Message was read by the President before a joint session of the Senate and the House of Representatives, April 2, 1917.

after instance in the progress of the cruel and unmanly business, but a certain degree of restraint was observed.

The new policy has swept every restriction aside. Vessels of every kind, whatever their flag, their character, their cargo, their destination, their errand, have been ruthlessly sent to the bottom without warning and without thought of help or mercy for those on board, the vessels of friendly neutrals along with those of belligerents. Even hospital ships and ships carrying relief to the sorely bereaved and stricken people of Belgium, though the latter were provided with safe conduct through the proscribed areas by the German Government itself and were distinguished by unmistakable marks of identity, have been sunk with the same reckless lack of compassion or of principle.

I was for a little while unable to believe that such things would in fact be done by any Government that had hitherto subscribed to humane practices of civilized nations. International law had its origin in the attempt to set up some law which would be respected and observed upon the seas, where no nation has right of dominion and where lay the free highways of the world. By painful stage after stage has that law been built up, with meagre enough results, indeed, after all was accomplished that could be accomplished, but always with a clear view, at least, of what the heart and conscience of mankind demanded.

This minimum of right the German Government has swept aside, under the plea of retaliation and necessity and because it had no weapons which it could use at sea except these, which it is impossible to employ, as it is employing them, without throwing to the wind all scruples of humanity or of respect for the understandings that were supposed to underlie the intercourse of the world.

I am not now thinking of the loss of property involved, immense and serious as that is, but only of the wanton and wholesale destruction of the lives of noncombatants, men, women, and children, engaged in pursuits which have always, even in the darkest periods of modern history, been deemed innocent and legitimate. Property can be paid for; the lives of peaceful and innocent people cannot be.

The present German submarine warfare against commerce is a warfare against mankind. It is a war against all nations. American ships have been sunk, American lives taken, in ways which it has stirred us very deeply to learn of, but the ships and people of other neutral and friendly nations have been sunk and overwhelmed in the waters in the same way. There has been no discrimination. The challenge is to all mankind. Each nation must decide for itself how it will meet it. The choice we make for ourselves must be made with a moderation of counsel and a temperateness of judgment befitting our character and our motives as a nation. We must put excited feeling away. Our motive will not be revenge or the victorious assertion of the physical might of the Nation, but only the vindication of right, of human right, of which we are only a single champion.

When I addressed the Congress on the 26th of February last I thought that it would suffice to assert our neutral rights with arms, our right to use the seas against unlawful interference, our right to keep our people safe against unlawful violence. But armed neutrality, it now appears, is impracticable. Because submarines are in effect outlaws, when used as the German submarines have been used against merchant shipping, it is impossible to defend ships against their attacks, as the law of nations has assumed that merchantmen would defend themselves against privateers or cruisers, visible craft giving chase upon the open sea. It is common prudence in such circumstances, grim necessity, indeed, to endeavor to destroy them before they have shown their own intention. They must be dealt with upon sight, if dealt with at all.

The German Government denies the right of neutrals to use arms at all within the areas of the sea which it has proscribed, even in the defense of rights which no modern publicist has ever before questioned their right to defend. The intimation is conveyed that the armed guards which we have placed on our merchant ships will be treated as beyond the pale of law and subject to be dealt with as pirates would be. Armed neutrality is ineffectual enough at best; in such circumstances and in the face of such pretensions it is worse than ineffectual; it is likely only to produce what it was meant to prevent; it is practically certain to draw us into the war without either the rights or the effectiveness of belligerents. There is one choice we cannot make, we are incapable of making: we will not choose the path of submission and suffer the most sacred rights of our Nation and our people to be ignored or violated. The wrongs against which we now array ourselves are not common wrongs; they cut to the very roots of human life.

With a profound sense of the solemn and even tragical character of the step I am taking and of the grave responsibilities which it involves, but in unhesitating obedience to what I deem my constitutional duty, I advise that the Congress declare the recent course of the Imperial German Government to be in fact nothing less than war against the Government and people of the United States; that it formally accept the status of belligerent which has thus been thrust upon it; and that it take immediate steps not only to put the country in a more thorough state of defense, but also to exert all its power and employ all its resources to bring the Government of the German Empire to terms and end the war.

What this will involve is clear. It will involve the utmost

practicable coöperation in counsel and action with the Governments now at war with Germany, and, as incident to that, the extension to those Governments of the most liberal financial credits, in order that our resources may so far as possible be added to theirs.

It will involve the organization and mobilization of all the material resources of the country to supply the materials of war and serve the incidental needs of the nation in the most abundant and yet the most economical and efficient way possible.

It will involve the immediate full equipment of the navy in all respects, but particularly in supplying it with the best means of dealing with the enemy's submarines.

It will involve the immediate addition to the armed forces of the United States, already provided for by law in case of war, of at least five hundred thousand men who should, in my opinion, be chosen upon the principle of universal liability to service, and also the authorization of subsequent additional increments of equal force so soon as they may be needed and can be handled in training.

It will involve also, of course, the granting of adequate credits to the Government, sustained, I hope, so far as they can equitably be sustained by the present generation, by well-conceived taxation.

I say sustained so far as may be equitable by taxation, because it seems to me that it would be most unwise to base the credits, which will now be necessary, entirely on money borrowed. It is our duty, I most respectfully urge, to protect our people, so far as we may, against the very serious hardships and evils which would be likely to arise out of the inflation which would be produced by vast loans.

In carrying out the measures by which these things are to be accomplished, we should keep constantly in mind the wisdom of interfering as little as possible in our own preparation and in the equipment of our own military forces with the duty — for it will be a very practical duty — of supplying the nations already at war with Germany with the materials which they can obtain only from us or by our assistance. They are in the field and we should help them in every way to be effective there.

I shall take the liberty of suggesting, through the several executive departments of the Government, for the consideration of your committees, measures for the accomplishment of the several objects I have mentioned. I hope that it will be your pleasure to deal with them as having been framed after very careful thought by the branch of the Government upon whom the responsibility of conducting the war and safeguarding the Nation will most directly fall.

While we do these things, these deeply momentous things, let us be very clear, and make very clear to all the world, what our motives and our objects are. My own thought has not been driven from its habitual and normal course by the unhappy events of the last two months, and I do not believe that the thought of the Nation has been altered or clouded by them. I have exactly the same things in mind now that I had in mind when I addressed the Senate on the 22d of January last; the same that I had in mind when I addressed the Congress on the 3d of February and on the 26th of February. Our object now, as then, is to vindicate the principles of peace and justice in the life of the world as against selfish and autocratic power, and to set up among the really free and self-governed peoples of the world such a concert of purpose and of action as will henceforth insure the observance of those principles.

Neutrality is no longer feasible or desirable where the peace of the world is involved and the freedom of its peoples, and the menace to that peace and freedom lies in the existence of autocratic Governments, backed by organized force which is controlled wholly by their will, not by the will of their people. We have seen the last of neutrality in such circumstances. We are at the beginning of an age in which it will be insisted that the same standards of conduct and of responsibility for wrong done shall be observed among nations and their Governments that are observed among the individual citizens of civilized States.

We have no quarrel with the German people. We have no feeling toward them but one of sympathy and friendship. It was not upon their impulse that their Government acted in entering this war. It was not with their previous knowledge or approval. It was a war determined upon as wars used to be determined upon in the old, unhappy days, when peoples were nowhere consulted by their rulers and wars were provoked and waged in the interest of dynasties or of little groups of ambitious men who were accustomed to use their fellowmen as pawns and tools.

Self-governed nations do not fill their neighbor States with spies or set the course of intrigue to bring about some critical posture of affairs which will give them an opportunity to strike and make conquest. Such designs can be successfully worked out only under cover and where no one has the right to ask questions. Cunningly contrived plans of deception or aggression, carried, it may be, from generation to generation, can be worked out and kept from the light only within the privacy of courts or behind the carefully guarded confidences of a narrow and privileged class. They are happily impossible where public opinion commands and insists upon full information concerning all the Nation's affairs.

A steadfast concert for peace can never be maintained except by a partnership of democratic nations. No autocratic Government could be trusted to keep faith within it or observe its covenants. It must be a league of honor, a partnership of opinion. Intrigue would eat its vitals away; the plottings of inner circles who could plan what they would and render account to no one would be a corruption seated at its very heart. Only free peoples can hold their purpose and their honor steady to a common end and prefer the interests of mankind to any narrow interest of their own.

Does not every American feel that assurance has been added to our hope for the future peace of the world by the wonderful and heartening things that have been happening within the last few weeks in Russia? Russia was known by those who knew it best to have been always in fact democratic at heart, in all the vital habits of her thought, in all the intimate relationships of her people that spoke their natural instinct, their habitual attitude toward life. The autocracy that crowned the summit of her political structure, long as it had stood and terrible as was the reality of its power, was not in fact Russian in origin, character, or purpose; and now it has been shaken off and the great, generous Russian people have been added, in all their native majesty and might, to the forces that are fighting for freedom in the world, for justice, and for peace. Here is a fit partner for a league of honor.

One of the things that has served to convince us that the Prussian autocracy was not and could never be our friend is that from the very outset of the present war it has filled our unsuspecting communities, and even our offices of government, with spies and set criminal intrigues everywhere afoot against our National unity of counsel, our peace within and without, our industries and our commerce. Indeed, it is now evident that its spies were here even before the war began; and it is unhappily not a matter of conjecture, but a fact proved in our courts of justice, that the intrigues, which have more than once come perilously near to disturbing the peace and dislocating the industries of the country, have been carried on at the instigation, with the support, and even under the personal direction of official agents of the Imperial Government, accredited to the Government of the United States.

Even in checking these things and trying to extirpate them we have sought to put the most generous interpretation possible upon them because we knew that their source lay, not in any hostile feeling or purpose of the German people toward us (who were, no doubt, as ignorant of them as we ourselves were), but only in the selfish designs of a Government that did what it pleased and told its people nothing. But they have played their part in serving to convince us at last that the Government entertains no real friendship for us, and means to act against our peace and security at its convenience. That it means to stir up enemies against us at our very doors the intercepted note to the German Minister at Mexico City is eloquent evidence.

We are accepting this challenge of hostile purpose because we know that in such a Government, following such methods, we can never have a friend; and that in the presence of its organized power, always lying in wait to accomplish we know not what purpose, can be no assured security for the democratic Governments of the world. We are now about to accept the gage of battle with this natural foe to liberty and shall, if necessary, spend the whole force of the nation to check and nullify its pretensions and its power. We are glad, now that we see the facts with no veil of false pretense about them, to fight thus for the ultimate peace of the world and for the liberation of its peoples, the German people included; for the rights of nations, great and small, and the privilege of men everywhere to choose their way of life and of obedience. The world must be made safe for democracy. Its peace must be planted upon the tested foundations of political liberty.

We have no selfish ends to serve. We desire no conquest,

no dominion. We seek no indemnities for ourselves, no material compensation for the sacrifices we shall freely make. We are but one of the champions of the rights of mankind. We shall be satisfied when those rights have been made as secure as the faith and the freedom of nations can make them.

Just because we fight without rancor and without selfish object, seeking nothing for ourselves but what we shall wish to share with all free peoples, we shall, I feel confident, conduct our operations as belligerents without passion and ourselves observe with proud punctilio the principles of right and of fair play we profess to be fighting for.

I have said nothing of the Governments allied with the Imperial Government of Germany because they have not made war upon us or challenged us to defend our right and our honor. The Austro-Hungarian Government has, indeed, avowed its unqualified endorsement and acceptance of the reckless and lawless submarine warfare, adopted now without disguise by the Imperial German Government, and it has therefore not been possible for this Government to receive Count Tarnowski, the Ambassador recently accredited to this Government by the Imperial and Royal Government of Austria-Hungary; but that Government has not actually engaged in warfare against citizens of the United States on the seas, and I take the liberty, for the present at least, of postponing a discussion of our relations with the authorities at Vienna. We enter this war only where we are clearly forced into it because there are no other means of defending our right.

It will be all the easier for us to conduct ourselves as belligerents in a high spirit of right and fairness because we act without animus, not with enmity toward a people or with the desire to bring any injury or disadvantage upon them, but only an armed opposition to an irresponsible Government which has thrown aside all considerations of humanity and of right and is running amuck.

We are, let me say again, the sincere friends of the German people, and shall desire nothing so much as the early re-establishment of intimate relations of mutual advantage between us, however hard it may be for them for the time being to believe that this is spoken from our hearts. We have borne with their present Government through all these bitter months because of that friendship, exercising a patience and forbearance which would otherwise have been impossible.

We shall happily still have an opportunity to prove that friendship in our daily attitude and actions toward the millions of men and women of German birth and native sympathy who live among us and share our life, and we shall be proud to prove it toward all who are in fact loyal to their neighbors and to the Government in the hour of test. They are most of them as true and loyal Americans as if they had never known any other fealty or allegiance. They will be prompt to stand with us in rebuking and restraining the few who may be of a different mind and purpose. If there should be disloyalty, it will be dealt with with a firm hand of stern repression; but, if it lifts its head at all, it will lift it only here and there and without countenance except from a lawless and malignant few.

It is a distressing and oppressive duty, gentlemen of the Congress, which I have performed in thus addressing you. There are, it may be, many months of fiery trial and sacrifice ahead of us. It is a fearful thing to lead this great, peaceful people into war, into the most terrible and disastrous of all wars, civilization itself seeming to be in the balance.

But the right is more precious than peace, and we shall fight for the things which we have always carried nearest our hearts — for democracy, for the right of those who submit to authority to have a voice in their own Governments, for the rights and liberties of small nations, for a universal dominion of right by such a concert of free peoples as shall bring peace and safety to all nations and make the world itself at last free.

To such a task we can dedicate our lives and our fortunes, everything that we are and everything that we have, with the pride of those who know that the day has come when America is privileged to spend her blood and her might for the principles that gave her birth and happiness and the peace which she has treasured.

God helping her, she can do no other.

V
FOREIGN OPINION OF THE UNITED STATES

TO OLD–WORLD CRITICS [1]

WALT WHITMAN

HERE first the duties of to-day, the lessons of the concrete,
Wealth, order, travel, shelter, products, plenty;
As of the building of some varied, vast, perpetual edifice,
Whence to arise inevitable in time, the towering roofs, the lamps,
The solid-planted spires tall shooting to the stars.

[1] Included in "Sands at Seventy," *Leaves of Grass.* Reprinted with the generous permission of Mr. Horace Traubel.

THE SOVEREIGNTY OF THE PEOPLE [1]

ALEXIS DE TOCQUEVILLE

WHENEVER the political laws of the United States are to be discussed, it is with the doctrine of the sovereignty of the people that we must begin.

The principle of the sovereignty of the people, which is to be found, more or less, at the bottom of almost all human institutions, generally remains concealed from view. It is obeyed without being recognized, or if for a moment it be brought to light, it is hastily cast back into the gloom of the sanctuary.

"The will of the nation" is one of those expressions which have been most profusely abused by the wily and the despotic of every age. To the eyes of some it has been represented by the venal suffrages of a few of the satellites of power; to others, by the votes of a timid or an interested minority; and some have even discovered it in the silence of a people, on the supposition that the fact of submission established the right of command.

In America, the principle of the sovereignty of the people is not either barren or concealed, as it is with some other nations; it is recognized by the customs and proclaimed by the laws; it spreads freely, and arrives without impediment at its most remote consequences. If there be a country in the world where the doctrine of the sovereignty of the people can be fairly appreciated, where it can be studied in its ap-

[1] Tocqueville, after a two years' visit, described and interpreted the United States of his day in *De la Démocratie en Amérique*, 1835, from which this and the two following selections are taken.

plication to the affairs of society, and where its dangers and its advantages may be foreseen, that country is assuredly America.

I have already observed that, from their origin, the sovereignty of the people was the fundamental principle of the greater number of the British colonies in America. It was far, however, from then exercising as much influence on the government of society as it now does. Two obstacles, the one external, the other internal, checked its invasive progress.

It could not ostensibly disclose itself in the laws of the colonies, which were still constrained to obey the mother-country; it was therefore obliged to spread secretly, and to gain ground in the provincial assemblies, and especially in the townships.

American society was not yet prepared to adopt it with all its consequences. The intelligence of New England, and the wealth of the country to the south of the Hudson (as I have shown in the preceding chapter), long exercised a sort of aristocratic influence, which tended to limit the exercise of social authority within the hands of a few. The public functionaries were not universally elected, and the citizens were not all of them electors. The electoral franchise was everywhere placed within certain limits, and made dependent on a certain qualification, which was exceedingly low in the north, and more considerable in the south.

The American Revolution broke out, and the doctrine of the sovereignty of the people, which had been nurtured in the townships, took possession of the State; every class was enlisted in its cause; battles were fought, and victories obtained for it; until it became the law of laws.

A scarcely less rapid change was effected in the interior of society, where the law of descent completed the abolition of local influences.

At the very time when this consequence of the laws and of the Revolution became apparent to every eye, victory was irrevocably pronounced in favor of the democratic cause. All power was, in fact, in its hands, and resistance was no longer possible. The higher orders submitted without a murmur and without a struggle to an evil which was thenceforth inevitable. The ordinary fate of falling powers awaited them; each of their several members followed his own interest; and as it was impossible to wring the power from the hands of a people which they did not detest sufficiently to brave, their only aim was to secure its good-will at any price. The most democratic laws were consequently voted by the very men whose interests they impaired; and thus, although the higher classes did not excite the passions of the people against their order, they accelerated the triumph of the new state of things; so that, by a singular change, the democratic impulse was found to be most irresistible in the very States where the aristocracy had the firmest hold.

The State of Maryland, which had been founded by men of rank, was the first to proclaim universal suffrage, and to introduce the most democratic forms into the conduct of its government.

When a nation modifies the elective qualification, it may easily be foreseen that sooner or later that qualification will be entirely abolished. There is no more invariable rule in the history of society: the farther electoral rights are extended, the more is felt the need of extending them; for after each concession the strength of the democracy increases, and its demands increase with its strength. The ambition of those who are below the appointed rate is irritated in exact proportion to the great number of those who are above it. The exception at last becomes the rule, concession follows concession, and no stop can be made short of universal suffrage.

At the present day the principle of the sovereignty of the

people has acquired, in the United States, all the practical development which the imagination can conceive. It is unencumbered by those fictions which have been thrown over it in other countries, and it appears in every possible form according to the exigency of the occasion. Sometimes the laws are made by the people in a body, as at Athens; and sometimes its representatives, chosen by universal suffrage, transact business in its name, and almost under its immediate control.

In some countries a power exists which, though it is in a degree foreign to the social body, directs it, and forces it to pursue a certain track. In others the ruling force is divided, being partly within and partly without the ranks of the people. But nothing of the kind is to be seen in the United States; there society governs itself for itself. All power centers in its bosom; and scarcely an individual is to be met with who would venture to conceive, or, still more, to express, the idea of seeking it elsewhere. The Nation participates in the making of its laws by the choice of its legislators, and in the execution of them by the choice of the agents of the Executive Government; it may almost be said to govern itself, so feeble and so restricted is the share left to the Administration, so little do the authorities forget their popular origin and the power from which they emanate.

GENERAL TENDENCY OF THE LAWS

ALEXIS DE TOCQUEVILLE

THE defects and the weaknesses of a democratic government may very readily be discovered; they are demonstrated by the most flagrant instances, while its beneficial influence is less perceptibly exercised. A single glance suffices to detect its evil consequences, but its good qualities can only be discerned by long observation. The laws of the American democracy are frequently defective or incomplete; they sometimes attack vested rights, or give a sanction to others which are dangerous to the community; but even if they were good, the frequent changes which they undergo would be an evil. How comes it, then, that the American Republics prosper and maintain their position?

In the consideration of laws a distinction must be carefully observed between the end at which they aim and the means by which they are directed to that end; between their absolute and their relative excellence. If it be the intention of the legislator to favor the interests of the minority at the expense of the majority, and if the measures he takes are so combined as to accomplish the object he has in view with the least possible expense of time and exertion, the law may be well drawn up, although its purpose be bad; and the more efficacious it is, the greater is the mischief which it causes.

Democratic laws generally tend to promote the welfare of the greatest possible number; for they emanate from a majority of the citizens, who are subject to error, but who cannot have an interest opposed to their own advantage. The laws of an aristocracy tend, on the contrary, to concentrate wealth and power in the hands of the minority, because an aristocracy, by its very nature, constitutes a minority. It may therefore be asserted, as a general proposition, that the purpose of a democracy, in the conduct of its legislation, is useful to a greater number of citizens than that of an aristocracy. This is, however, the sum total of its advantages.

Aristocracies are infinitely more expert in the science of legislation than democracies ever can be. They are possessed of a self-control which protects them from the errors of a temporary excitement; and they form lasting designs which they mature with the assistance of favorable opportunities. Aristocratic government proceeds with the dexterity of art; it understands how to make the collective force of all its laws converge at the same time to a given point. Such is not the case with democracies, whose laws are almost always ineffective or inopportune. The means of democracy are therefore more imperfect than those of aristocracy, and the measures which it unwittingly adopts are frequently opposed to its own cause; but the object it has in view is more useful.

Let us now imagine a community so organized by nature, or by its constitution, that it can support the transitory action of bad laws, and that it can await, without destruction, the general tendency of the legislation: we shall then be able to conceive that a democratic government, notwithstanding its defects, will be most fitted to conduce to the prosperity of this community. This is precisely what has occurred in the United States; and I repeat, what I have before remarked, that the great advantage of the Americans consists in their being able to commit faults which they may afterward repair.

An analogous observation may be made respecting public officers. It is easy to perceive that the American democracy frequently errs in the choice of the individuals to whom it en-

trusts the power of the Administration; but it is more difficult to say why the State prospers under their rule. In the
first place, it is to be remarked, that if in a democratic State
the governors have less honesty and less capacity than elsewhere, the governed, on the other hand, are more enlightened and more attentive to their interests. As the people in
democracies is more incessantly vigilant in its affairs, and
more jealous of its rights, it prevents its representatives
from abandoning that general line of conduct which its own
interest prescribes. In the second place, it must be remembered that if the democratic magistrate is more apt to misuse
his power, he possesses it for a shorter period of time. But
there is yet another reason which is still more general and
conclusive. It is no doubt of importance to the welfare of
nations that they should be governed by men of talents and
virtue; but it is perhaps still more important that the interests of those men should not differ from the interests of
the community at large; for if such were the case, virtues of
a high order might become useless, and talents might be
turned to a bad account.

I say that it is important that the interests of the persons
in authority should not conflict with or oppose the interests
of the community at large; but I do not insist upon their
having the same interests as the *whole* population, because I
am not aware that such a state of things ever existed in any
country.

No political form has hitherto been discovered, which is
equally favorable to the prosperity and the development of
all the classes into which society is divided. These classes
continue to form, as it were, a certain number of distinct
nations in the same nation; and experience has shown that it
is no less dangerous to place the fate of these classes exclusively in the hands of any one of them, than it is to make one
people the arbiter of the destiny of another. When the rich

alone govern, the interest of the poor is always endangered; and when the poor make the laws, that of the rich incurs very serious risks. The advantage of democracy does not consist, therefore, as has been sometimes asserted, in favoring the prosperity of all, but simply in contributing to the well-being of the greatest possible number.

The men who are entrusted with the direction of public affairs in the United States are frequently inferior, both in point of capacity and of morality, to those whom aristocratic institutions would raise to power. But their interest is identified and confounded with that of the majority of their fellow-citizens. They may frequently be faithless, and frequently mistake; but they will never systematically adopt a line of conduct opposed to the will of the majority; and it is impossible that they should give a dangerous or an exclusive tendency to the Government.

The maladministration of a democratic magistrate is a mere isolated fact, which only occurs during the short period for which he is elected. Corruption and incapacity do not act as common interests, which may connect men permanently with one another. A corrupt or an incapable magistrate will not concert his measures with another magistrate, simply because that individual is as corrupt and as incapable as himself; and these two men will never unite their endeavors to promote the corruption and inaptitude of their remote posterity. The ambition and manœuvers of the one will serve, on the contrary, to unmask the other. The vices of a magistrate, in democratic States, are usually peculiar to his own person.

But under aristocratic Governments public men are swayed by the interests of their order, which, if it is sometimes confounded with the interests of the majority, is very frequently distinct from them. This interest is the common and lasting bond which unites them together; it induces them to coalesce, and to combine their efforts in order to attain an end which does not always ensure the greatest happiness of the greatest number; and it serves not only to connect the persons in authority, but to unite them to a considerable portion of the community, since a numerous body of citizens belongs to the aristocracy, without being invested with official functions. The aristocratic magistrate is therefore constantly supported by a portion of the community, as well as by the Government of which he is a member.

The common purpose which connects the interest of the magistrates in aristocracies with that of a portion of their contemporaries, identifies it with that of future generations; their influence belongs to the future as much as to the present. The aristocratic magistrate is urged at the same time toward the same point, by the passions of the community, by his own, and I may almost add, by those of his posterity. It is, then, wonderful that he does not resist such repeated impulses? And, indeed, aristocracies are often carried away by the spirit of their order without being corrupted by it; and they unconsciously fashion society to their own ends, and prepare it for their own descendants.

The English aristocracy is perhaps the most liberal which ever existed, and no body of men has ever, uninterruptedly, furnished so many honorable and enlightened individuals to the government of a country. It cannot, however, escape observation, that in the legislation of England the good of the poor has been sacrificed to the advantage of the rich, and the rights of the majority to the privileges of the few. The consequence is, that England, at the present day, combines the extremes of fortune in the bosom of her society; and her perils and calamities are almost equal to her power and her renown.

In the United States, where the public officers have no interests to promote connected with their caste, the general and constant influence of the Government is beneficial, although the individuals who conduct it are frequently unskillful and sometimes contemptible. There is, indeed, a secret tendency in democratic institutions to render the exertions of the citizens subservient to the prosperity of the community, notwithstanding their private vices and mistakes; while in aristocratic institutions there is a secret propensity, which, notwithstanding the talents and the virtues of those who conduct the Government, leads them to contribute to the evils which oppress their fellow-creatures. In aristocratic Governments public men may frequently do injuries which they do not intend; and in democratic States they produce advantages which they never thought of.

THE ACTIVITY OF THE BODY POLITIC

ALEXIS DE TOCQUEVILLE

ON passing from a country in which free institutions are established to one where they do not exist, the traveler is struck by the change; in the former all is bustle and activity, in the latter everything is calm and motionless. In the one, melioration and progress are the general topics of inquiry; in the other, it seems as if the community only aspired to repose in the enjoyment of the advantages which it has acquired. Nevertheless, the country which exerts itself so strenuously to promote its welfare is generally more wealthy and more prosperous than that which appears to be so contented with its lot; and when we compare them together, we can scarcely conceive how so many new wants are daily felt in the former, while so few seem to occur in the latter.

If this remark is applicable to those free countries in which monarchical and aristocratic institutions subsist, it is still more striking with regard to democratic republics. In these States it is not only a portion of the people which is busied with the melioration of its social condition, but the whole community is engaged in the task; and it is not the exigencies and the convenience of a single class for which a provision is to be made, but the exigencies and the convenience of all ranks of life.

It is not impossible to conceive the surpassing liberty which the Americans enjoy; some idea may likewise be formed of the extreme equality which subsists among them; but the political activity which pervades the United States must be seen in order to be understood. No sooner do you set foot upon the American soil than you are stunned by a kind of tumult; a confused clamor is heard on every side; a thousand simultaneous voices demand the immediate satisfaction of their social wants. Everything is in motion around you; here, the people of one quarter of a town are met to decide upon the building of a church; there, the election of a representative is going on; a little farther, the delegates of a district are posting to the town in order to consult upon some local improvements; or, in another place, the laborers of a village quit their ploughs to deliberate upon the project of a road or a public school. Meetings are called for the sole purpose of declaring their disapprobation of the line of conduct pursued by the Government; while in other assemblies the citizens salute the authorities of the day as the fathers of their country. Societies are formed which regard drunkenness as the principal cause of the evils under which the State labors, and which solemnly bind themselves to give a constant example of temperance.

The great political agitation of the American legislative bodies, which is the only kind of excitement that attracts the attention of foreign countries, is a mere episode or a sort of continuation of that universal movement which originates in the lowest classes of the people and extends successively to all the ranks of society. It is impossible to spend more efforts in the pursuit of enjoyment.

The cares of political life engross a most prominent place in the occupation of a citizen in the United States; and almost the only pleasure of which an American has any idea, is to take a part in the Government, and to discuss the part he has taken. This feeling pervades the most trifling habits of life; even the women frequently attend public meetings, and listen to political harangues as a recreation after their household labors. Debating clubs are to a certain extent a substitute for theatrical entertainments: an American cannot converse, but he can discuss; and when he attempts to talk he falls into a dissertation. He speaks to you as if he were addressing a meeting; and if he should warm in the course of the discussion, he will infallibly say, "Gentlemen," to the person with whom he is conversing.

In some countries the inhabitants display a certain repugnance to avail themselves of the political privileges with which the law invests them; it would seem that they set too high a value upon their time to spend it on the interests of the community; and they prefer to withdraw within the exact limits of a wholesome egotism, marked out by four sunk fences and a quickset hedge. But if an American were condemned to confine his activity to his own affairs, he would be robbed of one half of his existence; he would feel an immense void in the life which he is accustomed to lead, and his wretchedness would be unbearable. I am persuaded that if ever a despotic government is established in America, it will find it more difficult to surmount the habits which free institutions have engendered than to conquer the attachment of the citizens to freedom.

This ceaseless agitation which democratic government has introduced into the political world, influences all social intercourse. I am not sure that upon the whole this is not the greatest advantage of democracy; and I am much less inclined to applaud it for what it does than for what it causes to be done.

It is incontestable that the people frequently conducts public business very ill; but it is impossible that the lower orders should take a part in public business without extending the circle of their ideas, and without quitting the ordinary routine of their mental acquirements. The humblest individual who is called upon to coöperate in the government of society, acquires a certain degree of self-respect; and as he possesses authority, he can command the services of minds much more enlightened than his own. He is canvassed by a multitude of applicants, who seek to deceive him in a thousand different ways, but who instruct him by their deceit. He takes a part in political undertakings which did not originate in his own conception, but which give him a taste for undertakings of the kind. New meliorations are daily pointed out in the property which he holds in common with others, and this gives him the desire of improving that property which is more peculiarly his own. He is perhaps neither happier nor better than those who came before him, but he is better informed and more active. I have no doubt that the democratic institutions of the United States, joined to the physical constitution of the country, are the cause (not the direct, as is so often asserted, but the indirect cause) of the prodigious commercial activity of the inhabitants. It is not engendered by the laws, but the people learns how to promote it by the experience derived from legislation.

When the opponents of democracy assert that a single individual performs the duties which he undertakes much better than the government of the community, it appears to me that they are perfectly right. The government of an individual, supposing an equality of instruction on either side, is more consistent, more persevering, and more accurate than that of a multitude, and it is much better qualified judiciously to discriminate the characters of the men it employs. If any deny what I advance, they have certainly never seen a democratic government, or have formed their opinion upon very partial evidence. It is true that even when local circumstances and the disposition of the people allow democratic institutions to subsist, they never display a regular and methodical system of government. Democratic liberty is far from accomplishing all the projects it undertakes, with the skill of an adroit despotism. It frequently abandons them before they have borne their fruits, or risks them when the consequences may prove dangerous; but in the end it produces more than any absolute government, and if it do fewer things well, it does a great number of things. Under its sway, the transactions of the public administration are not nearly so important as what is done by private exertion. Democracy does not confer the most skillful kind of government upon the people, but it produces that which the most skillful governments are frequently unable to awaken, namely, an all-pervading and restless activity, a superabundant force, and an energy which is inseparable from it, and which may, under favorable circumstances, beget the most amazing benefits. These are the true advantages of democracy.

In the present age, when the destinies of Christendom seem to be in suspense, some hasten to assail democracy as its foe while it is yet in its early growth; and others are ready with their vows of adoration for this new duty which is springing forth from chaos; but both parties are very imperfectly acquainted with the object of their hatred or of their desires; they strike in the dark, and distribute their blows by mere chance.

We must first understand what the purport of society and the aim of government are held to be. If it be your intention to confer a certain elevation upon the human mind, and to teach it to regard the things of this world with generous feelings; to inspire men with a scorn of mere temporal advantage; to give birth to living convictions, and to keep alive the spirit of honorable devotedness; if you hold it to be a good thing to refine the habits, to embellish the manners, to cultivate the arts of a nation, and to promote the love of poetry, of beauty, and of renown; if you would constitute a people not unfitted to act with power upon all other nations; nor unprepared for those high enterprises, which, whatever be the result of its efforts, will leave a name forever famous in time — if you believe such to be the principal object of society, you must avoid the government of democracy, which would be a very uncertain guide to the end you have in view.

But if you hold it to be expedient to divert the moral and intellectual activity of man to the production of comfort, and to the acquirement of the necessaries of life; if a clear understanding be more profitable to men than genius; if your object be not to stimulate the virtues of heroism, but to create habits of peace; if you had rather behold vices than crimes, and are content to meet with fewer noble deeds, provided offenses be diminished in the same proportion; if, instead of living in the midst of a brilliant state of society, you are contented to have prosperity around you; if, in short, you are of opinion that the principal object of a government is not to confer the greatest possible share of power and of glory upon the body of the nation, but to insure the greatest degree of enjoyment, and the least degree of misery, to each of the individuals who compose it — if such be your desires, you can have no surer means of satisfying them than by equalizing the condition of men, and establishing democratic institutions.

But if the time be past at which such a choice was possible, and if some superhuman power impel us toward one or the other of these two governments without consulting our wishes, let us at least endeavor to make the best of that which is allotted to us; and let us so inquire into its good and its evil propensities as to be able to foster the former, and repress the latter to the utmost.

THE GERMAN AND THE AMERICAN TEMPER [1]

KUNO FRANCKE

PERHAPS the most fundamental, or shall I say elementary, difference between the German temper and the American may be expressed by the word "slowness." Is there any possible point of view from which slowness might appear to an American as something desirable? I think not. Indeed, to call a thing or a person slow seems to spread about them an atmosphere of complete and irredeemable hopelessness. Compare with this the reverently sturdy feelings likely to be aroused in a German breast by the words *langsam und feierlich* inscribed over a religious or patriotic hymn, and imagine a German Männerchor singing such a hymn, with all the facial and tonal symptoms of joyful and devout slowness of cerebral activity — and you have in brief compass a specimen-demonstration of the difference in *tempo* in which the two national minds habitually move.

It has been said that the *langsamer Schritt* of the German military drill was in the last resort responsible for the astounding victories which in 1870 shook the foundations of Imperial France. Similarly, it might be said that slowness of movement and careful deliberateness are at the bottom of

---

[1] As a native German and an American citizen and patriot, Professor Francke is peculiarly fitted to recognize the merits and defects of both the German and the American temper. The article from which these extracts are derived — "German Literature and the American Temper," printed in the *Atlantic Monthly*, November, 1914, and again in *The German Spirit*, 1916 — was written in the spring preceding the outbreak of war. It is here reprinted through the generous permission of Henry Holt & Co.

most things in which Germans have excelled. To be sure, the most recent development of Germany, particularly in trade and industry, has been most rapid, and the whole of German life of to-day is thoroughly American in its desire for getting ahead and for working under high pressure. But this is a condition forced upon Germany from without through international competition and the exigencies of the world-market rather than springing from the inner tendency of German character itself. And it should not be forgotten that it was the greatest German of modern times, Goethe, who, anticipating the present era of speed, uttered this warning: "Railways, express posts, steamships, and all possible facilities for swift communication, — these are the things in which the civilized world is now chiefly concerned, and by which it will over-civilize itself and arrive at mediocrity." . . .

A striking consequence of this difference of tempo in which the American mind and the German naturally move, and perhaps the most conspicuous example of the practical effect of this difference upon National habits, is the German regard for authority and the American dislike of it. For the slower circulation in the brain of the German makes him more passive and more easily inclined to accept the decisions of others for him, while the self-reliant and agile American is instinctively distrustful of any decision which he has not made himself.

Here, then, is another sharp distinction between the two National tempers, another serious obstacle to the just appreciation of the German spirit by the American.

I verily believe that it is impossible for an American to understand the feelings which a loyal German subject, particularly of the conservative sort, entertains toward the State and its authority. That the State should be anything more than an institution for the protection and safeguarding of the happiness of individuals; that it might be considered as a spiritual, collective personality, leading a life of its own, beyond and above the life of individuals; that service for the State, therefore, or the position of a state official, should be considered as something essentially different from any other kind of useful employment, — these are thoughts utterly foreign to the American mind, and very near and dear to the heart of a German. The American is apt to receive an order or a communication from a public official with feelings of suspicion and with a silent protest; the German is apt to feel honored by such a communication and fancy himself elevated thereby to a position of some public importance.

The American is so used to thinking of the police as the servant, and mostly a very poor servant, of his private affairs, that on placards forbidding trespassing upon his grounds he frequently adds an order, "Police take notice"; the German, especially if he does not look particularly impressive himself, will think long before he makes up his mind to approach one of the impressive-looking *Schutzleute* to be found at every street corner, and deferentially ask him the time of day. The American dislikes the uniform as an embodiment of irksome discipline and subordination, he values it only as a sort of holiday outfit and for parading purposes; to the German the "King's Coat" is something sacrosanct and inviolable, an embodiment of highest national service and highest national honor. . . .

Closely allied with this German sense of authority, and again in sharp contrast with American feeling, is the German distrust of the average man. In order to realize the fundamental polarity of the two National tempers in this respect also, one need only think of the two great representatives of American and German political life in the nineteenth century: Lincoln and Bismarck. Lincoln in every fiber of his being a son of the people, an advocate of the common man, an ideal type of the best instincts of the masses, a man who could express with the simplicity of a child his ineradicable belief in the essential right-mindedness of the plain folk. Bismarck with every pulse-beat of his heart the chivalric vassal of his imperial master; the invincible champion of the monarchical principle; the caustic scorner of the crowd; the man who, whenever he notices symptoms in the crowd that he is gaining popularity with it, becomes suspicious of himself and feels inclined to distrust the justice of his own cause; the merciless cynic who characterizes the futile oratorical efforts of a silver-tongued political opponent by the crushing words, "He took me for a mass meeting."

But not only the political life of the two countries presents this difference of attitude toward the average man. The great German poets and thinkers of the last century were all of them aristocrats by temper. Goethe, Schiller, Kant, Schelling, Hegel, the Romanticists, Heine, Schopenhauer, Wagner, Nietzsche — is there a man among them who would not have begged off from being classed with the advocates of common sense or being called a spokesman of the masses? What a difference from two of the most characteristically American men of letters, Walt Whitman and Emerson: the one consciously and purposely a man of the street, glorying, one might say boastfully, in his comradeship with the crudest and roughest of tramps and dock-hands; the other a philosopher of the field, a modern St. Francis, a prophet of the homespun, an inspired interpreter of the ordinary, — perhaps the most enlightened apostle of democracy that ever lived. Is it not natural that a people which, although with varying degrees of confidence, acknowledges such men as Lincoln, Walt Whitman, and Emerson as the spokesmen of its convictions on the value of the ordinary intellect, should on the whole have no instinctive sympathy with a people whose intellectual leaders are men like Bismarck, Goethe, and Richard Wagner?

To be sure, there is another, a democratic side to German life, and this side naturally appeals to Americans. But German democracy is still in the making, it has not yet achieved truly great things, it has not yet found a truly great exponent either in politics or in literature. In literature its influence has exhausted itself largely, on the one hand, in biting satire of the ruling classes, such as is practiced to-day most successfully by the contributors to *Simplizissimus* and similar papers, sympathizing with Socialism; on the other hand, in idyllic representations of the healthy primitiveness of peasant life and the humble contentedness and respectability of the artisan class, the small tradespeople and subaltern officials — I am thinking, of course, of such sturdy and charming stories of provincial Germany as have been written by Wilhelm Raabe, Fritz Reuter, Peter Rosegger, and Heinrich Seidel. It may be that all these men have been paving the way for that great epoch of German democracy; it may be that some time there will arise truly constructive minds that will unite the whole of the German people in an irresistible movement for popular rights, which would give the average man the same dominating position which he enjoys in this country. But clearly this time has not yet come. In Germany, expert training still overrules common sense and dilettanteism.

The German distrust of the average intellect has for its logical counterpart another National trait which it is hard for Americans to appreciate — the German bent for vague intuitions of the infinite. It seems strange in this age of cold observation of facts, when the German scientist and the German captain of industry appear as the most striking embodiments of National greatness, to speak of vague intuitions of the infinite as a German characteristic. Yet throughout the

centuries this longing for the infinite has been the source of
much of the best and much of the poorest in German intellectual achievements. From this longing for the infinite
sprang the deep inwardness and spiritual fervor which impart such a unique charm to the contemplative thought of
the German Mystics of the fourteenth century. In this
longing for the infinite lay Luther's greatest inspiration and
strength. It was the longing for the infinite which Goethe
felt when he made his Faust say, —

" The thrill of awe is man's best quality."

This longing for the infinite was the very soul of German
Romanticism; and all its finest conceptions, the *Blue Flower*
of Novalis, Fichte's *Salvation by the Will*, Hegel's *Self-revela-
tion of the Idea*, Schopenhauer's *Redemption from the Will*,
Nietzsche's *Revaluation of all Values*, are nothing but ever
new attempts to find a body for this soul.

But while there has thus come a great wealth of inspiration and moral idealism from this German bent for reveling
in the infinite, there has also come from it one of the greatest National defects: German vagueness, German lack of
form, the lack of sense for the shape and proportion of finite
things. Here, then, we meet with another discrepancy between the American and the German character. For nothing
is more foreign to the American than the mystic and the
vague, nothing appeals more to him than what is clear-cut,
easy to grasp, and well proportioned; he cultivates "good
form" for its own sake, not only in his social conduct, but
also in his literary and artistic pursuits, and he usually at-
tains it easily and instinctively, often at the expense of the
deeper substance. To the German, on the contrary, form is a
problem. He is principally absorbed in the subject-matter,
the idea, the inner meaning; he struggles to give this subject-
matter, this inner meaning, an adequate outer form; and he

often fails. To comfort himself, he has invented a technical
term designed to cover up his failure: he falls back on the
"inner form" of his productions. . . .

I have reserved for the last place in this review of differences of German and American temper another trait inti-
mately connected with the German craving for the infinite;
I give the last place to the consideration of this trait, because
it seems to me the most un-American of all. I mean the passion for self-surrender.

I think I need not fear any serious opposition if I designate
self-possession as the cardinal American virtue, and consequently as the cardinal American defect also. It is impossible to imagine that so unmanly a proverb as the German —

> *"Wer niemals einen Rausch gehabt*
> *Der ist kein rechter Mann"* —

should have originated in New England or Ohio. But it is
impossible also to conceive that the author of *Werthers Lei-
den* should have obtained his youthful impressions and in-
spirations in New York City. *"Conatus sese conservandi
unicum virtutis fundamentum"* — this Spinozean motto
may be said to contain the essence of the American deca-
logue of conduct. Always be master of yourself; never betray any irritation, or disappointment, or any other weakness; never slop over; never give yourself away; never make
yourself ridiculous — what American would not admit that
these are foremost among the rules by which he would like
to regulate his conduct?

It can hardly be denied that this habitual self-mastery,
this habitual control over one's emotions, is one of the chief
reasons why so much of American life is so uninteresting
and so monotonous. It reduces the number of opportunities for intellectual friction, it suppresses the manifestation
of strong individuality, often it impoverishes the inner life

itself. But, on the other hand, it has given the American that sureness of motive, that healthiness of appetite, that boyish frolicsomeness, that purity of sex-instincts, that quickness and litheness of manners, which distinguish him from most Europeans; it has given to him all those qualities which insure success and make their possessor a welcome member of any kind of society.

If, in contradistinction to this fundamental American trait of self-possession, I designate the passion for self-surrender as perhaps the most significant expression of National German character, I am well aware that here again, I have touched upon the gravest defects as well as the highest virtues of German National life.

The deepest seriousness and the noblest loyalty of German character is rooted in this passion.

> " *Sich hinzugeben ganz und eine Wonne*
> *Zu fühlen die ewig sein muss,*
> *Ewig, ewig"* —

that is German sentiment of the most unquestionable sort. Not only do the great names in German history — as Luther, Lessing, Schiller, Bismarck, and so many others — stand in a conspicuous manner for this thoroughly German devotion, this absorption of the individual in some great cause or principle, but countless unnamed men and women are equally typical representatives of this German virtue of self-surrender: the housewife whose only thought is for her family; the craftsman who devotes a lifetime of contented obscurity to his daily work; the scholar who foregoes official and social distinction in unremitting pursuit of his chosen inquiry; the official and the soldier, who sink their personality in unquestioning service to the State.

But a German loves not only to surrender himself to a great cause or a sacred task, he equally loves to surrender himself to whims. He loves to surrender to feelings, to hysterias of all sorts; he loves to merge himself in vague and formless imaginings, in extravagant and reckless experience, in what he likes to call "living himself out." And thus this same passion for self-surrender which has produced the greatest and noblest types of German earnestness and devotion, has also led to a number of paradoxical excrescences and grotesque distortions of German character. Nobody is more prone to forget his better self in this so-called "living himself out" than the German. Nobody can be a cruder materialist than the German who has persuaded himself that it is his duty to unmask the "lie of idealism." Nobody can be a more relentless destroyer of all that makes life beautiful and lovely, nobody can be a more savage hater of religious beliefs, of popular tradition, of patriotic instincts, than the German who has convinced himself that by the uprooting of all these things he performs the sacred task of saving society.

THE "DIVINE AVERAGE" [1]

G. LOWES DICKINSON

THE great countries of the East have each a civilization
that is original, if not independent. India, China, Japan,
each has a peculiar outlook on the world. Not so America,
at any rate in the north. America, we might say, does not
exist; there exists instead an offshoot of Europe. Nor does
an "American spirit" exist; there exists instead the spirit
of the average Western man. Americans are immigrants
and descendants of immigrants. Putting aside the negroes
and a handful of Orientals, there is nothing to be found here
that is not to be found in Western Europe; only here what
thrives is not what is distinctive of the different European
countries, but what is common to them all. What America
does, not, of course, in a moment, but with incredible rapid-
ity, is to obliterate distinctions. The Scotchman, the Irish-
man, the German, the Scandinavian, the Italian, even, I
suppose, the Czech, drops his costume, his manner, his
language, his traditions, his beliefs, and retains only his
common Western humanity. Transported to this continent
all the varieties developed in Europe revert to the original
type, and flourish in unexampled vigor and force. It is not
a new type that is evolved; it is the fundamental type, growing in a new soil, in luxuriant profusion. Describe the average Western man and you describe the American; from east
to west, from north to south, everywhere and always the
same — masterful, aggressive, unscrupulous, egotistic, at
once good-natured and brutal, kind if you do not cross him,

[1] *Appearances*, part IV, chapter I. Reprinted through the generous permission of the author and of Doubleday, Page & Co.

ruthless if you do, greedy, ambitious, self-reliant, active for the sake of activity, intelligent and unintellectual, quick-witted and crass, contemptuous of ideas but amorous of devices, valuing nothing but success, recognizing nothing but the actual, Man in the concrete, undisturbed by spiritual life, the master of methods and slave of things, and therefore the conqueror of the world, the unquestioning, the un-doubting, the child with the muscles of a man, the European stripped bare, and shown for what he is, a predatory, unre-flecting, naïf, precociously accomplished brute.

One does not then find in America anything one does not find in Europe; but one finds in Europe what one does not find in America. One finds, as well as the average, what is below and what is above it. America has, broadly speak-ing, no waste products. The wreckage, everywhere evident in Europe, is not evident there. Men do not lose their self-re-spect, they win it; they do not drop out, they work in. This is the great result not of American institutions or ideas, but of American opportunities. It is the poor immigrant who ought to sing the praises of this continent. He alone has the proper point of view; and he, unfortunately, is dumb. But often, when I have contemplated with dreary disgust, in the outskirts of New York, the hideous, wooden shanties planted askew in wastes of garbage, and remembered Naples or Genoa or Venice, suddenly it has been borne in upon me that the Italians living there feel that they have their feet on the ladder leading to paradise; that for the first time they have before them a prospect and a hope; and that while they have lost, or are losing, their manners, their beauty, and their charm, they have gained something which, in their eyes, and perhaps in reality, more than compensates for losses they do not seem to feel, they have gained self-respect, independence, and the allure of the open horizon. "The vi-sion of America," a friend writes, "is the vision of the lifting up of the millions." This, I believe, is true, and it is America's great contribution to civilization. I do not forget it; but neither shall I dwell upon it; for though it is, I suppose, the most important thing about America, it is not what I come across in my own experience. What strikes more often and more directly home to me is the other fact that America, if she is not burdened by masses lying below the average, is also not inspired by an élite rising above it. Her distinction is the absence of distinction. No wonder Walt Whitman sang the "Divine Average." There was nothing else in America for him to sing. But he should not have called it divine; he should have called it "human, all too human."

Or *is* it divine? Divine somehow in its potentialities? Divine to a deeper vision than mine? I was writing this at Brooklyn, in a room that looks across the East River to New York. And after putting down those words, "human, all too human," I stepped out on to the terrace. Across the gulf before me went shooting forward and back interminable rows of fiery shuttles; and on its surface seemed to float blazing basilicas. Beyond rose into the darkness a dazzling tower of light, dusking and shimmering, primrose and green, up to a diadem of gold. About it hung galaxies and constellations, outshining the firmament of stars; and all the air was full of strange voices, more than human, ingeminating Babylonian oracles out of the bosom of night. This is New York. This it is that the average man has done, he knows not why; this is the symbol of his work, so much more than himself, so much more than what seems to be itself in the common light of day. America does not know what she is doing, neither do I know, nor any man. But the impulse that drives her, so mean and poor to the critic's eye, has perhaps more significance in the eye of God; and the optimism of this continent, so seeming-frivolous, is justified, may be, by reason lying beyond its ken.

THE FRAME OF NATIONAL GOVERNMENT [1]

JAMES BRYCE

THE account which has been so far given of the working of the American Government has been necessarily an account rather of its mechanism than of its spirit. Its practical character, its temper and color, so to speak, largely depend on the party system by which it is worked, and on what may be called the political habits of the people. These will be described in later chapters. Here, however, before quitting the study of the constitutional organs of government, it is well to sum up the criticisms we have been led to make, and to add a few remarks, for which no fitting place could be found in preceding chapters, on the general features of the National Government.

I. No part of the Constitution cost its framers so much time and trouble as the method of choosing the President. They saw the evils of a popular vote. They saw also the objections to placing in the hands of Congress the election of a person whose chief duty it was to hold Congress in check. The plan of having him selected by judicious persons, specially chosen by the people for that purpose, seemed to meet both difficulties, and was therefore recommended with confidence. The Presidential electors have, however, turned out mere ciphers, and the President is practically chosen by the people at large. The only importance which the elaborate machinery provided in the Constitution retains, is that it prevents a simple popular vote in which the majority of the Nation should prevail, and makes the

[1] *The American Commonwealth* (Revised Edition), part I, chapter XXVI. Reprinted through the generous permission of The Macmillan Company.

issue of the election turn on the voting in certain "pivotal" States.

II. The choice of the President, by what is now practically a simultaneous popular vote, not only involves once in every four years a tremendous expenditure of energy, time, and money, but induces of necessity a crisis which, if it happens to coincide with any passion powerfully agitating the people, may be dangerous to the Commonwealth.

III. There is always a risk that the result of a Presidential election may be doubtful or disputed on the ground of error, fraud, or violence. When such a case arises, the difficulty of finding an authority competent to deal with it, and likely to be trusted, is extreme. Moreover, the question may not be settled until the preëxisting Executive has, by effluxion of time, ceased to have a right to the obedience of the citizens. The experience of the election of 1876 illustrates these dangers. Such a risk of interregna is incidental to all systems, monarchic or republican, which make the executive head elective, as witnesses the Romano-Germanic Empire of the Middle Ages, and the Papacy. But it is more serious where he is elected by the people than where, as in France and Switzerland, he is chosen by the Chambers.

IV. The change of the higher executive officers, and of many of the lower executive officers also, which usually takes place once in four years, gives a jerk to the machinery, and causes a discontinuity of policy, unless, of course, the President has served only one term, and is reëlected. Moreover, there is generally a loss either of responsibility or of efficiency in the executive chief magistrate during the last part of his term. An outgoing President may possibly be a reckless President, because he has little to lose by misconduct, little to hope from good conduct. He may therefore abuse his patronage, or gratify his whims with impunity. But more often he is a weak President. He has little influence with

Congress, because his patronage will soon come to an end, little hold on the people, who are already speculating on the policy of his successor. His Secretary of State may be unable to treat boldly with foreign powers, who perceive that he has a diminished influence in the Senate, and know that the next secretary may have different views.

The question whether the United States, which no doubt needed a President in 1789 to typify the then created political unity of the Nation, might not now dispense with one, has never been raised in America, where the people, though dissatisfied with the method of choice, value the office because it is independent of Congress and directly responsible to the people. Americans condemn any plan under which, as lately befell in France, the legislature can drive a President from power and itself proceed to choose a new one.

V. The Vice-President's office is ill-conceived. His only ordinary function is to act as chairman of the Senate, but as he does not appoint the committees of that House, and has not even a vote (except a casting vote) in it, this function is of little moment. If, however, the President dies, or becomes incapable of acting, or is removed from office, the Vice-President succeeds to the Presidency. What is the result? The place being in itself unimportant, the choice of a candidate for it excites little interest, and is chiefly used by the party managers as a means of conciliating a section of their party. It becomes what is called "a complimentary nomination." The man elected Vice-President is therefore rarely if ever a man then in the front rank. But when the President dies during his term of office, which has happened to five out of the twenty Presidents, this possibly second-class man steps into a great place for which he was never intended. Sometimes, as in the case of Mr. Arthur, he fills the place respectably. Sometimes, as in that of Andrew Johnson, he throws the country into confusion.

He is *aut nullus aut Cæsar.*

VI. The defects in the structure and working of Congress, and in its relations to the Executive, have been so fully dwelt on already that it is enough to refer summarily to them. They are —

The discontinuity of Congressional policy.

The want of adequate control over officials.

The want of opportunities for the Executive to influence the Legislature.

The want of any authority charged to secure the passing of such legislation as the country needs.

The frequency of disputes between three coördinate powers, the President, the Senate, and the House.

The maintenance of a continuous policy is a difficulty in all popular governments. In the United States it is specially so, because —

The Executive head and his Ministers are necessarily (unless when a President is reëlected) changed once every four years.

One House of Congress is changed every two years.

Neither House recognizes permanent leaders.

No accord need exist between Congress and the Executive.

There may not be such a thing as a party in power, in the European sense of the term, because the party to which the Executive belongs may be in a minority in one or both Houses of Congress, in which case it cannot do anything which requires fresh legislation, — may be in a minority in the Senate, in which case it can take no administrative act of importance.

There is little true leadership in political action, because the most prominent man has no recognized party authority. Congress was not elected to support him. He cannot threaten disobedient followers with a dissolution of Parliament like an English Prime Minister. He has not even the French

President's right of dissolving the House with the consent of the Senate.

There is often no general and continuous Cabinet policy, because the Cabinet has no authority over Congress, may perhaps have no influence with it.

There is no general or continuous legislative policy, because the legislature, having neither recognized leaders, nor a guiding committee, acts through a large number of committees, independent of one another, and seldom able to bring their measures to maturity. What continuity exists is due to the general acceptance of a few broad maxims, such as that of non-intervention in the affairs of the Old World, and to the fact that a large nation does not frequently or lightly change its views upon leading principles. In minor matters of legislation there is little settled policy, for the Houses trifle with questions, take them up in one session and drop them the next, seem insensible to the duty of completing work once begun, and are too apt to yield to the pressure which sections, or even influential individuals in their constituencies, exert upon them to arrest some measure the public interest demands. Neither is there any security that Congress will attend to such defects in the administrative system of the country as may need a statute to correct them. In Europe the daily experience of the administrative departments discloses faults or omissions in the law which involve needless trouble to officials, needless cost to the treasury, needless injustice to classes of the people. Sometimes for their own sakes, sometimes from that desire to see things well done which is the life breath of a good public servant, the permanent officials call the attention of their parliamentary chief, the minister, to the defective state of the law, and submit to him the draft of a bill to amend it. He brings in this bill, and if it involves no matter of political controversy (which it rarely does), he gets it passed. As an

American Minister has no means (except by the favor of a committee) of getting anything he proposes attended to by Congress, it is a mere chance if such amending statutes as these are introduced or pass into law. And it sometimes happens that when he sees the need for an improvement he cannot carry it, because selfish interests oppose it, and he has not that command of a majority by means of which a European minister is able to effect reforms.

These defects are all reducible to two. There is an excessive friction in the American system, a waste of force in the strife of various bodies and persons created to check and balance one another. There is a want of executive unity, and therefore a possible want of executive vigor. Power is so much subdivided that it is hard at a given moment to concentrate it for prompt and effective action. In fact, this happens only when a distinct majority of the people are so clearly of one mind that the several coördinate organs of government obey this majority, uniting their efforts to serve its will.

VII. The relations of the people to the legislature are in every free country so much the most refined and delicate, as well as so much the most important part of the whole scheme and doctrine of government, that we must not expect to find perfection anywhere. But comparing America with Great Britain since 1832, the working of the representative system in America seems somewhat inferior.

There are four essentials to the excellence of a representative system: —

That the representatives shall be chosen from among the best men of the country, and, if possible, from its natural leaders.

That they shall be strictly and palpably responsible to their constituents for their speeches and votes.

That they shall have courage enough to resist a momentary impulse of their constituents which they think mischievous; i.e., shall be representatives rather than mere delegates.

That they individually, and the chamber they form, shall have a reflex action on the people; i.e., that while they derive authority from the people, they shall also give the people the benefit of the experience they acquire in the chamber, as well as of the superior knowledge and capacity they may be presumed to possess.

Americans hold, and no doubt correctly, that of these four requisities, the first, third, and fourth are not attained in their country. Congressmen are not chosen from among the best citizens. They mostly deem themselves mere delegates. They do not pretend to lead the people, being, indeed, seldom specially qualified to do so.

That the second requisite, responsibility, is not fully realized seems surprising in a democratic country, and indeed almost inconsistent with that conception of the representative as a delegate, which is supposed, perhaps erroneously, to be characteristic of democracies. Still the fact is there. One cause, already explained, is to be found in the committee system. Another is the want of organized leadership in Congress. In Europe, a member's responsibility takes the form of his being bound to support the leader of his party on all important divisions. In America, this obligation attaches only when the party has "gone into caucus," and there resolved upon its course. Not having the right to direct, the leader cannot be held responsible for the action of the rank and file. As a third cause we may note the fact that owing to the restricted competence of Congress many of the questions which chiefly interest the voter do not come before Congress at all, so that its proceedings are not followed with the close and keen attention which the debates and divisions of European chambers excite, and some may think that a fourth cause is found in the method by which candidates for membership of Congress are selected. That method is described in later chapters. Its effect has been to make Congressmen (including Senators) be, and feel themselves to be, the nominees of the party organizations rather than of the citizens, and thus it has interposed what may for some purposes be called a sort of non-conducting medium between the people and their representatives.

In general the reciprocal action and reaction between the electors and Congress, what is commonly called the "touch" of the people with their agents, is not sufficiently close, quick, and delicate. Representatives ought to give light and leading to the people, just as the people give stimulus and momentum to their representative. This incidental merit of the parliamentary system is among its greatest merits. But in America the action of the voter fails to tell upon Congress. He votes for a candidate of his own party, but he does not convey to that candidate an impulse toward the carrying of particular measures, because the candidate when in Congress will be practically unable to promote those measures, unless he happens to be placed on the committee to which they are referred. Hence the citizen, when he casts his ballot, can seldom feel that he is advancing any measure or policy, except the vague and general policy indicated in his party platform. He is voting for a party, but he does not know what the party will do, and for a man, but a man whom chance may deprive of the opportunity of advocating the measures he cares most for.

Conversely, Congress does not guide and illuminate its constituents. It is amorphous, and has little initiative. It does not focus the light of the Nation, does not warm its imagination, does not dramatize principles in the deeds and characters of men. This happens because, in ordinary times, it lacks great leaders. and the most obvious cause why it lacks them, is its disconnection from the Executive. As it is often devoid of such men, so neither does the country habitually come to it to look for them. In the old days, neither Hamilton, nor Jefferson, nor John Adams; in later days, neither Stanton, nor Grant, nor Tilden, nor Cleveland, nor Roosevelt, ever sat in Congress. Lincoln sat for two years only, and owed little of his subsequent eminence to his career there.

VIII. The independence of the Judiciary, due to its holding for life, has been a conspicuous merit of the Federal system, as compared with the popular election and short terms of judges in most of the States. Yet even the Federal Judiciary is not secure from the attacks of the two other powers, if combined. For the Legislature may by statute increase the number of Federal Justices, increase it to any extent, since the Constitution leaves the number undetermined, and the President may appoint persons whom he knows to be actuated by a particular political bias, perhaps even prepared to decide specific questions in a particular sense. Thus he and Congress together may obtain such a judicial determination of any constitutional question as they join in desiring, even although that question has been heretofore differently decided by the Supreme Court. The only safeguard is in the disapproval of the people.

It is worth remarking that the points in which the American frame of National Government has proved least successful are those which are most distinctly artificial; i.e., those which are not the natural outgrowth of old institutions and well-formed habits, but devices consciously introduced to attain specific ends. The election of the President and Vice-President by electors appointed *ad hoc* is such a device. The functions of the Judiciary do not belong to this category; they are the natural outgrowth of the common-law doctrines and of the previous histories of the colonies and States; all that is novel in them, for it can hardly be called artificial, is the creation of courts coextensive with the sphere of the National Government.

All the main features of American Government may be deduced from two principles. One is the sovereignty of the people, which expresses itself in the fact that the supreme law — the Constitution — is the direct utterance of their will, that they alone can amend it, that it prevails against every other law, that whatever powers it does not delegate are deemed to be reserved to it, that every power in the State draws its authority, whether directly, like the House of Representatives, or in the second degree, like the President and the Senate, or in the third degree, like the Federal Judiciary, from the people, and is legally responsible to the people, and not to any one of the other powers.

The second principle, itself a consequence of this first one, is the distrust of the various organs and agents of Government. The States are carefully safeguarded against aggression by the Central Government. So are the individual citizens. Each organ of Government, the Executive, the Legislature, the Judiciary, is made a jealous observer and restrainer of the others. Since the people, being too numerous, cannot directly manage their affairs, but must commit them to agents, they have resolved to prevent abuses by trusting each agent as little as possible, and subjecting him to the oversight of other agents, who will harass and check him if he attempts to overstep his instructions.

Some one has said that the American Government and Constitution are based on the theology of Calvin and the philosophy of Hobbes. This at least is true, that there is a hearty Puritanism in the view of human nature which pervades the instrument of 1787. It is the work of men who believed in original sin, and were resolved to leave open for transgressors no door which they could possibly shut. Compare this spirit with the enthusiastic optimism of the

Frenchmen of 1789. It is not merely a difference of race temperaments; it is a difference of fundamental ideas.

With the spirit of Puritanism there is blent a double portion of the spirit of legalism. Not only is there no reliance on ethical forces to help the Government to work; there is an elaborate machinery of law to preserve the equilibrium of each of its organs. The aim of the Constitution seems to be not so much to attain great common ends by securing a good government as to avert the evils which will flow, not merely from a bad government, but from any government strong enough to threaten the preëxisting communities or the individual citizen.

The spirit of 1776, as it speaks to us from the Declaration of Independence and the glowing periods of Patrick Henry, was largely a revolutionary spirit, revolutionary in its faith in abstract principles, revolutionary also in its determination to carry through a tremendous political change in respect of grievance which the calm judgment of history does not deem intolerable, and which might probably have been redressed by less trenchant methods. But the spirit of 1787 was an English spirit, and therefore a conservative spirit, tinged, no doubt, by the hatred to tyranny developed in the revolutionary struggle, tinged also, by the nascent dislike to inequality, but in the main an English spirit, which desired to walk in the old paths of precedent, which thought of government as a means of maintaining order and securing to every one his rights, rather than as a great ideal power, capable of guiding and developing a nation's life. And thus, though the Constitution of 1789 represented a great advance on the still oligarchic system of contemporary England, it was yet, if we regard simply its legal provisions, the least democratic of democracies. Had the points which it left undetermined, as for instance the qualifications of congressional electors, been dealt with in an aristocratic spirit, had the legislation of Congress and of the several States taken an aristocratic turn, it might have grown into an aristocratic system. The democratic character which it now possesses is largely the result of subsequent events, which have changed the conditions under which it had to work, and have delivered its development into the hands of that passion for equality which has become a powerful factor in the modern world everywhere.

He who should desire to draw an indictment against the American scheme of government might make it a long one, and might for every count in it cite high American authority and adduce evidence from American history. Yet a European reader would greatly err were he to conclude that this scheme of government is a failure, or is, indeed, for the purpose of the country, inferior to the political system of any of the great nations of the Old World.

All governments are faulty; and an equally minute analysis of the Constitution of England, or France, or Germany would disclose mischiefs as serious, relatively to the problems with which those states have to deal, as those we have noted in the American system. To any one familiar with the practical working of free governments it is a standing wonder that they work at all. The first impulse of mankind is to follow and obey; servitude rather than freedom is their natural state. With freedom, when it emerges among the more progressive races, there come dissension and faction; and it takes many centuries to form those habits of compromise, that love of order, and that respect for public opinion which make democracy tolerable. What keeps a free government going is the good sense and patriotism of the people, or of the guiding class, embodied in usages and traditions which it is hard to describe, but which find, in moments of difficulty, remedies for the inevitable faults of the system. Now, this good sense and that power of subordinating sectional to national interests which we call patriotism, exist in higher measure in America, than in any of the great states of Europe. And the United States, more than any other country, are governed by public opinion, that is to say, by the general sentiment of the mass of the nation, which all the organs of the National Government and of the State Governments look to and obey.

A philosopher from Jupiter or Saturn who should examine the Constitution of England or that of America would probably pronounce that such a body of complicated devices, full of opportunities for conflict and deadlock, could not work at all. Many of those who examined the American Constitution when it was launched did point to a multitude of difficulties, and confidently predicted its failure. Still more confidently did the European enemies of free government declare in the crisis of the War of Secession that "the republican bubble had burst." Some of these censures were well grounded, though there were also defects which had escaped criticism, and were first disclosed by experience. But the Constitution has lived on in spite of all defects, and seems stronger now than at any previous epoch.

Every Constitution, like every man, has "the defects of its good qualities." If a nation desires perfect stability, it must put up with a certain slowness and cumbrousness; it must face the possibility of a want of action where action is called for. If, on the other hand, it seeks to obtain executive speed and vigor by a complete concentration of power, it must run the risk that that power will be abused and irrevocable steps too hastily taken. "The liberty-loving people of every country," says Judge Cooley, "take courage from American freedom, and find augury of better days for themselves from American prosperity. But America is not so much an example in her liberty as in the covenanted and enduring securities which are intended to prevent liberty degenerating into license, and to establish a feeling of trust and repose under a beneficent government, whose excellence, so obvious in its freedom, is still more conspicuous in its careful provision for permanence and stability." Those faults on which I have laid stress, the waste of power by friction, the want of unity and vigor in the conduct of affairs by Executive and Legislature, are the price which the Americans pay for the autonomy of their States, and for the permanence of the equilibrium among the various branches of their Government. They pay this price willingly, because these defects are far less dangerous to the body politic than they would be in a European country. Take, for instance, the shortcomings of Congress as a legislative authority. Every European country is surrounded by difficulties which legislation must deal with, and that promptly. But in America, where those relics of mediæval privilege and injustice that still cumber most parts of the Old World either never existed, or were long ago abolished, where all the conditions of material prosperity exist in ample measure, and the development of material resources occupies men's minds, where nearly all social reforms lie within the sphere of State action, — in America there has generally been less desire than in Europe for a perennial stream of Federal legislation. People are contented if things go on fairly well as they are. Political philosophers, or philanthropists, perceive not a few improvements which Federal statutes might effect, but the mass of the Nation has not greatly complained and the wise see Congress so often on the point of committing mischievous errors that they do not deplore the barrenness of session after session.

Every European State has to fear not only the rivalry but the aggression of its neighbors. Even Britain, so long safe in her insular home, has lost some of her security by the growth of steam navies, and has in her Indian and colonial posses-

sions given pledges to Fortune all over the globe. She, like
the powers of the European continent, must maintain her
system of government in full efficiency for war as well as for
peace, and cannot afford to let her armaments decline, her
finances become disordered, the vigor of her Executive authority be impaired, sources of internal discord continue to
prey upon her vitals. But America has lived in a world of
her own, *ipsa suis pollens opibus, nihil indigna nostri.* Safe
from attack, safe even from menace, she hears from afar the
warring cries of European races and faiths, as the gods of
Epicurus listened to the murmurs of the unhappy earth
spread out beneath their golden dwellings,

"Sejuncta a rebus nostris remotaque longe."

Had Canada or Mexico grown to be a great power, had
France not sold Louisiana, or had England, rooted on the
American continent, become a military despotism, the
United States could not indulge the easy optimism which
makes them tolerate the faults of their Government. As it
is, that which might prove to a European State a mortal disease is here nothing worse than a teasing ailment. Since the
War of Secession ended, no serious danger has arisen either
from within or from without to alarm transatlantic statesmen. Social convulsions from within, warlike assaults from
without, seem now as unlikely to try the fabric of the American Constitution as an earthquake to rend the walls of the
Capitol. This is why the Americans submit, not merely pa-
tiently but hopefully, to the defects of their Government.
The vessel may not be any better built, or found, or rigged
than are those which carry the fortunes of the great nations
of Europe. She is certainly not better navigated. But for
the present, at least — it may not always be so — she sails
upon a summer sea.

It must never be forgotten that the main object which
the framers of the Constitution set before themselves has

been achieved. When Sieyès was asked what he had done during the Reign of Terror, he answered, "I lived." The Constitution as a whole has stood and stands unshaken. The scales of power have continued to hang fairly even. The President has not corrupted and enslaved Congress: Congress has not paralyzed and cowed the President. The legislative may have sometimes appeared to be gaining on the executive department; but there are also times when the people support the President against the Legislature, and when the Legislature are obliged to recognize the fact. Were George Washington to return to earth, he might be as great and useful a President as he was more than a century ago. Neither the Legislature nor the Executive has for a moment threatened the liberties of the people. The States have not broken up the Union, and the Union has not absorbed the States. No wonder that the Americans are proud of an instrument under which this great result has been attained, which has passed unscathed through the furnace of civil war, which has been found capable of embracing a body of Commonwealths more than three times as numerous, and with twenty fold the population of the original States, which has cultivated the political intelligence of the masses to a point reached in no other country, which has fostered and been found compatible with a larger measure of local self-government than has existed elsewhere. Nor is it the least of its merits to have made itself beloved. Objections may be taken to particular features, and these objections point, as most American thinkers are agreed, to practical improvements which would preserve the excellences and remove some of the inconveniences. But reverence for the Constitution has become so potent a conservative influence, that no proposal of fundamental change seems likely to be entertained. And this reverence is itself one of the most wholesome and hopeful elements in the character of the American people.

CRITICISM OF THE FEDERAL SYSTEM [1]

JAMES BRYCE

ALL Americans have long been agreed that the only possible form of government for their country is a Federal one. All have perceived that a centralized system would be inexpedient, if not unworkable, over so large an area, and have still more strongly felt that to cut up the continent into absolutely independent States would not only involve risks of war but injure commerce, and retard in a thousand ways the material development of every part of the country. But regarding the nature of the Federal tie that ought to exist there have been keen and frequent controversies, dormant at present, but which might break out afresh should there arise a new question of social or economic change capable of bringing the powers of Congress into collision with the wishes of any State or group of States. The general suitability to the country of a Federal system is therefore accepted, and need not be discussed. I pass to consider the strong and weak points of that which exists.

The faults generally charged on federations as compared with unified governments are the following: —

1. Weakness in the conduct of foreign affairs.
2. Weakness in home government, that is to say, deficient authority over the component States and the individual citizens.
3. Liability to dissolution by the secession or rebellion of States.
4. Liability to division into groups and factions by the

[1] *The American Commonwealth* (Revised Edition), part I, chapter XXIX. Reprinted through the generous permission of The Macmillan Company.

formation of separate combinations of the component States.

5. Want of uniformity among the States in legislation and administration.

6. Trouble, expense, and delay due to the complexity of a double system of legislation and administration.

The first four of these are all due to the same cause, viz., the existence within one government, which ought to be able to speak and act in the name and with the united strength of the Nation, of distinct centers of force, organized political bodies into which part of the Nation's strength has flowed, and whose resistance to the will of the majority of the whole Nation is likely to be more effective than could be the resistance of individuals, because such bodies have each of them a government, a revenue, a militia, a local patriotism to unite them, whereas individual recalcitrants, however numerous, would be unorganized, and less likely to find a legal standing ground for opposition. The gravity of the first two of the four alleged faults has been exaggerated by most writers, who have assumed, on insufficient grounds, that Federal Governments are necessarily weak. Let us, however, see how far America has experienced such troubles from these features of a Federal system.

I. In its early years, the Union was not successful in the management of its foreign relations. Few popular Governments are, because a successful foreign policy needs in a world such as ours conditions which popular Governments seldom enjoy. In the days of Adams, Jefferson, and Madison, the Union put up with a great deal of ill-treatment from France as well as from England. It drifted rather than steered into the War of 1812. The conduct of that war was hampered by the opposition of the New England States. The Mexican War of 1846 was due to the slaveholders; but as the combination among the Southern leaders which entrapped the Nation into that conflict might have been equally successful in a unified country, the blame need not be laid at the door of Federalism. The principle of abstention from Old World complications has been so heartily and consistently adhered to that the capacities of the Federal system for the conduct of foreign affairs have been seldom seriously tried, so far as concerned European powers; and the likelihood of any danger from abroad is so slender that it may be practically ignored. But when a question of external policy arises which interests only one part of the Union (such for instance as the immigration of Asiatic laborers), the existence of States feeling themselves specially affected is apt to have a strong and probably an unfortunate influence. Only in this way can the American Government be deemed likely to suffer in its foreign relations from its Federal character.

II. For the purposes of domestic government the Federal authority is now, in ordinary times, sufficiently strong. However, as was remarked in the last chapter, there have been occasions when the resistance of even a single State disclosed its weakness. Had a man less vigorous than Jackson occupied the Presidential chair in 1832, South Carolina would probably have prevailed against the Union. In the Kansas troubles of 1855–56 the National Executive played a sorry part; and even in the resolute hands of President Grant it was hampered in the reëstablishment of order in the reconquered Southern States by the rights which the Federal Constitution secured to those States. The only general conclusion on this point which can be drawn from history is that while the Central Government is likely to find less and less difficulty in enforcing its will against a State or disobedient subjects, because the prestige of its success in the Civil War has strengthened it and the facilities of communication make the raising and moving of troops more easy, nevertheless recalcitrant States, or groups of States, still enjoy certain advantages for resistance, advantages due partly to the legal position, partly to their local sentiment, which rebels might not have in unified countries like England, France, or Italy.

III. Everybody knows that it was the Federal system, and the doctrine of State sovereignty grounded thereon, and not expressly excluded, though certainly not recognized, by the Constitution, which led to the secession of 1861, and gave European powers a plausible ground for recognizing the insurgent minority as belligerents. Nothing seems now less probable than another secession, not merely because the supposed legal basis for it has been abandoned, and because the advantages of continued union are more obvious than ever before, but because the precedent of the victory won by the North will discourage like attempts in the future. This is so strongly felt that it has not even been thought worth while to add to the Constitution an amendment negativing the right to secede. The doctrine of the legal indestructibility of the Union is now well established. To establish it, however, cost thousands of millions of dollars and the lives of a million of men.

IV. The combination of States into groups was a familiar feature of politics before the war. South Carolina and the Gulf States constituted one such, and the most energetic, group; the New England States frequently acted as another, especially during the War of 1812. At present, though, there are several sets of States whose common interests lead their representatives in Congress to act together, it is no longer the fashion for States to combine in an official way through their State organizations, and their doing so would excite reprehension. It is easier, safer, and more effective to act through the great National parties. Any considerable State interest (such as that of the silver-miners or cattle-men, or

Protectionist manufacturers) can generally compel a party to conciliate it by threatening to forsake the party if neglected. Political action runs less in State channels than it did formerly, and the only really threatening form which the combined action of States could take, that of using for a common disloyal purpose State revenues and the machinery of State Governments, has become, since the failure of secession, most improbable.

It has been a singular piece of good fortune that lines of religious difference have never happened to coincide with State lines; nor has any particular creed ever dominated any group of States. The religious forces which in some countries and times have given rise to grave civil discord, have in America never weakened the Federal fabric.

V. Towards the close of the nineteenth century two significant phenomena began to be seen. One was the increasing power of incorporated companies and combinations of capitalists. It began to be felt that there ought to be a power of regulating corporations, and that such regulation cannot be effective unless it proceeds from Federal authority and applies all over the Union. At present the power of Congress is deemed to be limited to the operations of inter-State commerce, so that the rest of the work done by corporations, with the law governing their creation and management, belongs to the several States. The other phenomenon was the growing demand for various social reforms, some of which (such as the regulation of child labor) are deemed to be neglected by the more backward States, while others cannot be fully carried out except by laws of general application. The difficulty of meeting this demand under existing conditions has led to many complaints, and while some call for the amendment of the Constitution, others have gone so far as to suggest that the courts ought now to construe the Constitution as conferring powers it has not hitherto been deemed to include.

VI. The want of uniformity in private law and methods of administration is an evil which different minds will judge by different standards. Some may think it a positive benefit to secure a variety which is interesting in itself and makes possible the trying of experiments from which the whole country may profit. Is variety within a country more a gain or a loss? Diversity in coinage, in weights and measures, in the rules regarding bills and checques and banking and commerce generally is obviously inconvenient. Diversity in dress, in food, in the habits and usages of society, is almost as obviously a thing to rejoice over, because it diminishes the terrible monotony of life. Diversity in religious opinion and worship excited horror in the Middle Ages, but now passes unnoticed, except where Governments are intolerant. In the United States the possible diversity of laws is immense. Subject to a few prohibitions contained in the Constitution, each State can play whatever tricks it pleases with the law of family relations, of inheritance, of contracts, of torts, of crimes. But the actual diversity is not great, for all the States, save Louisiana, have taken the English common and statute law of 1776 as their point of departure, and have adhered to its main principles. A more complete uniformity as regards marriage and divorce is desirable, for it is particularly awkward not to know whether you are married or not, nor whether you have been or can be divorced or not; and several States have tried bold experiments on divorce laws. But, on the whole, far less inconvenience than could have been expected seems to be caused by the varying laws of different States, partly because commercial law is the department in which the diversity is smallest, partly because American practitioners and judges have become expert in applying the rules for determining which law, where those of different States are in question, ought to be deemed to govern a given case. However, some States have taken steps to reduce this diversity by appointing Commissions, instructed to meet and confer as to the best means of securing uniform State legislation on some important subjects, and progress in this direction has been made.

He who is conducted over an iron-clad warship, and sees the infinite intricacy of the machinery and mechanical appliances which it contains and by which its engines, its guns, its turrets, its torpedoes, its apparatus for anchoring and making sail, are worked, is apt to think that it must break down in the rough practice of war. He is told, however, that the more is done by machinery, the more safely and easily does everything go on, because the machinery can be relied on to work accurately, and the performance by it of the heavier work leaves the crew free to attend to the general management of the vessel and her armament. So in studying the elaborate devices with which the Federal system of the United States has been equipped, one fancies that with so many authorities and bodies whose functions are intricately interlaced, and some of which may collide with others, there must be a great risk of break-downs and deadlocks, not to speak of an expense much exceeding that which is incident to a simple centralized government. In America, however, smoothness of working is secured by elaboration of device; and complex as the mechanism of the government may appear, the citizens have grown so familiar with it that its play is smooth and easy, attended with less trouble, and certainly with less suspicion on the part of the people, than would belong to a scheme which vested all powers in one administration and one legislature. The expense is admitted, but is considered no grave defect when compared with the waste which arises from untrustworthy officials and legislators whose depredations would, it is thought, be greater were their sphere of action wider, and the checks upon them fewer. He who examines a system of government from with-

out is generally disposed to overrate the difficulties in working which its complexity causes. Few things, for instance,
are harder than to explain to a person who has not been a
student in one of the two ancient English universities the
nature of their highly complex constitution and the relation
of the college to the university. If he does apprehend it he
pronounces it too intricate for the purposes it has to serve.
To those who have grown up under it, nothing is simpler
and more obvious.

There is a blemish characteristic of the American federation which Americans seldom notice because it seems to
them unavoidable. This is the practice, in selecting candidates for Federal office, of regarding not so much the merits
of the candidate as the effect which his nomination will have
upon the vote of the State to which he belongs. Second-rate
men are run for first-rate posts, not because the party which
runs them overrates their capacity, but because it expects
to carry their State either by their local influence or through
the pleasure which the State feels in the prospect of seeing
one of its own citizens in high office. This of course works in
favor of the politicians who come from a large State. No
doubt the leading men of a large State are *prima facie* more
likely to be men of high ability than those of a small State,
because the field of choice is wider and the competition
keener. One is reminded of the story of the leading citizen
in the isle of Seriphus who observed to Themistocles, "You
would not have been famous had you been born in Seriphus,"
to which Themistocles replied, "Neither would you had you
been born in Athens." The two great States of Virginia and
Massachusetts reared one-half of the men who won distinction in the first fifty years of the history of the Republic.
Nevertheless it often happens that a small State produces a
first-rate man, whom the country ought to have in one of its
highest places, but who is passed over because the Federal

system gives great weight to the voice of a State, and because State sentiment is so strong that the voters of a State which has a large and perhaps a doubtful vote to cast in national elections, prefer an inferior man in whom they are directly interested to a superior one who is a stranger. It is also unfortunate that the President's liberty of choice in forming his Cabinet should be restricted by the doctrine that he must not have in it, if possible, two persons from the same State.

I have left to the last the gravest reproach which Europeans have been wont to bring against Federalism in America. They attributed to it the origin, or at least the virulence, of the great struggle over slavery which tried the Constitution so severely. That struggle created parties which, though they had adherents everywhere, no doubt tended more and more to become identified with States, controlling the State organizations and bending the State Governments to their service. It gave tremendous importance to legal questions arising out of the differences between the law of the Slave States and the Free States, questions which the Constitution had either evaded or not foreseen. It shook the credit of the Supreme Court by making the judicial decision of those questions appear due to partiality to the Slave States. It disposed the extreme men on both sides to hate the Federal Union which bound them in the same body with their antagonists. It laid hold of the doctrine of State rights and State sovereignty as entitling a Commonwealth which deemed itself aggrieved to shake off allegiance to the National Government. Thus at last it brought about secession and the great Civil War. Even when the war was over, the dregs of the poison continued to haunt and vex the system and bred fresh disorders in it. The constitutional duty of reëstablishing the State Governments of the conquered States on the one hand, and on the other hand the practical danger of doing so while their people remained disaffected, produced the Military Governments, the "Carpet-bag" Governments, the Ku Klux Klan outrages, the gift of suffrage to a negro population unfit for such a privilege, yet apparently capable of being protected in no other way. All these mischiefs, it has often been argued, are the results of the Federal structure of the Government, which carried in its bosom the seeds of its own destruction, seeds sure to ripen so soon as there arose a question that stirred men deeply.

It may be answered not merely that the National Government has survived this struggle and emerged from it stronger than before, but also that Federalism did not produce the struggle, but only gave to it the particular form of a series of legal controversies over the Federal pact followed by a war of States against the Union. Where such vast economic interests were involved, and such hot passions roused, there must anyhow have been a conflict, and it may well be that a conflict raging within the vitals of a centralized government would have proved no less terrible and would have left as many noxious *sequelæ* behind.

In blaming either the conduct of a person or the plan and scheme of a government for evils which have actually followed, men are apt to overlook those other evils, perhaps as great, which might have flowed from different conduct or some other plan. All that can fairly be concluded from the history of the American Union is that Federalism is obliged by the law of its nature to leave in the hands of States powers whose exercise may give to political controversy a peculiarly dangerous form, may impede the assertion of National authority, may even, when long-continued exasperation has suspended or destroyed the feeling of a common patriotism, threaten National unity itself. Against this danger is to be set the fact that the looser structure of a

Federal Government and the scope it gives for diversities of legislation in different parts of a country may avert sources of discord, or prevent local discord from growing into a contest of national magnitude.

MERITS OF THE FEDERAL SYSTEM [1]

JAMES BRYCE

I DO not propose to discuss in this chapter the advantages of Federalism in general, for to do this we should have to wander off to other times and countries, to talk of Achaia and the Hanseatic League and the Swiss Confederation. I shall comment on those merits only which experience of the American Union illustrates.

There are two distinct lines of argument by which their Federal system was recommended to the framers of the Constitution, and upon which it is still held forth for imitation to other countries. These lines have been so generally confounded that it is well to present them in a precise form.

The first set of arguments point to Federalism proper, and are the following: —

1. That Federalism furnishes the means of uniting commonwealths into one nation under one National Government without extinguishing their separate administrations, legislatures, and local patriotisms. As the Americans of 1787 would probably have preferred complete State independence to the fusion of their States into a unified government, Federalism was the only resource. So when the new Germanic Empire, which is really a Federation, was established in 1871, Bavaria and Würtemberg could not have been brought under a national government save by a Federal scheme. Similar suggestions, as every one knows, have been made for re-setting the

[1] *The American Commonwealth* (Revised Edition), part I, chapter XXX. Reprinted through the generous permission of The Macmillan Company.

relations of Ireland to Great Britain, and of the self-governing British colonies to the United Kingdom. There are causes and conditions which dispose independent or semi-independent communities, or peoples living under loosely compacted governments, to form a closer union in a Federal form. There are other causes and conditions which dispose the subjects of one government, or sections of these subjects, to desire to make their governmental union less close by substituting a Federal for a unitary system. In both sets of cases, the centripetal or centrifugal forces spring from the local position, the history, the sentiments, the economic needs of those among whom the problem arises; and that which is good for one people or political body is not necessarily good for another. Federalism is an equally legitimate resource whether it is adopted for the sake of tightening or for the sake of loosening a pre-existing bond.

2. That Federalism supplies the best means of developing a new and vast country. It permits an expansion whose extent, and whose rate and manner of progress, cannot be foreseen to proceed with more variety of methods, more adaptation of laws and administration to the circumstances of each part of the territory, and altogether in a more truly natural and spontaneous way, than can be expected under a centralized government, which is disposed to apply its settled system through all its dominions. Thus the special needs of a new region are met by the inhabitants in the way they find best: its laws can be adapted to the economic conditions which from time to time present themselves: its special evils can be cured by special remedies, perhaps more drastic than

an old country demands, perhaps more lax than an old country would tolerate; while at the same time the spirit of self-reliance among those who build up these new communities is stimulated and respected.

3. That Federalism prevents the rise of a despotic central government, absorbing other powers, and menacing the private liberties of the citizen. This may now seem to have been an idle fear, so far as America was concerned. It was, however, a very real fear among the ancestors of the present Americans, and nearly led to the rejection even of so undespotic an instrument as the Federal Constitution of 1789. Congress (or the President, as the case may be) is still sometimes described as a tyrant by the party which does not control it, simply because it is a central government: and the States are represented as bulwarks against its encroachments.

The second set of arguments relate to and recommend not so much Federalism as local self-government. I state them briefly because they are familiar: —

4. Self-government stimulates the interest of people in the affairs of their neighborhood, sustains local political life, educates the citizen in his daily round of civic duty, teaches him that perpetual vigilance and the sacrifice of his own time and labor are the price that must be paid for individual liberty and collective prosperity.

5. Self-government secures the good administration of local affairs by giving the inhabitants of each locality due means of overseeing the conduct of their business.

That these two sets of grounds are distinct appears from the fact that the sort of local interest which local self-government evokes is quite a different thing from the interest men feel in the affairs of a large body like an American State. So, too, the control over its own affairs of a township, or even a small county, where everybody can know what is going on, is quite different from the control exercisable over the affairs of a commonwealth with a million of people. Local self-government may exist in a unified country like England, and may be wanting in a Federal country like Germany. And even in the United States, while some States, as in New England, possessed an admirably complete system of local government, others, such as Virginia, the old champion of State sovereignty, were imperfectly provided with it. Nevertheless, through both sets of arguments there runs the general principle, applicable in every part and branch of government, that, where other things are equal, the more power is given to the units which compose the Nation, be they large or small, and the less to the Nation as a whole and to its central authority, so much the fuller will be the liberties and so much greater the energy of the individuals who compose the people. This principle, though it had not been then formulated in the way men formulate it now, was heartily embraced by the Americans. Perhaps it was because they agreed in taking it as an axiom that they seldom referred to it in the subsequent controversies proceeded on the basis of the Constitution as a law rather than on considerations of general political theory. A European reader of the history of the first seventy years of the United States is surprised how little is said, through the interminable discussions regarding the relation of the Federal government to the States, on the respective advantages of centralization or localization of powers as a matter of historical experience and general expediency.

Three further benefits to be expected from a Federal system may be mentioned, benefits which seem to have been unnoticed or little regarded by those who established it in America: —

6. Federalism enables a people to try experiments in legislation and administration which could not be safely tried in a large centralized country. A comparatively small commonwealth like an American State easily makes and unmakes its laws; mistakes are not serious, for they are soon corrected; other States profit by the experience of a law or a method which has worked well or ill in the State that has tried it.

7. Federalism, if it diminishes the collective force of a nation, diminishes also the risks to which its size and the diversities of its parts expose it. A nation so divided is like a ship built with water-tight compartments. When a leak is sprung in one compartment, the cargo stowed there may be damaged, but the other compartments remain dry and keep the ship afloat. So, if social discord or an economic crisis has produced disorders or foolish legislation in one member of the Federal body, the mischief may stop at the State frontier instead of spreading through and tainting the Nation at large.

8. Federalism, by creating many local legislatures with wide powers, relieves the National Legislature of a part of that large mass of functions which might otherwise prove too heavy for it. Thus business is more promptly despatched, and the great central council of the Nation has time to deliberate on those questions which most nearly touch the whole country.

All of these arguments recommending Federalism have proved valid in American experience.

To create a Nation while preserving the States was the main reason for the grant of powers which the National

Government received; an all-sufficient reason, and one which holds good to-day. The several States have changed greatly since 1789, but they are still commonwealths whose wide authority and jurisdiction practical men are agreed in desiring to maintain.

Not much was said in the Convention of 1787 regarding the best methods of extending government over the unsettled territories lying beyond the Alleghany Mountains. It was, however, assumed that they would develop as the older colonies had developed, and in point of fact each district, when it became sufficiently populous, was formed into a self-governing State, the less populous divisions still remaining in the status of semi-self-governing Territories. Although many blunders have been committed in the process of development, especially in the reckless contraction of debt and the wasteful disposal of the public lands, greater evils might have resulted had the creation of local institutions and the control of new communities been left to the Central Government. Congress would have been not less improvident than the State Governments, for it would have been even less irresistible, the growth of order and civilization probably slower. It deserves to be noticed that, in granting self-government to all those of her colonies whose population is of English race, England has practically adopted the same plan as the United States have done with their western territory. The results have been generally satisfactory, although England, like America, has found that her colonists have in some regions been disposed to treat the aboriginal inhabitants, whose lands they covet and whose persons they hate, with a harshness and injustice which the mother country would gladly check.

The argument which set forth the advantages of local self-government were far more applicable to the States of 1787 than to those of 1907. Virginia, then the largest State, had only half a million free inhabitants, less than the present population of Baltimore. Massachusetts had 450,000, Pennsylvania 400,000, New York 300,000; while Georgia, Rhode Island, and Delaware had (even counting slaves) less than 200,000 between them. These were communities to which the expression "local self-government" might be applied, for, although the population was scattered, the numbers were small enough for the citizens to have a personal knowledge of their leading men, and a personal interest (especially as a large proportion were land-owners) in the economy and prudence with which common affairs were managed. Now, however, when of the nearly fifty States twenty-nine have more than a million inhabitants, and six have more than three millions, the newer States, being, moreover, larger in area than most of the older ones, the stake of each citizen is relatively smaller, and generally too small to sustain his activity in politics, and the party chiefs of the State are known to him only by the newspapers or by their occasional visits on a stumping tour.

All that can be claimed for the Federal system under this head of the argument is that it provides the machinery for a better control of the taxes raised and expended in a given region of the country, and a better oversight of the public works undertaken there than would be possible were everything left to the Central Government. As regards the educative effect of numerous and frequent elections, it will be shown in a later chapter that elections in America are too many and come too frequently. Overtaxing the attention of the citizen and frittering away his interest, they leave him at the mercy of knots of selfish adventurers.

The utility of the State system in localizing disorders or discontents, and the opportunities it affords for trying easily and safely experiments which ought to be tried in legislation and administration, constitute benefits to be set off against the risk, referred to in the last preceding chapters, that evils may continue in a district, may work injustice to a minority and invite imitation by other States, which the wholesome stringency of the Central Government might have sup- pressed.

A more unqualified approval may be given to the division of legislative powers. The existence of the State Legisla- tures relieves Congress of a burden too heavy for its shoul- ders; for although it has far less foreign policy to discuss than the Parliaments of England, France, or Italy, and although the separation of the executive from the legislative depart- ment gives it less responsibility for the ordinary conduct of the Administration than devolves on those chambers, it could not possibly, were its competence as large as theirs, deal with the multiform and increasing demands of the dif- ferent parts of the Union. There is great diversity in the material conditions of different parts of the country, and at present the people, particularly in the West, are eager to have their difficulties handled, their economic and social needs satisfied, by the State and the law. It would be ex- tremely difficult for any central legislature to pass measures suited to these dissimilar and varying conditions. How little Congress could satisfy them appears by the very imperfect success with which it cultivates the field of legislation to which it is now limited.

These merits of Federal system of government which I have enumerated are the counterpart and consequences of that limitation of the central authority whose dangers were indicated in the last chapter. They are, if one may reverse the French phrase, the qualities of Federalism's defects. The problem which all federalized nations have to solve is how to secure an efficient central government and preserve National unity, while allowing free scope for the diversities, and free play to the authorities, of the members of the federation. It is, to adopt that favorite astronomical metaphor which no American panegyrist of the Constitution omits, to keep the centrifugal and centripetal forces in equilibrium, so that neither the planet States shall fly off into space, nor the sun of the Central Government draw them into its consuming fires. The characteristic merit of the American Constitution lies in the method by which it has solved this problem. It has given the National Government a direct authority over all citizens, irrespective of the State Governments, and has therefore been able safely to leave wide powers in the hands of those Governments. And by placing the Constitution above both the National and the State Governments, it has referred the arbitrament of disputes between them to an independent body, charged with the interpretation of the Constitution, a body which is to be deemed not so much a third authority in the Government as the living voice of the Constitution, the unfolder of the mind of the people whose will stands expressed in that supreme instrument.

The application of these two principles, unknown to, or at any rate little used by, any previous federation, has contributed more than any thing else to the stability of the American system, and to the reverence which its citizens feel for it, a reverence which is the best security for its permanence. Yet even these devices would not have succeeded but for the presence of a mass of moral and material influences, stronger than any political devices, which have maintained the equilibrium of centrifugal and centripetal forces. On the one hand, there has been the love of local independence and self-government; on the other, the sense of community in blood, in language, in habits and ideas, a common pride in the National history and the National flag.

Quid leges sine moribus? The student of institutions, as well as the lawyer, is apt to overrate the effect of mechanical contrivances in politics. I admit that in America they have had one excellent result; they have formed a legal habit in the mind of the Nation. But the true value of a political contrivance resides not in its ingenuity, but in its adaptation to the temper and circumstances of the people for whom it is designed, in its power of using, fostering and giving a legal form to those forces of sentiment and interest which it finds in being. So it has been with the American system. Just as the passions which the question of slavery evoked strained the Federal fabric, disclosing unforeseen weaknesses, so the love of the Union, the sense of the material and social benefits involved in its preservation, appeared in unexpected strength, and manned with zealous defenders the ramparts of the sovereign Constitution. It is this need of determining the suitability of the machinery for the workmen and its probable influence upon them, as well as the capacity of the workmen for using and their willingness to use the machinery, which makes it so difficult to predict the operation of a political contrivance, or, when it has succeeded in one country, to advise its imitation in another. The growing strength of the National Government in the United States is largely due to sentimental forces that were weak a century ago, and to a development of internal communications which was then undreamt of. And the devices which we admire in the Constitution might prove unworkable among a people less patriotic and self-reliant, less law-loving and law-abiding, than are the English of America.

THE COÖPERATION OF ENGLISH-SPEAKING PEOPLES [1]

ARTHUR JAMES BALFOUR

MR. PRESIDENT, GENTLEMEN OF THE CHAMBER: The noble words to which we have just listened struck, I am well convinced, a sympathetic chord in the heart of every one in your audience, but I don't think that in all the multitude gathered here to-day there was one to whom they went more home than to myself. Mr. President, I have had as the dream of my life a hope that before I died the union between the English-speaking, freedom-loving branches of the human race should be drawn far closer than in the past, and that all temporary causes of difference which may ever have separated two great peoples would be seen in its true and just proportion, and that we should all realize, on whatever side of the Atlantic fortune had place us, that the things wherein we have differed in the past sink into absolute insignificance compared with those vital agreements which at all times, but never at such a time as the present, unite us in one great spiritual whole.

My friend Mr. Choate, in a speech that he delivered yesterday at the City Hall, told his audience that as Ambassador to Great Britain he had been in close official relations with me through many years, and that during all of these years I had stood solid — I think that was his phrase — for American friendship. That is strictly and absolutely true, and the feelings that I have this great opportunity of

---

[1] Speech made before the New York Chamber of Commerce, May 12, 1917, by the head of the British Mission to the United States.

expressing are not born, believe me, of the necessities of the
Great War; they are not the offspring of recent events;
they are based upon my most enduring convictions, convictions of which I cannot remember the beginning, which
I have held with unalterable fidelity through the political
life which is now a long life, and which, I am quite sure, I
shall cherish to the end.

You, Mr. President, have referred to the preparations
that were made only, I suppose, a little more than two years
and a half ago — though how long those two and a half years
seem to all of us! — preparations that were made two and a
half years ago to celebrate the one hundred years of peace
between our two countries. I ardently supported that movement, and yet the very phrases in which its objects were expressed show how inadequate it was to reach the real truth
and heart of the matter. It is true that one hundred years
have passed, and many hundreds of years, I hope, were to
pass, before any overt act of war should divide those whom,
as you said in your final words, should never be asunder.
But, after all, normal and official peace is but a small thing
compared with that intimate mutual comprehension which
ought always to bind the branches of the English-speaking
peoples together. You have absorbed in your midst many
admirable citizens drawn from all parts of Europe, whom
American institutions and American ways of thought have
moulded and are moulding into one great people. I rejoice
to think it should be so. A similar process on a smaller scale
is going on in the self-governing dominions of the British
Empire. It is a good process; it is a noble process. Let us
never forget that wherever be the place in which that great
and beneficent process is going on, whether it be in Canada,
whether it be in Australia, or whether on the largest scale of
all it be in the United States of America, the spirit which the
immigrant absorbs is a spirit in all these places largely due to

a historic past in which your forefathers and my forefathers, gentlemen, all had their share.

You incidentally mentioned, Mr. President, that this very body I am addressing dates the origin of its society to a charter, I think you said of 1758. Is not that characteristic and symbolic of what happens on both sides of the Atlantic? We strike our roots into a distant past. We have known how through revolutions, in spite of revolutions, sometimes because of revolutions, and through revolutions, we have known how to weld the past and the present into one organic whole, and I see around me in a country which calls itself and is, in one sense, a new country — I everywhere see signs of these roots which draw their nourishment and their strength from epochs far removed from us, and I feel when I talk to those who are born and bred under the American flag, who have absorbed all their political ideas from American institutions — I feel, and I think I speak for my friends here that they also feel — I feel that I am speaking to those brought up, as it were, under one influence, in one house, under one set of educational conditions. I require no explanations of what they think, and I am required to give no explanations of what I think, because our views of great questions seem to be shared; born, as it were, of common knowledge which we know instinctively, and which we do not require explicitly to expound or to define.

This is a great heritage to have in common, and I think, nay, I am sure, that you, Mr. President, struck a true note when you told us that all the sentiments which I have imperfectly tried to express this afternoon will receive a double significance, and infinitely increased significance from the fact that we are now not merely sharing a common political ideal in some speculative fashion, but that all of us are committed to sacrificing everything that we hold most dear to carry these ideals into practical execution.

There will be a bond of union between our peoples which nothing will ever be able to shake, and which I believe to be the securest guarantee for the future of the world, for the future peace and freedom of the world.

Mr. President, I have already detained you too long, but there was one word which fell from you toward the end of your speech upon post-war problems and you indicated your view — a view which I personally entirely share — that when this tremendous conflict has drawn to its appointed close, and when, as I believe, victory shall have crowned our joint efforts, there will arise not merely between nations, but within nations, a series of problems which will tax all our statesmanship to deal with. I look forward to that time, not, indeed, wholly without anxiety, but in the main with hope and with confidence; and one of the reasons for that hope and one of the foundations of that confidence is to be found in the fact that your nation and my nation will have so much to do with the settlement of the questions. I do not think anybody will accuse me of being insensible to the genius and to the accomplishments of other nations. I am one of those who believe that only in the multitude of different forms of culture can the completed movement of progress have all the variety in unity of which it is capable; and, while I admire other cultures, and while I recognize how absolutely all-important they are to the future of mankind, I do think that among the English-speaking peoples is especially and peculiarly to be found a certain political moderation in all classes, which gives one the surest hope of dealing in a reasonable progressive spirit with social and political difficulties. And without that reasonable moderation interchanges are violent also, and the smooth advance of humanity is seriously interfered with. I believe that on this side of the Atlantic, and I hope on the other side of the Atlantic, if and when these great problems have actively to be dealt with, it will not be beyond the reach of your statesmanship or of our own, to deal with them in such a manner that we cannot merely look back upon this great war as the beginning of a time of improved international relations, of settled peace, of deliberate refusal to pour out oceans of blood to satisfy some notion of domination; but that in addition to those blessings the war may prove to be the beginning of a revivified civilization, which will be felt in all departments of human activity, which will not merely touch the material but also the spiritual side of mankind, and which will make the second decade of the twentieth century memorable in the history of mankind.